Marlon Quintero

Innovation for Media Content Creation

Tools and Strategies for Delivering Successful Content

Marlon Quintero

Copyright ©2015 by Marlon Quintero

ISBN-13: 978-1-60427-104-1

Printed and bound in the U.S.A. Printed on acid-free paper
10 9 8 7 6 5 4 3 2 1

Library of Congress Cataloging-in-Publication Data
Quintero, Marlon, 1970-
Innovation for media content creation : tools and strategies for
delivering successful content / Marlon Quintero.
  pages cm
  Includes index.
  ISBN 978-1-60427-104-1 (hardcover : alk. paper) 1. Television
broadcasting. 2. Television programs. 3. Mass media. 4. Creation
(Literary, artistic, etc.) I. Title.
  PN1992.55.Q56 2015
  791.45--dc23

                                                    2014048610

Phone: (954) 727-9333
Fax: (561) 892-0700
Web: www.jrosspub.com

To my wife, Cristina, my son, Guillermo, and my daughter, Anna,
the loves of my life
Thank you for believing in me and letting me pursue my dream.
Without your support, I wouldn't have been able to write a single word.

To my parents and my siblings for their unconditional love and support

Professionals in Entertainment Series

Branded Entertainment: Dealmaking Strategies and Techniques for
Industry Professionals
by Damaris Valero
ISBN: 978-1-60427-094-5, 248 pages, 2014

Innovation for Media Content Creation: Tools and Strategies for
Delivering Successful Content
by Marlon Quintero
ISBN: 978-1-60427-104-1, 344 pages, 2015

CONTENTS

STEP 5: EMBRACE THE ENTIRE METHODOLOGY THROUGH THE CIRCLE OF CONTENT INNOVATION

ACKNOWLEDGMENTS

Thanks to those who I have had the good fortune to work with—I have learned from all of you, but the experience of creating something together has been the biggest reward for me. You are the main source of inspiration for this book and the stories I have to tell.

Thanks to Dr. Ron Compesi and Dr. Herb Zettl, professors at San Francisco State University. You always believed in me and welcomed this book initiative as yours. Thanks also to Dr. Sanjeev Chaterjee, Professor at the University of Miami, and to Dr. Jack Lewis, former Associate Dean of the International Business Education and Research Program, Marshall School of Business, at the University of Southern California. You have always been strong supporters of my educational initiative.

Thanks to all the clients, supervisors, and the companies I have had the honor of working for. You gave me the chance to become inspired by your brands. Thank you for supporting this book initiative.

Special thanks to Gino Berrios, Ramon Leon, Karen Barroeta, Carlos R. Bardasano, Ligiah Villalobos, Ricardo Ehrsam, Tony Fadel, Maria Gabriela Silva, and Chris Bilton. You are relentless, true believers in outstanding work and have collaborated in various ways. Thanks to my wife Cristina who was key in making my ideas sound clear.

And finally, thanks to Carolyn Lea, my editor, for polishing my work and Steve Buda, my publisher, for being the engine behind my dream. You made it a reality, my friend.

Although many others are not mentioned here, you still impacted me throughout my career. You were key in providing encouragement and motivation. Thank you all.

INTRODUCTION

The television industry generates content to entertain the masses through different platforms of exposition and is constantly in search of the next breakthrough hit. The need for innovation, originality, and creativity is intrinsic to this industry. Creative geniuses are responsible for the magic, but guaranteeing that their operations will ensure that magic—all the time—is not easy for industry professionals. Only by understanding the importance of strategy, the real meaning of creativity, and the specific activities that define the process of innovation will more professionals be ready for this challenge.

As a creative individual, producer, and executive, I always strive for excellence in content and have had the good fortune to work in many different creative environments that have allowed me to implement efficient and strategic ways to create, develop, and produce television shows. I have been able to work with local channels, U.S. television networks, and ultimately in the international global market to generate creative solutions for broadcasters in the form of content. I have been responsible for more than 4500 hours of television fiction and non-fiction content that has aired in the United States, Latin America, and Europe. I have learned from my successes and failures and have managed to maintain a constantly prolific operation and pipeline of concepts and shows ready for the opportunities ahead.

To achieve these moments of success and a high level of productivity, I have developed a strategic business and creative sensitivity that has allowed me to acquire clear direction and set goals to light not only my way but also the ways of those I lead. After many years of producing content and managing creative and production operations, I have come to understand the applicability of concepts such as *strategy* and *innovation*, concepts which I first heard about during my engineering and business school days—days that are far from the creative environment where I work but concepts that are closer than ever to the creative environment where I currently am. Years ago, in a quest to coexist with both my business and creative sides, I decided to gain understanding of the applicability of the concepts of strategy and innovation in the creative world of entertainment in order to produce a framework of operation that would drive my actions in the industry in a very solid way. That is how strategy became my rule, creativity became my strength, and innovation became my goal. I have merged these three concepts into a process and mastered its implementation in media content creation.

In my quest for understanding, I noticed that the concepts of strategy and innovation were topics that had been fleshed out in books and research papers in the academic world and in the overall market—all intended for different industries—but none specifically addressed media content as being an object of applicability. I also found that the concept of creativity had been explained through different sciences as being the fundamental fuel for the creation of products for any industry and for the expression of the arts, but I did not find a single theory or book that explained being creative in the media in a precise way. So I extrapolated the meanings of these concepts for the media industry, more specifically for the generation of content in the new multiplatform television landscape, and mixed them with the know-how I had gathered during my career to create a working philosophy that would respond to change and allow success to occur steadily.

Throughout my experience and investigations, I have found that innovation is a term widely used in the entertainment industry but that the term is used differently than in other industries such as manufacturing. In these other industries, innovation is a process; it is a full operational division; it is a philosophy; and it is core to the business strategy of implementation. Procter & Gamble, 3M, Apple, and Google are living proof of that. I have also noticed that innovation is a recurring term used in the entertainment industry to describe successful shows or the nature of a risky work that has breakthrough potential. The term innovation in this sense describes rather than represents the value chain of the activities required to produce content. Yet it would be shallow analysis to say that the entertainment industry does not operate based on innovation—that would be absolutely false. I would have no examples to present or success stories to tell if that were the case. The wonderful works coming from producers and creators around the world clearly illustrate why the entertainment industry is an innovative one. Hollywood has always been the epicenter of attention and has exported thousands of hours of innovative content globally. The United Kingdom, Spain, Argentina, Mexico, Colombia, Japan, and Holland, to name just a few, are key sources of creativity and risk takers who provide innovative content to the world.

My point concerning innovation has to do with *learning* the concept, *utilizing* it in our day-to-day work, and *implementing* it as a process and implied methodology. Despite the successful creative processes of the entertainment industry, innovation is not a term commonly used to describe the product being made or the process being used to come up with particular media content. In the entertainment industry, usually there are no actual innovation processes but instead processes of development and production—and that is terrific because these two processes *are* processes of innovation. Innovative companies in the entertainment industry use development and production processes that have defined validation and feedback stages that yield great content. The point, the key value added, that I am trying to make is that in the entertainment industry the process of innovation encompasses both development and production *and* it also adds another layer of strategic understanding and creative resources that provide an extra dimension to the processes that already exist.

We all pursue innovation, but has anyone ever taught us what innovation really means? The entertainment industry dreams with innovation. Its implementation is rather intuitive. Although innovation already exists, we all still continue to pursue it. In this book, more than trying to teach something to those who are already creating media content successfully, I instead will extrapolate the experiences and results of highly successful content creators to describe a process of innovation that could revise the methods used to create and produce outstanding content. I have found a different way to describe how creators of content succeed. I have reviewed the concept of innovation and projected it over the entertainment industry to give a different perspective to the art of content creation. I am not reinventing the wheel or creating a revolutionary method that no one has ever seen before. Instead I have contextualized the process of creation in the entertainment industry and organized it within the notion of innovation to provide an understanding of what the concept really means and how to use in the industry. What I will do in this book is explore what is behind the intuitive line of thought and explain how this can become more of a philosophy implemented than just an adjective used in a sentence.

In my experience, few media companies have a functional department called the department of content innovation that is dedicated to the procurement of innovation in content. Few have implemented the concept or the philosophy of innovation at the core of their content creation processes as manufacturing and pharmaceutical firms do. I have also found that innovation is often seen as a term associated only with technology, cutting its applicability to the field of content creation. In fact, when thinking about my seminars on innovation in media content creation, the first thing that comes to mind about describing to a person in the entertainment industry what the seminars will entail is that I need to explain that the discussion will be about creating innovative stories and characters, not just about technology applications in media. People just relate innovation with technology.

Although the entertainment industry has creative development processes to procure the proliferation of ideas that later will become television shows or other types of media forms, some of these development processes do not necessarily follow innovation criteria closely enough to ensure creative diversity at the source, quality, sustainability, and evolution all the time. Some companies have innovation embedded in their processes and concentrate on finding breakthroughs, whereas others concentrate so much on sticking to some rule that they fail to break it, thus reducing risks but also reducing the possibilities to innovate. Even though the entertainment industry is highly innovative and always pursuing innovation, if you want to enter this field you have to understand the meaning of innovation and the methodology behind its implementation to avoid droughts in ideas and breakthrough possibilities.

This book might lead to new roles and positions to manage the implementation of innovation within the entertainment industry. Existing roles such as chief creative officer might become chief innovation officer with a focus on content, not just a focus on technological applications. Vice presidents, directors, and heads of development might have innovation added to their titles. Ultimately, however, innovation is not about titles. The titles can stay just as they are now. What is important is to *know how* to implement innovation successfully throughout an entire creative organization or a team. Everyone has to be innovative, not just the leader, so everyone has to know what innovation is all about—that precisely is my goal.

THE TELEVISION INDUSTRY

In the last 40 years, the television industry has changed before my eyes—from a black and white television with a long V antenna in my living room to the flat television screens with internet, 3D, and smart capabilities now available in stores. The television viewing experience has changed as well. I cannot only watch my favorite show on television but also, thanks to digital video recording equipment, see that show anytime. Thanks to excellent internet connections, I can watch television content on my computer or, better yet, via wireless on one of the multiple devices that allows me to do so while on the go!

All of this sounds overwhelming. As creative individuals, many find themselves lost in a jungle of technological options, but guess what, in the end it's all about content. Content is what is important, not the technology. It's all about how engaging you are with the stories you tell and how opportunistic the industry is in bringing, at the right time, something, some type of content, an audience is hungry for. Understanding this landscape is not easy. It will never be, but having a notion about how to uncover the state of the market and then stay current is what will allow you to be on top of your creative and innovative game.

The intent of this book is to provide tools to creative professionals so they can understand the importance of knowing the characteristics of their competitive environment and the value chain of activities that will help them to stay grounded and yet still have a clearer horizon in order to be as creative, strategic, and innovative as possible. Strategy, creativity, and innovation are as crucial to the creation of media content as they are to the creation of any product in any industry in existence (health, sports, manufacturing, apparel, etc.).

Content generation is the heart of the entertainment business and all its sectors. From a very simplistic standpoint, what sets a particular content apart and makes it stand out is how successful that content is in the marketplace. This level of success is ultimately measured by audience reaction and whatever milestones the media industry sets as determinants of success, determinants that are expressed as revenue, goals, or records to beat. Some of these metrics are objective and others are more subjective, but all are a means to determine how successful the content has been. Some of these metrics include:

- Number of albums sold (music industry)
- Weekend box office receipts (film industry)
- Show ratings (television industry)
- Number of positive reviews critics gave a film (television, box offices, etc.)
- Awards a show receives (television)
- Viral reactions on the internet or on any digital mobile platform
- Degree of pop culture influence that leads to the creation of fashions, apps, merchandise, conversations, and even other shows of the same type

Before a show becomes a success, before it reaches an audience, a show has to be innovative and creative according to some basic standard of reference. Media industry experts define that standard based on what they know, the target audience, and what the market wants.

The entertainment industry in general is hit-driven (Aris & Bughin, 2005). To come up with as many hits as possible, absolutely key is to be innovative and creative, yet to do so with a purpose, and to have a market, audience, and ultimately a strategy in mind. These requirements become the fuel that ignites the industry in its quest for finding the next big thing, the next big show, or the next big hit that will revolutionize the world.

The process of generating ideas for a hit, however, is not random. The process is well thought out and relevant to the context defined by the industry and the audience within. The process requires knowledge and market awareness. It is a process that does not occur suddenly and individualistically. Team work and validation are required. Even though no one can predict the exact moment when the next big idea is going to "hit our brain," we can nurture an environment that encourages ideas to occur and that then guarantees quality in execution and the conversion of an idea into a product. The process is therefore none other than a process of innovation, with an objective of nurturing creativity and with an end result that we call innovation. A process of innovation, when well implemented, leads to a higher rate of hits and success in the market, making the investment process more efficient, with a positive return.

Every year new hits come from the glut of television shows that inundate the programming grids in the Guide feature of the remote control devices for our televisions. *Lost, American Idol, Survivor, Desperate Housewives, The Office, Grey's Anatomy, The Sopranos,* and *The Walking Dead* are examples of successful shows that fuel our notion of the possibility of hitting the jackpot of entertainment—of securing investments and funding that guarantees that the process of innovation does not stop in our quest to find the next hit on television. These television shows are innovations that have gone from being watched by millions of people sitting in front of single television sets in their living rooms across the world to millions who are watching these shows across many platforms at their own convenience. This experience with television has proven that over time the television industry will be ever evolving and demanding creativity and innovative content to satisfy the need for more hits—innovation that is the result of strategies that rule the creative process within the value chain of innovation and is the object of ultimate validation by the audience. The hit-making process is a delicate one that if not renewed will be very difficult to sustain over time. The challenge is not to be a one-hit wonder but to be a continual industry wonder all the time. This book will give you a methodology and the tools to achieve that professional goal.

BOOK SUMMARY

The methodology in this book is a summary of my research findings (literature review) and professional experiences organized in a five-step model to implement the process of innovation for media content creation. This five-step methodology is aimed at students, creative professionals, executives, and anyone who intends to develop a career creating content in the entertainment industry. The methodology addresses strategy, creativity, and innovation and the importance of discovery and delivery in the process of creation of media for different digital outlets and platforms reaching an audience.

This book targets creative professionals who want to create good content in a constant and sustained fashion and to find processes and ways to work strategically and efficiently, aiming to achieve creativity and innovation year after year, project after project. It is intended to give these creative professionals the means, tools, and fundamentals to help them form strategies, to manage resources and processes, and to establish a clear goal and vision to deliver quality content with success. This book is not about learning how to write or how to produce. It is about learning how to be strategic in the process of creating innovative content. In other words, this book is about innovation in the delivery of media content.

The methodology, which is based on five steps that compose the model, defines the structure of the book:

Step 1: Understand strategy, creativity, and innovation.

Step 2. Create the conditions for innovation to occur.

Step 3. Adopt discovery as your core.

Step 4. Implement the value chain of content innovation.

Step 5. Embrace the entire methodology through the circle of content innovation.

The five-step model starts with understanding the basic concepts that define the working philosophy. The next step provides recommendations for setting up the best possible environment to nurture innovation. The third step deals with the adoption of discovery as the heart of the entire operation, which precedes the value chain of innovation, or fourth step of the model and the ultimate set of activities to deliver results. All key takeaways of the book are recapped in the fifth step in a framework called the circle of content innovation to provide a practical reference for everyone involved in the search for the next big hit.

Step 1: Understand Strategy, Creativity, and Innovation is broken-down into three parts: *Part I: Strategy, Part II: Creativity,* and *Part III: Innovation.*

Part I: Strategy provides notions that need to be taken into account to be strategic and to generate a macro strategy based on an honest assessment of *who* you are, *where* you are as a creative individual, and *what* resources you have to achieve your goals as a content creator.

- Chapter 1, *The Importance of Being Strategic in the Process of Innovation,* explains why being strategic is of utmost importance in the entertainment industry and describes the meaning of strategy and how to define it by assessing *who* you are as a creative professional, *where* in the industry you want to work, and *what* assets you possess to create content.
- Chapter 2, *Defining Who You Are: Creative Individual or Creative Executive,* is a classification of the types of creative professionals in the industry and is presented to orient or guide you in deciding if you are (or want to be) an independent creative individual (writer, producer,

director) or a creative executive within a corporation. This chapter explains the responsibilities and functionalities that each role entails.

- Chapter 3, *Finding Where You Are*, is an overview of the industry provided to understand its inner dynamics. This chapter describes the media industry and how the television landscape has evolved to the multiplatform world that it is today. The chapter also introduces the concept of television development cycles and how content travels through the new multiplatform dynamic for exposition.
- Chapter 4, *Assessing What You Have*, deals with the assessment required to determine the resources you own that define your edge and leverage to enter and transit the media industry. Resources are material (money, equipment, and software), intellectual (know-how and experience), and emotional (inner drive, aptitude for feedback, leadership, diva and arrogance control, and frustration management).

Part II: Creativity is about understanding the concept of creativity applied to the media industry to unveil how the dynamics within affect the potential success a concept may have.

- Chapter 5, *Understanding Creativity*, presents the definition, process, and resources necessary to achieve creativity. This chapter helps understand what makes a person creative and the difference between just being inventive. This chapter also addresses the relationship between leadership and creativity in the media industry as a key driver in the process of innovation.
- Chapter 6, *The Sociocultural Model of Creative Validation in Media*, is one of the most important chapters of the book. This chapter presents the model of sociocultural creative validation as the key filtering process for a concept and idea to travel through the industry until reaching an audience. This sociocultural creative validation model is explained through four dimensions: domain, field, individuals, and audience, which together represent the context and stages to assess and validate the potential an idea has to become a success—and thus an innovation.

Part III: Innovation deepens in the concepts of innovation applied to the media industry and orients the design of radical or incremental innovations. This section helps define a line of action to enter in the industry, either creating something absolutely radical or a derivative incremental concept. What type of product can you do? What are the key drivers for content innovations?

- Chapter 7, *Understanding Innovation*, presents the definition of innovation, how an audience adopts an innovative product, and the classification of innovation and its relationship with media. This chapter explores in detail the concepts of radical and incremental innovation, the S curve in program innovation, and the derivative process of innovation in media.
- Chapter 8, *Classification of Media Content Innovation According to Degree of Novelty*, presents how, according to degree of novelty, innovations are classified as radical and incremental. This chapter addresses through examples each classification and describes how television content has evolved through time based on these two types of innovation.
- Chapter 9, *Drivers for Content Innovation*, concentrates on the types of innovation in media specifically related to content (genre, conceptual, aesthetics, production value, storytelling, structure), services (cable, internet, mobile), and processes (production).

In *Step 2: Create the Conditions for Innovation to Occur*, Chapter 10, *Implementing the Process of Innovation*, explores the importance of setting strategic goals for the entire operation and addresses the how to create the right environment to innovate through leadership, learning, communication, collaboration, time and space, and the establishment of the right team.

In *Step 3: Adopt Discovery as Your Core*, Chapter 11, *The Discovery Circle*, establishes the importance of discovery as the main component of the entire innovation process. Discovery must be embedded in all of the activities required to generate innovation.

Step 4: Implement the Value Chain of Content Innovation explains how to implement a value chain of innovation for content creation.

- Chapter 12, *The Value Chain of Innovation*, identifies the value chain of innovation as the key aspect in the implementation of a process to generate a strategy for creating innovative content. This chapter explains in detail what the process of innovation entails and the importance of the activities to create innovation such as association, questioning, observation, experimenting, networking, and practice. Chapter 12 also explains specific components of a value chain of innovation and how a creative individual and an executive can implement it, e.g., with core activities, such as market and creative strategic research, exploration, concept development, pitch and marketing, and development and creative sustainability in production, and supporting activities, such as management, legal, accounting and finance, business affairs, physical production, and engineering. The chapter also explains how to leverage activities and assets (including creative human resources) and how to organize them into the overall process of innovation.

- Chapter 13, *Market and Strategic Research*, deals with market research, strategy formulation, and resource planning and concentrates on the importance of understanding the market and the competitive landscape before embarking on a think tank innovative operation. Once the macro-strategy is clear and defined and you see with clarity the kind of product (innovation) you want to create, you are ready to understand the different steps and activities that need to be undertaken to generate a specific strategy that will help yield continued creativity (approved and celebrated by others) and innovation (fulfilling an utilitarian purpose). Chapter 12 explains how to define the target market, addresses the importance of understanding the programming strategies of networks and channels, and discusses the art of timing and knowing when and how to pitch the show. In this chapter, different ways to develop disruptive thinking are explored, identifying orthodoxies within the industry, looking for discontinuities in the market, and trying to get into the audience's mind through empathic conversations that lead to uncovering hidden needs and, ultimately, realizing your mix of assets so you can decide what to do with them. This process leads to a strategy. Special emphasis is given to how disruptive thinking helps create strategies to procure differentiation and to be ahead of the competition. This chapter ultimately provides the reader with instructions to formulate the specific content strategic plan based on resources, goals, needs, technological evolution, and competition in the market and to organize the innovative team for content creation.
- Chapter 14, *Exploration*, explains the types, sources, submission process, evaluation process, and selection process for creative ideas; the importance of securing intellectual property rights; and database management of information. Once a strategy is in place, you need to know how to find the best possible ideas, how to manage references and trends, and ultimately how, if you are working for a corporation, to filter and evaluate in an efficient and educated way all of the creative submissions so you can generate an excellent pool of ideas that might eventually enter the concept development stage. After reading this chapter, you will also be able to differentiate between the kind of exploration process that a creative individual needs to pursue as an

independent generator of ideas and the process that production companies and networks undertake when looking for original material and formats.

- Chapter 15, *Concept Development*, presents in detail, strategic functionalities and activities that help decision makers, creative individuals, and executives create the substance or concept of a television show. What is it about? What genre is suitable for the concept? What is the story about? What is the idea for the game show? Different outcomes of this process are illustrated as necessary steps of preparation before selling/pitching the show in the market.

- Chapter 16, *Selling the Concept*, explains the importance of implementing solid customer relationship management strategies to guarantee efficient and successful sales. This chapter breaks down the commissioning process for creative individuals and executives.

- Chapter 17, *Development*, describes the development process and presents the different deliverables that this task entails once a show has been commissioned. In this chapter, you will learn how the value of a creative asset increases or decreases depending on the level of acceptance and on advancing to the production stage.

- Chapter 18, *Production*, explores the importance of costs and their effect on the creative process and end result, the franchise potential, and the process of reinvention and reengineering to innovate season after season. Once the show is on the air, producers must ensure sustainability through the constant injection of energy and high-impact events throughout the run of the show.

- Chapter 19, *Supporting Activities*, deals with the importance of knowledge, teamwork, networking, and staffing to cover different functional areas that permit a flow in the process of innovation. Creative individuals and executives need to pay special attention to these supporting activities to accomplish their goals. This chapter will walk you through legal, finance, accounting, and engineering areas and explain how they all contribute to achieve the creative vision of the writers/creators.

By the end of Step 4, you will be able to:

- Understand why innovation represents the intersection between a great idea and effective execution through a well-defined value chain of operations.

- Formulate a strategy to create a specific type content and design a process to execute and sustain this strategy.

In *Step 5: Embrace the Entire Methodology Through the Circle of Content Innovation*, Chapter 20, *The Full Circle of Innovation*, presents a full summary of the methodology using a comprehensive framework of reference. The full circle combines the discovery circle and the value chain of innovation together with the system of creative validation to represent the cyclical nature of the entire process of innovation. Information describes how to make the strategy and processes of creativity and innovation sustainable and renewable over time. This chapter also addresses how to implement an iterative process of feedback and collaboration to keep the value chain of innovation up to date; how to manage a creative team to keep it fresh, trained, empowered and confident; and how to work with innovation productivity indicators and guarantee flexibility, reinvention, reengineering, and reorganization. This chapter also addresses risk, change management, anticipating trends, and evolving with the industry to maintain competitive edge and growth.

By the end of the book, you will be able to set up a strategy for content creation and have a clear notion of all the necessary processes and resources needed to implement and maintain fresh that strategy. You can now consider yourself a creative strategic individual prepared to lead and manage a creative process that will yield innovation!

Believe in yourself. Believe in achieving. Believe in what you create. Believe that you can make others believe. This book is for all of you—for all of you who are pursuing the dream of creating the next big thing!

ABOUT THE AUTHOR

 Marlon Quintero is an international Emmy-nominated television producer and creative strategic global executive with experience in creating, developing, producing, and commissioning media content to ensure innovation, competitiveness, organizational development, brand positioning, audience success, value creation, and growth. Throughout his career, Marlon has established strong relationships with international creative communities. He has over 20 years of experience and has led or been involved in the production of more than 4500 hours of television programming in all genres and schedules and for different target audiences and channels.

Marlon is an industrial engineer with a Master of Arts in Television Production with honors from San Francisco State University. He has a Master in Business Administration from the University of Southern California Marshall School of Business with an emphasis in entertainment, marketing, and international business.

He began his career in 1994 with Radio Caracas Televisión Internacional (Venezuela) and subsequently became a production team member at 20th Century Fox, the Disney Channel, and Galan Entertainment in Los Angeles.

In 1998, Marlon joined Televen Corporation in Venezuela as Director of Image and Promotions (1998–2000) and then Director of Production (2000–2002), leading production and development for drama series, an original sitcom, and talk, variety, reality, and game shows. His team won four Promax Awards for on-air promotion excellence. He created *Futuro Seguro* (*Certain Future*), Televen's most successful original prime-time quiz show, and shepherded the writing and production of *Los Ultimos* (*The Last Ones*), Venezuela's first weekly original one-hour drama series shot in film.

In 2003, Marlon became Director of Programming Development for the Univision Network and was instrumental in implementing and managing all aspects of Univision's TV programming development process in all genres. He created, developed, and produced *Lo Veremos Todo* (*We Will See It All*), a celeb-reality series, which was the first of its kind in the Hispanic entertainment industry and the most successful original TV series in U.S. Hispanic markets in 2004. He supervised *Al Filo de la Ley* (*At the Edge of the Law*), the first weekly drama series produced by Univision, and created *Nuestra Belleza Latina* (*Latin Beauty*), the most successful reality beauty competition in the history of Hispanic TV.

Marlon joined Sony Pictures Television in 2006 as Vice President of Development and Current Programs to oversee the creative and production operations active in Latin America and the U.S. Hispanic market. He was responsible for the adaptation of *Los Simuladores* (*The Pretenders*), a comedy series for Mexico's Televisa, which earned an International Emmy Nomination as Best Comedy Series in 2010; for all creative and production aspects of Nickelodeon's *Isa TKM* (*Isa Te Quiero Mucho*) and *Isa TK+* (*Isa Te Quiero Más*), the first original telenovelas made for a cable channel; for *Niñas Mal* (*Bad Girls*), a teleseries based on a Sony film that was the first teleseries for MTV Latin America; and Executive in Charge of other hit telenovelas in the United States and Colombia. Marlon then became Vice President of Development and Programming Scripted for the worldwide production operation. He led initiatives in various territories.

In 2012, Marlon launched the Center for Innovation and Creativity in Media (CIC Media), a consulting and media production firm focusing on content innovation management, production, and training based in Miami, Florida. CIC Media has a global scope and targets clients in the United States, Latin America, and other major territories worldwide. Through CIC Media, Marlon is interested in continued implementation of his value chain of innovation model designed for media content creation. This model is to ensure creativity, innovation, and the proliferation of successful media content for multiple digital TV platforms in the media industry.

At CIC Media Marlon has developed and produced shows for Cisneros Media, Sony Entertainment Television, and SBS Broadcasting and designed the Hola TV prototype, the first cable channel based on the global magazine franchise *Hello* (*¡Hola!*). In 2014 NBC Universo chose his original drama series *Maria Among the Dead* (*Maria Entre Todos Los Muertos*) for development. He has also consulted for Zodiak Americas and provided creative services to Warner Brothers for the adaptation of the drama series *Nip/Tuck* in Colombia, *Gossip Girl* in Mexico and China, and *The OC* in Thailand. Other clients include Sony Music, HBO, and Televisa International. He is currently implementing an innovation lab for the global entertainment formats operation of Televisa International. Marlon has also successfully launched a series of seminars on innovation for media content creation that have been presented in Miami (the University of Miami), Mexico City (Instituto Tecnológico de Monterrey at Mexico City, DF), Caracas (Premium Theater), and San Francisco (San Francisco State University) and for private clients such as HBO.

Marlon may be reached at Facebook, Facebook.com/InnovationMCC; Twitter, @InnovationMCC; and Email: imccbook@cicmedia.tv.

Web
Added
Value™

At J. Ross Publishing we are committed to providing today's professional with practical, hands-on tools that enhance the learning experience and give readers an opportunity to apply what they have learned. That is why we offer free ancillary materials available for download on this book and all participating Web Added Value™ publications. These online resources may include interactive versions of material that appears in the book or supplemental templates, worksheets, models, plans, case studies, proposals, spreadsheets and assessment tools, among other things. Whenever you see the WAV™ symbol in any of our publications it means bonus materials accompany the book and are available from the Web Added Value™ Download Resource Center at www.jrosspub.com.

Downloads available for *Innovation for Media Content Creation: Tools and Strategies for Delivering Successful Content* consist of:

- A keynote presentation (from seminars) with real-world examples and references
- A team matrix to use in building and understanding the roles and necessary skill sets required for an innovative team
- The discovery circle representation in full color
- The circle of innovation representation in full color
- Worksheet templates for:
  - The innovation value chain
  - Exploration control
  - A sample evaluation database
  - Creative and production databases
- A sample submission release
- A pre-bible checklist for projects in development

STEP 1

UNDERSTAND STRATEGY, CREATIVITY, AND INNOVATION

PART I: STRATEGY

1

THE IMPORTANCE OF BEING STRATEGIC IN THE PROCESS OF INNOVATION

Consumption of media is growing at an accelerated rate thanks to multiplication of the TV platform in several exposition windows (computers, mobile phones, tablets, TV sets, etc.). This multiplication of the TV platform is defining and creating valuable opportunities for creative individuals who want to build a career producing content to entertain people, and these opportunities are generating a wave of content that defies structures and the old schools of thought, opening up new ways to tell stories and reach audiences in rather unexpected ways. Advertisers, TV networks, technology companies, user-enabled internet portals, movie rental corporations, electronic manufacturers, and mobile companies are adding to a growing melting pot of possibilities, all striving for content, which is nothing but good news for creative individuals. No matter how diverse the television experience becomes, and how the new concept of "transmedia" takes over, the importance of content will remain intact: audiences need to be entertained and writers need to bring relevant content to them. To secure relevancy in this new competitive environment, and to become a player and efficiently direct creative efforts to yield innovations, writers and creative professionals need to *be strategic* more than ever.

Developing a strategic notion (or perception) will allow you to be a more-intelligent and assertive creative individual and will help you to make better and more-educated career decisions. You will need a road map. You will need to develop a set of personal goals and then strive for them. You will also need to understand your strengths and weaknesses and then get the best out of them. You will need to team up with people and establish a network of contacts that will become your bridge to success. You will need to create a path and figure out how to walk it. To walk this path, you not only need to be intuitive, but you also need to know the terrain, and what to do, and to be clear about what comes next. Having a personal strategy will give you the inner motivation needed to pursue your path and help you match your creative interests with those of entertainment companies or entities to secure growth and mutual satisfaction.

Being strategic is a trait you must develop to be successful in the creative content business. Being strategic is not easy though. The road to success in entertainment has ups and downs, but in the end these ups and downs represent experiences that will help you to be stronger and to build the necessary knowledge to anticipate and better react to changes and obstacles. You must be flexible and alert and always willing to learn something new. Everything is a source of creativity. A well-processed concept might yield the always-expected innovation!

BEING STRATEGIC AND CREATIVE

The idealization of creating, producing, and owning "the show" everyone is talking about—the show that is able to attract advertisers and stay on the air for long periods of time or produce repeated downloads and streaming in different digital platforms—has writers, producers, and TV and media executives working tirelessly across the globe. Bilton (2007) stated that this notion has created two myths: the genius myth and the Hollywood myth. I would add a third, the new media myth. The *genius myth* is associated with the notion that it takes a lonely genius to come up with great and outstanding concepts; the *Hollywood myth* focuses on the illusion of hitting the Hollywood jackpot; and the *new media myth* leads us to believe that anybody can be the next Justin Bieber or pop sensation and be skyrocketed to terrestrial stardom thanks to the support of viral social networks of internet fans. There are, of course, few who actually do "make it" and find glory, strengthening the power of these myths, but fortunately this experience is not necessarily the "rule of the game." Those with real drive, strategic sense, and knowledge of the world they are in can succeed.

J.J. Abrams, Jerry Bruckheimer, David E. Kelly, and Shonda Rhimes have become solid references of successful creative and strategic individuals in the entertainment industry. Each of them has gone on from being a writer or a director with potential to become an enterprise and generator of content that pleases millions of viewers every week. They have been able to innovate and come up with a stable pipeline of content through time. Each of them embraced the industry, understood what was missing and what was needed, and brought to life a show that filled that void.

J.J. Abrams created *Felicity* (1998 – 2002) to serve a young audience in search of identity, reinvented science fiction (sci-fi) television with *Lost* (2004 – 2010), showed a new side to the world of undercover CIA agents in *Alias* (2001– 2006), and in 2008 brought us a post *The X-Files* investigative tale in *Fringe* (2008 – 2013) and later another lost world story in *Revolution* (2012 – 2014).

Jerry Bruckheimer has built a staple name in crime investigative shows (not to mention his successful and prolific film career). He produced one of the most successful drama series ever, *CSI*, and developed the TV franchise concept by creating *CSI Miami* and *CSI NY* without cannibalization between the two shows. He also produced *Without a Trace* and *Cold Case* and has led the production of *The Amazing Race*, one of the most successful reality shows ever.

David E. Kelly has dedicated his creative life to the exploration of human relations and behavior in the legal world. His shows *Ally McBeal*, *The Practice*, *Boston Legal*, and recently *Murphy's Law* are all unique thanks to the very peculiar characteristics of the leading characters and the way they practice law.

Shonda Rhimes broke through with *Grey's Anatomy* by showing a fresh and intimate youthful view of a hospital through the lives of resident doctors. After 6 years on the air, she continued innovating and then spun the show into *Private Practice* and more recently created *Off the Map*, a merge of *Survivor* with her own *Grey's Anatomy* series. After reinventing the medical drama genre, Shonda Rhimes continued showing us how love stories between real, diverse, and strong characters in chaotic and difficult work environments collided and mastered her offering by switching to Washington, DC, the most powerful place on earth, through her series *Scandal*.

These showbiz stars grew to be who they are and to specialize in what they do and they succeeded. They all started from scratch and built a path until hitting stardom. Their careers illustrate creativity, flexibility, knowledge, and consistency and a very specific content strategy. They are strategic in nature and always have been. They first worked to build a name: they understood the nature of the industry, developed their own competences, gathered knowledge and resources, and stayed consistent. For example, Kelly, Bruckheimer, and Rhimes never stop exploring characters, relationships, and different angles to show a new aspect of the world they live in (legal, investigative, and medical). J.J. Abrams is eclectic and radical in his proposals and prefers to come up with something new and different every time. Bruckheimer (fiction, film, TV, and reality) prefers to diversify his portfolio and try different genres. These creative individuals innovate in different ways, making their names into brands. Now they are institutions with innovative catalogs and complex operations to create content. We want to hear about "what's next" from them. They are trendsetters who help define the context of entertainment—the same context you have to understand today to figure out how to break into it and then create a new context with you in it.

In today's world, being innovative is not just related to coming out with awesome concepts but also to understanding how to bring to life ideas that matter and have a real purpose in the industry. To accomplish this goal, the same as our illustrious role models did, you need to be strategic—and to be strategic, you need to understand the forces behind the complex media industry to be able to implement a framework of operation that will allow you to make proper use of the resources at hand to ensure creativity and innovation over time.

THE MEANING OF STRATEGY: *WHO, WHERE,* AND *WHAT*

Common to hear from creative professionals is that the term *strategy* has nothing to do with them—that it is solely related to business people. And they are right in the sense that the business world moves based on strategies which are commonly prepared by business-savvy professionals working in the so-called strategic areas of corporations (business development, strategic planning, etc.). But guess what? You want to be a creative force that generates successful media content and money. Thus you want to be a business or to drive a business through the creation of content. Let's say that you want to have a creative business. As a result, no matter where you are in the chain of content generation, you are also part of the business. So, absolutely necessary is that you understand the meaning of strategy and then generate a strategy to succeed as a creative business force.

Strategy is about readiness and having a framework for action to embrace the future (Johnston & Bate, 2013). This framework provides direction and a capacity to respond to changes in the environment to continue growing and succeeding. Depending on the clarity of your framework, so that subsequently your strategy is clear as well, you will be able to sail through the changes.

There are two dimensions in the preparation of a strategy. One dimension is at a *macro* level and is called "corporate strategy." The second dimension corresponds to a *micro* level, which is more specific and results-driven, and is called "business strategy." The macro level serves to define what industry a company or a creative individual wants to compete in (telecommunications, electronics manufacturing, etc.). The more-specific micro level defines how the company or individual is going to compete to generate revenue (based on differentiation, cost advantage, or a combination). The mix of both levels defines the overall strategy.

Strategy provides a necessary sense of direction and identity (Grant, 2002). No matter whether you are leading the creative efforts in a company or deciding what kind of content you want to do in your own creative career, a crucial starting point is to define the macro-layer of your strategy by answering three basic questions: *who, where,* and *what*? *Who* represents your identity as creator or a creative entity. *Where* unveils the world you are going to compete in. *What* identifies your resources.

Part I will focus on the macro level (the *who*, *where*, and *what*) to define your core sense and macro-strategy as a creative entity. Then the remaining parts will walk you through how to generate and implement your specific creative strategy to achieve content innovation.

2

DEFINING *WHO* YOU ARE: CREATIVE INDIVIDUAL OR CREATIVE EXECUTIVE

The creative industry is managed by people and operated thanks to people. As a consequence, there are different layers of interaction in which people with different capacities and responsibilities work together to move the full machinery that will later yield a new show. The idea behind this chapter is for you to gain an understanding of the types of responsibilities of creative professionals to enable you to decide and define *who* you are.

CREATIVE PROFESSIONALS

Creative professionals are of two types: creative individuals and creative executives. Important is to recognize the roles of both. Creative individuals work together with creative executives who are the representatives of the industry that ignite the production of content. Creative individuals and executives need each other; they work in a system of interdependence. But how does that system work? How can these executives and generators of content understand each other so they can succeed in the process of media creation? How can executives and generators of content strive for innovation in creative industries? How can you understand these roles and decide where you fit in? What are the functionalities of creative professionals?

Creative individuals. Creative individuals are professionals who work directly in the crafting of a product. Writers, producers, and directors form this group. Creative individuals can be part of a corporation or work independently. Creative individuals present their projects to corporations that are looking for content or they are hired directly by corporations to render the necessary services to create a show. In the first case, individuals who present their projects to corporations, the creative individual negotiates the rights of their creation with a company that wants to acquire it. In the second case, individuals who are hired directly by corporations to render the necessary creative services, the creative individual usually does not own the property created, the company does. Creative individuals can also become show runners and manage large numbers of people and production teams. They might deliver a show and interact with the creative executives in the corporation. These creative individuals could then grow in their abilities to become creative companies (production companies, writing companies, etc.), such as Rhimes' *Shondaland* or Abrams' *Bad Robot*, or creative executives.

Creative executives. Creative executives are professionals who work in corporations to create, find, develop, and produce content. They acquire content rights and form creative teams to procure in-house generation of ideas that will then be taken to other creative executives for consideration (within the same company or another). Creative executives work in different aspects of the creation process (search, development, and production) and can be found in production companies, and TV networks, on the internet, and on mobile channels, etc. They are leaders who are capable of shepherding the process of creation and providing feedback and guidelines to creative individuals in their own companies. They also lead the processes of exploration and evaluation and make recommendations on what to do with concepts and ideas presented by creative individuals. A creative executive might hire creative individuals to further give substance and structure to an idea. A creative executive therefore not only identifies content but also creates content. Some creative executives cross over to become creative individuals or to form creative companies of their own. Creative executives can also be development executives at different levels (VP, director, manager, coordinator, content analysts, etc.). Anyone in a leadership position within a company, small or big, with the responsibility of finding or creating content for a firm is a creative executive.

What side are you on—or want to be on? Do you want to be a creative individual or do you want to be on the executive side? Not ready with an answer yet? Well, here is a little more context. Figure 2-1 represents the interaction dynamic between creative professionals in a studio and a commissioning broadcaster.

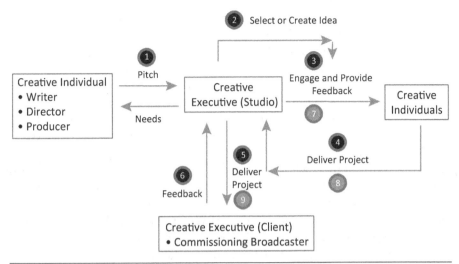

Figure 2-1. The interaction dynamic between creative professionals.

As indicated in Figure 2-1, the interaction between a creative individual and a creative executive starts with conversations about needs and the development/reception of a pitch (1). The material provided goes through a process of revision and if selected (2) goes through a process of interaction between the creative executive and the creative individual (3) until the project is delivered (4). The creative executive takes this project and presents it to a client (5), also called a commissioning broadcaster. The person on the client side is also a creative executive who provides feedback to the studio's creative executive (6). New feedback is then given to the creative individual (7) who will generate a revised project. The process repeats itself as necessary. This iteration allows the creative professionals involved to enhance the project until it is ready for the next step in the process of development (8, 9).

Interaction could also be directly between the creative individual and the creative executive at a TV channel. This situation happens more often when a broadcaster is vertically integrated and possesses a production infrastructure (very common in U.S. Hispanic and Latin American TV, e.g., Televisa, Telemundo Networks, and Fox channels).

INTERACTION BETWEEN CREATIVE PROFESSIONALS

Writers and producers often approach development creative executives asking, "What are you looking for?" The answer depends on whether the executive is working for a studio, a TV network, or a production company, and the answer could range from wide open to very specific. Studio executives provide diverse answers because they deal with multiple channels and genres and keep a multi-valent state of mind to decide what is good or not for a specific broadcaster. The answer, however, could also be more precise, if coming from a network executive who focuses on a specific channel or group of channels, time frame, or genre. In the case of executives working for production companies, the answer depends on their degree of specialization in genres (scripted, nonscripted, comedy, drama, movies, telenovelas, series, target audiences, etc.). The answer is rarely fixed.

Whatever the case, creative executives rely on a filtering process to find new and fresh ideas, from which usually only 5% or less make it to the next stage of development. Executives define the premises for the filtering process and rely on the judgment of groups of experts who evaluate the concepts and grade the property with a "pass" or a "consider." The effectiveness of this filtering process varies. Some filtering processes are very objective and rely on a solid system of internal checks and balances to fully evaluate a show from different perspectives (creative, marketing, programming, economic). If the result of the filtering process is positive, then the show moves into the next stage.

In some cases, however, the filtering process can be so unfocused that some of the ideas chosen might not even be what the entity acquiring the content really needs, which on occasion only comes to light too late in the process—after an audience has already seen the show and rejected it. This situation is part of the gamble and the risk, which I know sounds frustrating. You might be wondering, if a development executive does not have the right answers, then who does? If a development executive is the gatekeeper of the development process and decides what goes and what does not, and still makes a mistake, then who does not? Problems arise when an executive does not use a clear strategy and a fair system of content evaluation and is not aware of changes and needs in the market. Believe it or not, these situations happen. They are the result of biased creative environments that get stuck on notions that do not deliver innovative results. These notions encompass orthodoxies, past data (analytics), safe choices, and a lack of market knowledge. As a result, the strategic process of screening media content may be flawed, weak, and sometimes not even ready for the concept presented. Again, this is not always the case, but it can happen—that is what makes the process of selection so risky.

Media content production is risky for corporations because the investment is usually high. For that reason the process of selection has to be tight and rigorous, imposing hurdles and sometimes limited to creative ideas coming from already validated or known sources or "connections" that do not defy the status quo. Creative professionals, following the simple notion that connections are essential and the key driver to getting their shows read and ultimately produced, work their way through contacts within the studio system or they find a good agent to help them get noticed by creative executives. To avoid burning bridges, agents want to be sure that whatever they recommend is good. If the project fails, millions of dollars will be lost, and along with that jobs, and the companies involved will be at risk.

If you become relevant in the exploration process as a creative individual, you must make the best of every opportunity, and to do that you must be strategic. If you become a secure source of content, then you have made a "name" for yourself in the industry, a brand, and you will probably succeed. In the end though, it all depends on a creative executive's criteria for ruling out something "bad," even if it came from a friend or secure source.

Creative professionals, individuals and executives, need to understand their part in the system of interaction with the industry. If a creative individual presents an irrelevant or weak product for consideration, and if for some reason the show gets chosen as a result of a biased and flawed process and fails, this failure will most likely cause ultimate harm to the writer, the executive, and everyone involved—which could leave everyone associated with the failed show out of the system and consideration for future work.

Creative individuals need to learn how to be strategic and to implement their own creative processes to improve the probability of having a concept chosen and then succeed with an audience. If the written or produced content is weak, then the show will probably fail, but on the other hand, creative executives need to maintain fresh systems of exploration, research, and market analysis to constantly rejuvenate the process of content generation and stay on top of the innovative curve. They must be very precise about the needs of the network or the company they represent to better direct the work of creative individuals. A writer might be terrific, but if the writer receives the wrong indications, the work done might turn into something bad. Creative executives need to be open to new and out-of-the-box concepts that might become breakthroughs. The jobs of creative individuals and creative executives are fascinating and compelling. Working together they have the power to turn something good into something greater.

Simply put, creative executives (also called activators and facilitators in the process of media content creation) manage, lead, and provide strategic direction, whereas creative individuals are creators, executers, and developers. They deliver. So if you want to work for Sony Pictures or Google and someday become the chief creative officer of one of those corporations, then you want to be a creative executive (facilitator, activator). If you want to write scripts, direct a TV series, be the show runner for a TV show, or even act like Mindy Kaling (*The Mindy Project*), Tina Fey (*30 Rock*), or Lena Dunham (*Girls*), then you want to be a creative individual (creator and executor). (Chapter 10, *Implementing the Process of Innovation*, will explore further the different roles professionals have in the process of innovation.)

Now do you know what side of the equation you want to be on? Both positions are important and, of course, all manage risky situations. Whichever path you choose, the important aspect is that you do your job right. You want to find and bring forward creative solutions. You want to be an innovator and to succeed. To avoid unpleasant hurdles and a load of negative situations, you must be strategic. By being strategic, you understand how to address your creative adrenaline and how to put your creative solutions into operation. But first and foremost, you must understand the industry.

Once you know *who* you want to be, next is to understand the *where*—the world you are stepping into or are already in.

3

FINDING *WHERE* YOU ARE

THE MEDIA INDUSTRY

The media industry is part of the entertainment or creative industries. Its operation relies on specific media to generate revenue (Figure 3-1). The media industry is also a complex scenario composed of different sectors. These sectors are defined by the nature of the platform of exposition or the medium, primarily: TV, music, film, internet, theater, print, mobile, radio, games, and home entertainment. Each sector is also identified as an industry, with specific activities that allow the generation and packaging of media for consumption by different audiences, either in a mass or a boutique fashion.

Media is the content that is created, produced, and then delivered to audiences through platforms of exposition. Media comes in the form of news, music, books, music videos, movies, theater plays, TV shows, webisodes, mobisodes, etc. Media content is also referred to as intellectual property (IP). IP constitutes the main asset generated in the media industry, which bases all of its transactions on value.

According to Bilton (2007), director of the Master of Arts program in Creative and Media Enterprises at the University of Warwick in England, the economies of the media industry usually favor those who are exploiting IPs rather than those who are generating them. Exploiters of IP are studios, record companies, big media conglomerates, distribution firms, production companies, and agents. To exploit their properties, IP generators (writers, songwriters) usually go to studios and corporations with strong capital assets. These creative IP professionals are individuals who might be independent or part of a corporate creative process and

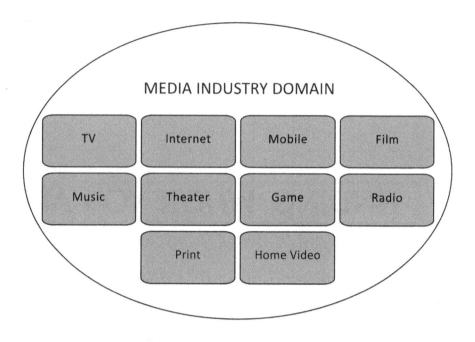

Figure 3-1. The entertainment industry domain.

who, depending on the leverage and degree of independence they have, are able to negotiate fair rights fees and revenue-sharing deals that ensure profit participation throughout the life cycle of the exploitation of the property.

The media industry operates as a function of three variables: capital, uncertainty, and risk. *Capital* has to do with resources (cash, media assets, infrastructure, and equipment) owned by a company to activate its processes to generate revenue and profits. *Uncertainty* has to do with the inability to predict the outcome of a specific action. *Risk* is related to the amount of capital assets that could be lost versus the benefits that could be obtained if the outcome of a specific action is negative or positive. In the media industry, capital assets are usually impressive and uncertainty and risks are high. Uncertainty follows a cycle of interdependence between the capital assets and the media content. Depending on the success of a particular media project, capital assets are activated and, if the project is successful, capital grows. For that reason, resources, employment, and continued work might be tenuous and unpredictable, sometimes with little chance of career progression or job certainty for creative professionals (Bilton, 2007).

For example, all of the major studios (Viacom, Sony Pictures, Warner Brothers, NBC Universal, News Corp, and Disney) possess vast capital assets represented by their overall infrastructure, profits, and value of the content library they represent (media assets). Their libraries of content generate revenue for their companies. So the more successful the content is, the more valuable it is and the more value the overall company achieves. As a result, studios invest their capital (represented by money) in the procurement of new successful media assets to continue their growth and to maintain their mammoth level of operation. This business model obviously not only works for the big majors but also for mid-size, small, and even individuals in the industry.

Executives in the industry value IPs through a process of exploration that contemplates creative analysis, market assessment, speculation, and corporate enthusiasm. This valuation process could create price wars and desperation on the corporate side, all under the expectation that the IPs will generate tremendous wealth. Creative individuals (should) benefit from this competitive valuation process by negotiating terms that ensure participation throughout, improving their chances to succeed and make a living from their creative work. (*Note:* Many creative individuals who lack negotiating and business skills, hire lawyers and agents or join unions to represent them when negotiating terms.)

The media industry is thus a complex scenario in which creative individuals work and give their best to satisfy audiences and corporations and to ultimately get paid. Corporations and creative individuals will continue to benefit from this model of exploitation, but to actively be part of it, and to get the best part from it, you must understand four key aspects of the media industry:

- The TV multiplatform landscape
- The economic nature of the traditional TV industry
- The TV development cycle
- The dynamic for exposition of content

THE TV MULTIPLATFORM LANDSCAPE

TV has been an industry since the late 1930s when it was created as an electronic medium to broadcast aural/visual images through a few channels. Toward the end of the twentieth century, convergence of the electronic and digital industries was inevitable, and the medium evolved to a digital multiplatform with sophisticated and diverse channel offerings that included a vast variety of content to satisfy different audience needs.

From TV, other forms of entertainment have derived, pretty much to let people enjoy the same content in different ways not necessarily live, but whenever they wanted to see the content. The advent of home video platforms such as VHS in the 1980s, DVDs in the 1990s, and more recently DVRs in the 2000s gave audiences the possibility of controlling and deciding when to watch content. The internet and the mobile spectrum of communication further catalyzed the digital revolution of platforms of exposition. Transmission and access of data through these new media platforms led to a proliferation of new options for watching content, such as Internet Protocol Television (IPTV) channels and mobile TV, and thus a new digital world to be considered by creative minds working on content.

Within the digital landscape, wireless and internet platforms are capable of bringing content ranging from user-generated videos to high-end TV shows and movies in high definition. Audiences today live in a multiplatform world of options and can now watch content anywhere through their computers, mobile phones, mobile TVs, tablets, and other types of mobile internet-enabled entertainment platforms or portable devices.

Only a few years ago, it seemed impossible to think of a way to deliver content in excellent quality through devices different from the regular TV or cable signal. In 1997, for example, all thoughts were on HDTV and the adoption of this technology. The internet was taking baby steps in processing multimedia. Today everything has merged. No longer is there a single-medium world, but instead the world is a multiplatform one with a diverse and segmented audience. Figure 3-2 presents this evolution.

Multimedia processing has to do with the ability of a device to bring the audience aural/visual content, music, written information, books, games, movies, etc. The internet has become a multimedia platform and has embedded all forms of media entertainment into one place. The internet has enhanced its multimedia capability to process incredibly large quantities of information and video via streaming and downloading at outstanding definition and audio quality, thus allowing viewers to add the option of viewing content through their computers. This convergence process has gone even further through game or multimedia internet-enabled consoles (e.g., Playstation, Wii, Xbox) that offer the possibility of bringing to a TV set an array of internet-based TV channels (IPTV) some of them tailor-made to the viewer's taste. This overwhelming and ever-growing number of digital choices has created the need to differentiate and stand out. Creators of content need to be innovative "smart" in understanding how branding, promotion, and marketing are done via the array of social networks, consoles, and cable boxes, combined with other existing media platforms of communication.

Technology will continue growing and evolving. The generation of content will invariably be adapting to trends and new conditions in the market. Content is king. Content will never go away. The TV industry will continue evolving as a medium to bring content to the masses. TV continues to be the best platform for visualizing content. Variations of TV platforms always end with the word TV: internet TV, Wireless TV, HDTV, 3DTV, etc. For that reason, no matter what platform content is on, the TV concept will be the same, and the creation of content that will be featured on those TV screens continues to be important. Important

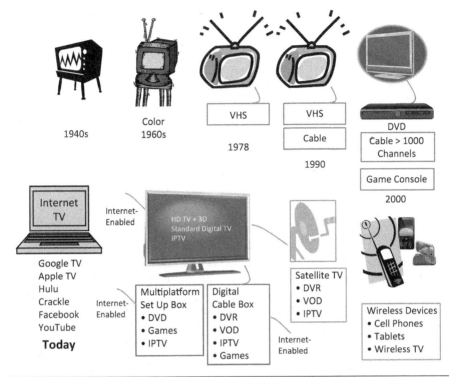

Figure 3-2. Television evolution.

to understand, however, is that there are different economic models to sustain the proliferation of traditional and nontraditional media.

THE ECONOMIC NATURE OF THE TRADITIONAL TV INDUSTRY

The TV industry is valued in billions of dollars and is composed of content providers, service providers, procurers, distributors, sponsors, and outlets or platforms of exposition. The interrelation of these players defines what is called the *business cycle for content generation* (Figure 3-3).

The business cycle for content generation starts as the result of interaction between a content provider and a procurer of content who finances the development and production of the show. Service providers are hired to secure the proper infrastructure and resources to produce the show. The TV content is then delivered to distributors in the form of a drama series, made-for-TV movie, sitcom, soap opera, newscast, reality show, sportscast, documentary, etc.

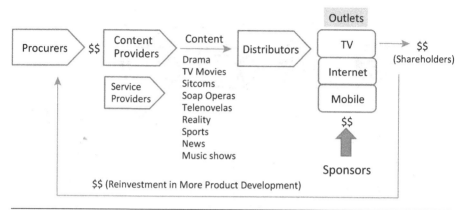

Figure 3-3. The TV industry players and business cycle for content generation.

The finished product is sold by distributors of content to outlets of exposition for airing. The outlet of exposition then offers advertisers the possibility of reaching an audience at a specific price. The money generated lets the outlets of exposition recoup their investment and provides profits that will benefit the circulation of money throughout the cycle and allow procurers of content to continue investing. Specific descriptions of the main players in this cycle are:

- Procurers: Financiers in the form of companies, such as TV networks, TV studios, and internet and mobile or telecommunication corporations; banks; or investors who secure funds for the creation and production of content

- Content providers: Writers, producers, and directors who are responsible for creating and producing content that will ultimately be exposed in a media platform

- Service providers: Individuals and organizations who secure equipment, infrastructure, and human resources to produce content

- Distributors: Individuals and organizations who ensure that content is acquired by platforms of exposition

- Outlets of exposition: Media outlets such as TV channels, internet channels, and mobile channels that are the ultimate means of reaching an end user or audience

- Sponsors: Individuals and organizations who take advantage of the relationship between the platform of exposition and the audience, buying time and access to the TV on-air schedule to expose their brands and products

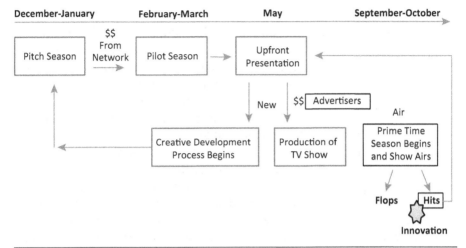

Figure 3-4. The development cycle in U.S. network TV.

THE TV DEVELOPMENT CYCLE

The quest for innovative content defines the cycles of creation and development of content in the TV industry. This quest keeps the industry moving tirelessly. Each country or market has a very specific development cycle. Figure 3-4 presents the development cycle for preparation of prime-time programming for free TV (networks) in the United States.

As illustrated in Figure 3-4, a show is first prepared to be pitched to executives in a network (Pitch Season, December and January). If the show receives a green light, the network secures funding for a pilot to be made during the months of February and March (Pilot Season). The pilots are then reviewed by executives who select the few that will make it to the Upfront Presentation in May. An upfront presentation consists of presentations to advertisers of shows that will be launched in the next season. During these presentations, advertisers provide support to the networks by investing their advertising money in the shows and time schedules they see as being strong. This revenue stream secures funds for the production of the TV shows which then start airing during the months of September and October (Air). If a show is a hit, it will receive a new season pick-up order and be presented as a returning hit in the next year's TV network line ups. If not, the show will be cancelled. The creative process for the next season starts right after the upfront presentations in May. While new shows are entering the production stage, developers of content start bringing new ideas to life so they can be pitched between December and January. The process then repeats itself.

Creative individuals must understand the cycles of the various industries they work in to better understand how content is procured and produced. For example, the cable industry has a different development cycle as do the multiple TV industries in the international marketplace. In the multiplatform world, the process of content preparation and exposition is more flexible and less structured than network or cable TV. Although content seems to pop up without specific timing, mobile and internet platforms of exposition are starting to analyze seasonal effects and audience behavior to better understand the best moment to grab people's attention and launch shows. Depending on audience behavior, multicasters of content then decide the best time of the year to put their content on a specific platform and sell that event to advertisers or a subscriber base. All of these dynamics generate new and specific cycles for content generation.

As an industry in evolution, TV content generators must understand the development cycles so they can respond and adjust to events. Having a capacity to respond to different developmental scenarios will determine the creative level required and the innovation potential of the team in charge of the creation of content.

The Dynamic for Exposition of Content

Content travels through different outlets of exposition at different instances in time. Each instance defines what is called a *window of exposition*. Each window of exposition has a very specific duration. The value to license a show to a window is defined by the success of the content when it was launched. Distribution companies control this exhibition and pricing dynamic.

An example of a traditional window dynamic of exposition is that for a movie:

- First window: Release in theaters
- Second window: Release in private, exclusive venues (e.g., airplanes)
- Third window: Release on premium pay-TV channels
- Fourth window: Video-on-demand release through cable/satellite boxes
- Fifth window: Home video release for purchase and rental (DVDs) and online services:
  - Internet distribution, geo-filtered (only available in the country of origin)
  - Release through online and mobile services (e.g., Netflix or Amazon).
- Sixth window: International distribution

In the case of TV content, the dynamic could be:

- First window: TV Network
- Second window: Almost simultaneous release:

- Private, exclusive venues such as hotels and airplanes
- Video-on-demand services through cable/satellite boxes
- Home video release for purchase and rental (DVDs) plus IPTV-OTT; online or mobile services (e.g., Netfilx or Amazon)
- Internet and mobile release through specialized services (e.g., iTunes, Hulu, Crackle)
- Third window: International distribution

In the case of the mobile and internet TV industries, the platforms present content to an audience in an on-demand fashion. Availability for streaming or downloading depends on the characteristics of the content:

- TV shows: The showcasing of TV shows over the internet and on mobile devices is still attached to the momentum determined by the channel (a free TV network or a cable channel) and the region of origin. TV networks allow free downloads (or downloads at very low prices) of an episode a few days after the show airs and for a limited time. After this short window, the content is unavailable until the formal home video release window allows users to acquire a full season at a price. The content is also limited to the country where the show originally aired and is blocked from international downloading or streaming to protect the international distribution of the show. This concept is also called *geo-filtering*.
- Original content for a platform: Digital platforms are now creating their own content and defining the particular dynamics for exposition. For example, online sites such as BBC Switch, Netflix, Amazon, Hulu, and Crackle are developing content that can only be seen on those internet platforms (via IPTV, a personal computer, or a mobile device). Netflix and Amazon are making available all episodes for a season at launch date.
- Library of movies and TV shows (archives of content): Platforms such as Netflix and Amazon have access to extensive libraries to showcase classics or content from the past.

Transmedia Windowing

Some internet and mobile platforms present content first in small episodes and then present it later on regular TV channels as half-hour or 1-hour shows that compile the short episodes into a longer form. Platforms that usually do this are TV networks that have a strong internet component. BBC, for example, has BBC Switch to showcase an internet series throughout the week composed of five 8-minute episodes; then BBC2 airs a full 1-hour episode made up of the five 8-minute online episodes. The windowing dynamic is:

- First window: Internet or mobile episodes (webisodes or mobisodes)
- Second window: TV (a weekly episode summary of internet or mobile episodes)
- Third window: Movie
- Fourth window: DVD and online sell-through systems

The series *Beat Girl*, which aired in the United Kingdom in 2013 through MTV's online platform as a 12-part webseries, is an example of transmedia. The full series was later turned into five half-hour episodes that aired on MTV's cable platform episodes. Afterward, a feature film version was assembled with all episodes and a special theatrical release was prepared for fans. The movie is now available on DVD and sells through Amazon and Hulu. The show also has a mobile application, a dedicated website, an e-book, a game, and a presence in all social media platforms (Bernardo, 2013).

Also in the transmedia context, complementing media is created to add value to the TV viewing experience. For example, in the United States, *Lost* aired as a TV episode every week. Internet viewers were able to see alternative stories depicting short situations involving the castaways that were not part of the main cast. The experience therefore became multidimensional, letting viewers see beyond the TV episode, i.e., through events occurring when the show was not on the air. Nowadays most shows have a multiplatform component. Examples include *The Office* and *The Walking Dead.*

The transmedia concept evolved to a higher level of interrelation among viewers thanks to the proliferation of content sites on social network platforms. Facebook has created the possibility for viewers to interact while watching a show and to even interact with the show's characters to acquire more knowledge about their inner thoughts and the motivations behind their actions. Through these social networks, viewers also have access to the TV show for limited periods of time.

The possibilities are endless. The transmedia world is finding its own structure. Multiplatform ways of exposition are allowing audiences to have multidimensional experiences and a very independent way of watching content whenever they want.

Try this activity:

- Pick a country and research the country. Then draw a map for the media industry development cycle in that country.
- Draw the development cycle for the cable industry in the United States.

- Draw the development cycle for the generation of content for mobile TV. Will it differ from the TV model?
- Draw the development cycle for the generation of IPTV content.
- Draw a window of the exposition dynamic for a TV series created exclusively for an iPad mobile device with an internet and TV component.
- Draw a window of the exposition dynamic for an internet miniseries with a TV summary component.

4

ASSESSING *WHAT* YOU HAVE

Now that you have an idea of *who* you are (a creative individual or creative executive) and *where* you are (how the multiplatform world of entertainment *is*), you need to assess *what*—what resources do you have? Resources can be classified as:

- Material
- Intellectual
- Emotional

MATERIAL RESOURCES

The material resources aspect is related to monetary resources, intellectual properties, and equipment.

Monetary resources. How much money do you (or don't you) have? The answer to this question will help you decide to either work on your own or for a company (either as a creative individual or as a creative executive). Access to money might come in different ways:

- Through a job position: Being hired to write for a company
- From investors: Finding individuals with money who are willing to support your creative work (These individuals could be producers or business developers with access to investors who are willing to create a company around your talent.)
- Through the licensing of your intellectual property rights: A transactional activity that will provide the funding you need to develop or produce content for a specific creative entity (a studio, TV network, etc.)

- From reinvesting personal earnings/savings in your creative activities: After a success and the receipt of a healthy income (being ready for the next step of reinvesting in yourself)

Intellectual properties. As a writer you might have already developed or written content that you own and that has been produced. These intellectual properties certainly have value and can be sold in the marketplace. As a producer you need to have content, stories, and scripts that you either own or have access to. The more of these resources you need, the more money you will have to raise or find to acquire or develop content.

Equipment. Equipment resources are computers, books, internet access, wireless tablets, applications, writing software, cable TV, subscriptions to creative or industry publications, etc. As a director, you might even need to have your own cameras and other resources to produce video or film shorts to showcase your talent.

INTELLECTUAL RESOURCES

The intellectual resources aspect is what you know. What are your key skills? Are you an academically trained writer or television producer? Weigh what you have learned at this point in your career and what you can potentially do with it. The intellectual aspect includes three different types of individuals: novice, mid-experienced, and accomplished.

Novice or beginner. These professionals are individuals who have just graduated from college and have the necessary knowledge to "get a foot in the door." They have rather generic skills. Their careers and specializing in a specific area are ahead of them. At this point, they are able to choose what they want to become—a creative individual or a creative executive. Some novices coming out of college already know that they will not be writers because they want to be producers, directors, or editors and to pursue the best paths that will align them with that career objective. Also in novice category are individuals coming from other backgrounds such as law, finance, etc. who are interested in changing careers and becoming creative professionals. These individuals usually consider enrolling in extension courses to obtain the necessary training or they pursue graduate certification to obtain know-how.

Mid-experienced. These individuals have been in the industry for 5+ years and have started to collect credits in the world of entertainment.

Accomplished. The accomplished category includes exceptionally creative professionals with 15+ years of experience in the industry who have succeeded in the development and production of content. They possess a proven track record (e.g., Shonda Rhimes, Jerry Bruckenheimer, and J.J. Abrams). More recently, creative professionals such as Mindy Kaling and Lena Dunham have achieved success at a young age. In less than 10 years they have become accomplished writers and producers: Mindy Kaling as an actress, comedian, writer, director, and producer and Lena Dunham as an actress/creator of *Girls*.

Note: Perhaps as a writer with 10 years of career experience you have developed extraordinary expertise in sitcoms or 1-hour action dramas. Perhaps you are an authority on sci-fi. Maybe you have spent 5 years evaluating and participating in the development of content. You may well be on the right career path for becoming an accomplished executive or maybe jumping to the independent side and becoming a producer or writer. This know-how is part of your intellectual resources. All of these resources should be made available in the form of a résumé or credit list. LinkedIn and IMDb are good sites to visit to get a sense of the types of intellectual resources creative individuals and executives have collected throughout their careers.

EMOTIONAL RESOURCES

The creative industry is a very passionate industry. Your ability to manage your emotions will play a very important role in securing access to this industry. You need to understand how you are emotionally "wired" to face challenges. You need to understand how well you are emotionally prepared for certain circumstances compared to others. You need to assess your strengths in this territory to understand how you will bring these inner assets to the industry, either as an individual working independently or within a company. Emotional resources can be broken down into four categories: inner drive, an aptitude for receiving and giving feedback, ego control, and frustration management.

Inner drive. Inner drive refers to your inner desires—your impetus to pursue what you want to do and be in the industry. Inner drive is all about having a positive attitude, motivation, confidence, leadership ability, desire, and an impetus to succeed. If you do not have motivation and do not believe in yourself, you will be unable to move forward in the creative industry. You will stall and freeze-up with your first move. You must always keep your inner desire alive to achieve a successful creative career intact. To do that, you need to understand *who* you are and *where* you are and to have your emotional resources in check, which will give you the confidence and ability to move forward as a winner.

An aptitude for receiving and giving feedback. The aptitude for giving and receiving feedback is a resource that concerns your willingness to interact with people. You must be willing to work with people. Creative work is all about teamwork. Part of teamwork concerns participating in feedback sessions. No matter whether you are an executive or a creative individual, your work will be exposed to criticism and feedback. Constructive criticism will help you improve. Greater interaction with the people around you will help you make your ideas stronger. Likewise, if you provide great feedback, consider that aspect of your abilities to be a very important trait. There is no substitute for constructive coaching or feedback when developing a TV show. The feedback process increases team morale and helps achieve the necessary level of trust required in the entire teamwork interaction.

Ego control. Keep diva behavior and arrogance to an absolute minimum. Divas and arrogant individuals are easily erased from a "go to" list of writers and producers. Keep yourself grounded and acknowledge every opportunity. Do not think of yourself as being bigger than other individuals. Remember: The creative industry is an industry that relies on creative teamwork. You need to be accessible and willing to collaborate—even if you are the leader or the most experienced person in the room.

Frustration management. As noted at the beginning of this section, the creative industry is a very passionate industry. Sometimes individuals develop a "crazy love" for what they do that makes them overreact. Everyone understands that the stakes are high. Success could represent a big career jump for the individuals involved or in the positioning of the company they work for. Failure could result in a fall into the abyss of the forgotten. These extreme realities sometimes drive emotions. They shouldn't. Keep in mind that the industry is made up of individuals who are in the industry to succeed, but sometimes they fail. Even though managing success is easier, it is best to have the capacity to manage stress, frustration, and failure. Having this ability is a real asset—it helps keep you in perspective, despite of the outcome of your last show or performance. Keep your perspective, no matter what the outcome is. Learn from it. Have clear sight on what is next. If you have that capability, then mark it as a valuable resource.

All of the emotional resources described apply to a creative individual, an executive, and even an entire corporation. Imagine a place packed with arrogant creative divas. Who wants to deal or work with them? Or imagine a place with low morale that is full of frustrated individuals with no impetus, drive, or motivation. Assess all of these aspects. Based on this assessment, focus on your strengths and pay special attention to your weaknesses. Do not let them ruin your possibilities in the industry.

Try this activity. Prepare a three-page document detailing your macro-strategy. Fill in each page:

- *Who* Are You?
- *Where* Are You? (*Where* Do You Work?)
- *What* Do You Have?

Fill in each page.

PART II: CREATIVITY

5

UNDERSTANDING CREATIVITY

Creativity is one of the most positive, life affirming traits of humanity, and people in all walks of life report that they feel at their peak and in flow when they are being the most creative.

—R. Keith Sawyer

DEFINITION

When creativity occurs, we feel that we are at our best. We feel happy and energized. Ideas surge and just keep coming. Adrenaline flows at high levels. We want to make things happen. Problems are resolved and a sense of accomplishment occurs. It is absolutely fulfilling.

Creativity starts with an individual and the ideas that come to mind. For example, when an artist believes in what he has created, all his senses are activated. Internally, excitement and the need to share his creation with the world build. The world then ultimately accepts or rejects his creation.

The concept of creativity has evolved over time. Initially, creativity was believed to have come from a superhuman force originated by a god or a divine intervention. Today, it is often impossible to view creativity based on individualistic conceptions as those in the nineteenth century did by referring to lonely poets and tormented composers or painters. Today the concept of creativity has a contextual explanation and considers social, cultural, and historical factors. According to Sawyer (2006), creativity is a social process, not just a result of individual talent or the sudden mysterious work of a genius.

The sociocultural approach brought to life by Teresa Amabile in the 1980s has become a powerful source to explain the concept of creativity in the entertainment industry. From a sociocultural standpoint, creativity is the process of generating ideas and bringing to life work that is novel, meaning a new product, a new original, or an unexpected concept that fits the task constraints but that will be useful, valuable, utilitarian, and appropriate for the audience, attaining some level of social recognition (Amabile, 1983; Sawyer, 2006; Bilton, 2007). Creativity therefore is not just a talent an individual has but also a goal-oriented process to yield innovation (Harvard Business Essentials, 2003).

From these descriptions of creativity, it is essential to remark that for a product to be creative, novelty alone is not sufficient. The product has to be appropriate and recognized as valuable by individuals in the community or society. This suitability of the product depends on the context in which the product is exposed and defined by social groups and culture. Suitability is also historically determined. For example, what is appropriate for individuals today is in great part different from what was accepted and found valuable in the 1960s. What individuals find appropriate at any given time is therefore deemed creative (Sawyer, 2006).

Creativity not only serves us to come up with ideas that no one has ever seen or to invent never-before-seen products, but creativity is also essential for enhancing products by adding features and applications, for amplifying the reach and the nature of experience and value, and for coming up with new business models, processes, and services. Creativity catalyzes the creation of media assets. Creativity is the fundamental competitive advantage that secures innovation in the media industry.

THE PROCESS OF CREATIVITY

The most important expressions of creativity today in media occur in the form of movies, TV shows, music videos, videogames, and music—all are the result of "joint cooperative activities of complex networks of skilled individuals" (Sawyer, 2006, p. 119). Creativity relies on people interacting, polishing ideas, and providing feedback until the final desired result is achieved. Creativity involves improvisation, collaboration, and communication (Sawyer, 2006). Creativity does not have to be the work of a sole individual. A genius could be the driving force, yes, but sometimes geniuses are unable to move beyond the initial idea to make it happen. All Steven Spielberg types have a team of knowledgeable people who are able to bring to life the visions of these individuals. Without the team, the idea does not come to full fruition and dies.

Creativity is found not only in personalities but also in products and the processes that make them. Creativity is a process. The output varies from industry to

Figure 5-1. Input to and output from the creative process.

industry. For example, in the media industry (Figure 5-1), the output of creativity is in the form of intellectual properties and profits, whereas the input is determined by the ideas, skills, and talents of individuals (Bilton, 2007). Individual creativity therefore does not refer to one individual, but to several skilled individuals who are able to accomplish a task. Individual creativity is key, but it is also well connected into a process.

Creative work takes time. Creative individuals also evolve with time. According to Hayes (1989), a 10-year rule represents the time that individuals spend preparing before they can accomplish true excellence ("expert" status) in any specific field or have a breakthrough. Kaufman & Baer (2004) also acknowledge that 10 years may be required "just to prepare one's self for the kind of paradigm-shifting creative work that may one day come to be called a work of genius."

Many successful young creative individuals might appear to be deviations from the 10-year rule, but even Mark Zuckerberg, a famous creative mind and the creator of Facebook, spent years understanding and mastering computer architecture and programming before having exposure to the social environment that was the driver for him to create such an extraordinary tool. Facebook did not just happen from one day to the next—with Zuckerberg having no background, knowledge, or technological understanding of the elements used to develop the social network we all now know. Facebook happened only after Zuckerberg spent 10 years of his life working with computers (even his initial exposure at age 13 counts).

Another example of a young creative individual is Steven Spielberg, a filmmaker who had a breakthrough at an early age, but then spent over 10 years experimenting with the art. Steven Spielberg, at the age of 12, was already making films with his friends. In 1968, 10 years later, Spielberg released *Amblin*, his first theatrical short film. By the time he was 25 (11 years after that small domestic film), Spielberg was directing a TV series—the rest is history.

So knowledge and experience are required, but ultimately what it is that causes a creative environment to be more productive and dynamic is the combination of knowledge and experience and the works of different types of individuals with various backgrounds and experiences. Creativity does not take place in a

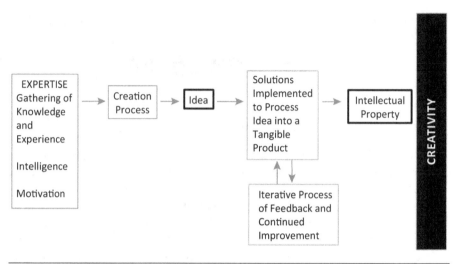

Figure 5-2. The process of creativity.

"zone of absolute freedom, characterized by chaos, irrationality and random innovation. Nor can it be only the result of carefully assembled and managed processes and people, characterized by order, logic and incremental progress" (Bilton, 2007, p. 5). Rather, creativity takes place at the "edges" of the two—absolute freedom and absolute order—or as a merger of both. Creativity is a flexible and dynamic process. Within the process, individuals strive for better ways to accomplish the end result. They find a problem and solve it within the scope of the functions and expertise of the process. As a process, creativity is composed of several activities that are creative in nature and that drive the making of a product.

Gathering of knowledge. As illustrated in Figure 5-2, creativity starts with the gathering of knowledge and experience, which defines the process of intelligence generation in creative individuals, a group, or organization. Once the base knowledge exists, the creation process occurs and yields the initial idea. This idea is then turned into something tangible. This creation process is also known as a creative operational solution implemented to mold an idea. The process is a complex operation that can take several iterations of feedback to ensure fitness and quality.

Iteration and feedback. During the iterative process of feedback, groups of individuals collaborate until they feel a solution is robust. For example, in the writing room for a TV sitcom, brainstorming with groups of 10 to 12 writers working on the scripts for episodes is crucial. Although the complete script is written by one individual, the input that all of these individuals bring to the discussion enriches the story in a way that an individual writer cannot. The brainstorming process also implies that there is a process of revision and feedback provided by creative executives from the commissioning network and the studio until the script is ready for the shoot. (*Note*: A story or script would stay on paper if other individuals beyond the writing room did not participate in the creative process. Creativity occurs in different layers of the entertainment process. Individuals with different competences all along the process intervene in making the show and ensuring its success.) Beyond the writing room, a group of producers then works to decide the most efficient way to make the show by lining up the utilization of resources and shooting the scenes in the most efficient order with the best production schedule possible (the creative solution). The director works with the actors to achieve the most realistic or appropriate representation of the story. The programming team assures the best time slot for the product. The promotions group watches the finished product and comes up with the best ideas to highlight the key selling aspects of the content. Distributors discuss strategic ways to sell the show to different broadcasters, assuring value added to their respective brands. The process is all about being creative all along the way: creative in the generation of the content, creative in how the show will technically be produced, creative in how the show will be financed, creative in the aesthetics of the show, and creative in how the show is to make money.

Intellectual property. The end result of the creativity process is intellectual property that, if it is suitable and if it finds acceptance in the audience, will then be considered a successful creative outcome of the process—a process that validates the power of teamwork and that a single person is not the only creative force used in making a product.

Groups bring a greater sum of competencies, insight, and energy to an effort than single individuals (Harvard Business Essentials, 2003). Especially today, the more diverse the groups are the better. Diversity relies on different thinking styles and professional competencies. According to Bilton (2007), nowadays creativity is more "based on processes or systems than [on] the search for the singularly gifted individual" (p. 23); "individual creativity needs to be integrated with organizational resources, capacities and systems" (p. xv); and "creativity is a multidimensional process, requiring a combination of thinking styles and a tolerance for contradiction and paradox" (p. 23).

Experts and novel talent must be mixed together to achieve this multidimensional line of thought in creativity by Bilton (2007). Experts may find it difficult to look at new things with fresh eyes, but they do know how to keep in perspective that creativity is not related to just breaking the rules or high risk taking. Experts play a role, but they are not the basis of the process. Having novel or disruptive talent in the process brings a new vision of the outside world—authentic information on what groups in society are experiencing that needs to be studied and adopted. A multidimensional creative process needs drivers and real engines to find balance and avoid chaos and anarchic environments, but the process of creativity also needs leadership to occur and prevail.

RESOURCES FOR CREATIVITY

Creativity is an indicator of productivity, adaptability, and the health of an industry, benefiting individuals, institutions, and societies. That value defines why individuals and enterprises are willing to take reasonable risks (Runco, 2004).

Sternberg & Lubart (1995a) stated that creativity requires a specific set of interrelated resources that will allow an investor get the best possible return. This theory, also called "the investment approach," perfectly applies to the entertainment industry in the sense that it proposes that a creative entity (an individual, company, network, etc.) "is one who possesses the necessary resources and uses these resources to 'buy low' (pursue ideas that are new or out of favor but have potential) and, after developing these ideas, 'sell high' in order for them to be produced and presented publicly at the right moment and at the best possible price."

Theresa Amabile (1998) described creativity as having three components: expertise, creative-thinking skills, and motivation, whereas Sternberg & Lubart (1995b) pointed out that knowledge, cognitive styles, intelligence, personality, and environmental context complete the list of resources for creativity. Using Amabile's (1998) and Sternberg & Lubart's (1995b) findings, creativity is therefore a function of components or resources:

- Expertise
  - Knowledge: Intellectual, procedural, or technical know-how skills to find solutions
  - Experience: Real life events throughout the lifetime of an individual
- Creative thinking
  - Cognitive style: The preference for novel ideas and thinking and an inductive or deductive approach when analyzing situations; the ability to go from details to the big picture
  - Intelligence: The ability to define and analyze problems in new ways; the analytic talent to identify which ideas are important to pursue; the practical skills to persuade others of the value of a new project; the ability to evaluate; the capacity to generate divergent thinking from a given starting idea

- Personality: Individuality, flexibility, perseverance, imagination, courage, risk, tolerance to ambiguity; an openness to novel experiences and ideas to approach problems
- Motivation: Drive coming from within or extrinsic coming from a strong leader who encourages individuals to work and stay focused (Is a person a strong motivator? Is a person easy or difficult to motivate?)
- Environmental: The physical and social stimuli that produce and incentivize the generation of ideas

The degree to which these resources or components are present in individuals or a team helps increase the possibility of a creative outcome. For example, an individual with a high degree of intelligence who is highly motivated might yield extraordinary results, whereas another individual with similar degree of strong knowledge might not be willing to open up to new lines of thought without external motivation (money talks!). The interrelation between intelligence and motivation is what drives creativity. Some resources are very domain-specific (such as knowledge), whereas others are generally applicable across resources (such as intelligence) and some have general attributes such as personality and cognitive styles.

The important matter here is that creative industries must rely on resources, strengths, and processes to help reduce the risk taken when investing in an intellectual property. Creative resources are absolutely necessary to guarantee a healthy process of creativity and a better control of risk.

WHO IS CREATIVE?

Individuals do not need to have a humanistic background to be creative. What really matters is to have the required knowledge and to be in an environment that needs ideas and different new ways to accomplish things, encourages everyone to be creative, and acknowledges that everyone is key in achieving creativity, thus innovation.

For some, being creative is all about being original. These individuals consider their originality to be a talent that few gifted individuals possess. Although creativity does involve originality, which is necessary but not all-sufficient, creativity is *not* a type of originality. According to Runco (2004), originality is usually defined in terms of "statistical infrequency"—uncommon, unique, or merely unusual things or a specific, out-of-the-box, different solution to a problem that makes the solution original, thus creative. Creativity is not the same as intelligence or giftedness either. Intelligence and giftedness are talents, but creativity involves problem finding in addition to problem solving, which makes creativity different from other types of talent. In other words, being creative means you are a problem finder *and* a problem solver. You solve a need or fulfill a need with something others will accept.

CREATIVE OR INVENTIVE?

An individual can either be creative or inventive. As previously defined by Bilton (2007), "to be creative the idea must be useful or valuable." Creativity accomplishes a result; inventiveness does not. Being inventive refers to coming up with ideas that are not necessarily going to "stick" or become a major product embraced by the market.

The media industry creates the context for cataloging an individual or a group as creative. The notion of being creative is also related to the number of breakthroughs and "hits" achieved in the market. In this context, being creative does not have to do with an individual or group and the things they create on their own but on how they relate to the world. If a concept is new to the world and provides a new solution, a new experience that people can benefit from, then this accomplishment validates how creative the person or the group who created the product is and validates the process through which the product is created. The accomplishment ultimately validates creativity and thus a hit is certified.

The number of hits and successes is what makes a company more creative than another—this measurement validates their creation process. Sony Pictures Television is seen as a creative company because many new and valuable media products have come out of its trenches. Sony Pictures has brought to the world some of the most successful and groundbreaking sitcoms of our time: *Married With Children, The Jeffersons, Mad About You,* and *Seinfeld* as well as a highly prolific pipeline of other hits that in recent years has added titles such as *Breaking Bad, Damages,* and *Community.* Creativity is high at Sony Pictures. Sony Pictures creates value for the customer and does it repeatedly, creating sustainability.

LEADERSHIP AND CREATIVITY IN THE MEDIA INDUSTRY

Leadership plays a very important role in fostering creativity. Without the clear vision of a leading force behind the creative process, creativity could become chaotic and nonproductive. Good leadership provides:

- Orientation
- Strategy
- Goals
- Premises

- Limitations
- Parameters
- Information
- Support
- Motivation

These elements of good leadership are the basis for creative minds to create something interesting, new, unexpected, surprising, entertaining, and pleasing. The role of a leader is to make all of these aspects clear to the team to ensure results. Leaders are managers, people with the ability to move processes forward to get results. A leading creative force could well be represented by the overall philosophy of a company, but it takes actual people to put a philosophy into practice. Within the creative process each activity needs to have individuals empowered to give the best possible result. Creativity is then a competitive advantage that is the result of a team effort pushed by a strong leading force. A creative company or division is one that embraces creativity through leaders and teams that make things happen.

In media production, the leading creative force relies on creative individuals or executives to make decisions throughout the production process. Throughout the process, a series of leaders arise, each of them maintaining the creative vision and finding solutions to accomplish the plan. In the case of a TV show, the executive producer (sometimes the creator of the show) is also called the "show runner" and is the leading creative engine for the production team. Even though the executive producer is the leading creative for the show, the executive producer reports into a higher authority in the network who ultimately approves the show and gives specific directions on what the TV network needs the show to be.

Leaders are not only producers, executives, creators, or show runners but also head writers, directors, engineers, art directors, set designers, directors of photography, etc. (Figure 5-3). A leader must manage resources to find the best possible talent: expert and experienced or novel and eager. A leader must find players with the necessary skill sets to assemble a powerful team that is able to craft good ideas with market potential, out of the box or within the box. Strong management is key to achieving creativity (Harvard Business Essentials, 2003).

In the media industry, creativity relies on all individuals interacting through the process of development, production, and business. Creativity is a team effort. "Creativity is the result of a combination of thinking styles, not spontaneous invention or divine inspiration" (Bilton, 2007). Writers, readers, evaluators, development executives, directors, etc. provide input for the evolution of a concept from its initial stage to the final production and interact in specific ways with savvy businessmen, sales reps, and engineers to ultimately sell and process the

Asks for Creativity
(Premises) ⟷ Ensures Creativity

PRODUCTION
HOUSE

Leader

Leader

Creative
Executive

Show Runner / Executive Producer

Leader

Leader

Headwriter

TV NETWORK

Writers

Actors

TV Crew

Figure 5-3. Leadership in media creation.

product to reach the biggest and right audience, but without leadership, creativity cannot happen.

6

THE SOCIOCULTURAL
MODEL OF CREATIVE
VALIDATION IN MEDIA

Creativity has been explained by scientists and researchers in different dimensions:

- One that is individualistic and explores the mental and individual processes behind the creation of new ideas '
- One that is more driven by external factors that help the proliferation of new ideas or determine how novel, unique, or original an idea is

Both dimensions try to explain when and how an idea is generated. External factors, however, define the context. Context is a key determinant framework for labeling an idea as being creative or not. Context is composed of economic, social, and political events that shape the environment we live in. Context aligns our thoughts based on a common ground in which new ideas stand out.

According to Lubart (1994), *novel* refers to going beyond replication, or a copy of a product, or referencing something already in existence. The notion of novelty is directly connected to originality and the context against which the originality is being assessed. Novelty is determined by how original a work is and can vary from being original only for the individual who came up with the idea to being original for a limited group of individuals or the entire world (Lubart & Guignard, 2004). Novelty is found in breakthroughs and also in incremental enhancements or variations to an original idea (Sternberg, Kaufman & Pretz, 2002).

Amabile (1982) and Csikszentmihalyi (1988) agreed that creativity is a social and a cultural phenomenon. Creativity exists thanks to individuals who are part

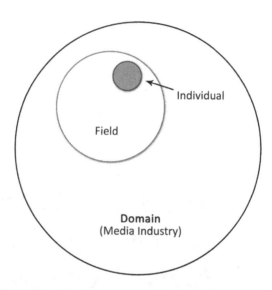

Figure 6-1. The traditional three-level sociocultural model. (Adapted from a reference in Sawyer (2006).)

of a society driven by the cultural and historical aspects of their surroundings. Culture changes and evolves over time and with that the knowledge, experiences, and tastes of the individuals in society who give ultimate approval to the work of creative individuals. Amabile also stated that creativity is determined when experts in an industry agree on a matter—not by an individual. Creativity is therefore socially, culturally, and historically driven. Based on these findings, creativity researchers developed the sociocultural model of creative validation (Sawyer, 2006).

The sociocultural model of creative validation is composed of three interdependent levels of interaction: individual, field, and domain (Abuhamdeh & Csikszentmihalyi, 2004; Sawyer, 2006). Figure 6-1 is a graphic representation of the three-level traditional sociocultural model. In this model, an *individual* creates content which is then taken to experts who ultimately green-light (or not) the making of the product that will then become part of the media industry domain. The product is media content in the form of TV shows or videos delivered via multiplatforms. These experts are social groups that are culturally and historically determined and evolve with time. The experts who decide on the appropriateness of the product represent the *field*, whereas the products accepted by the field are the *domain* (Sawyer, 2006).

In Figure 6-2 another level of interaction has been added, the *audience*, which is the layer that surrounds the industry and represents the individuals who ultimately experience and validate its output. Thus, for the purposes of this book,

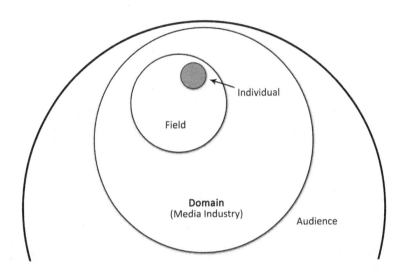

Figure 6-2. The four levels of the updated sociocultural model of creative validation.

the four levels that constitute the system of validation and form the sociocultural model of creativity are the individual, field, domain, and audience. The process of interaction between these four levels defines the constraints that an individual needs to consider during the creation of a novel product.

Amabile (1982) stated that the sociocultural approach of creativity, or what she called "creativity in context," relies on the assumption that a creative work must be *novel* and *suitable* to some realm of human activity. These two aspects become the main objects of evaluation of creative work within the system of creative validation. They rely on the fact that a creator or an individual on their own cannot decide that their product is a breakthrough. Breakthroughs are validated only through the consensus of experts and input from the public, as shown in the adjusted model in Figure 6-2—in other words, by the *field* and the *audience*.

A system of validation then becomes the best way to mitigate risk in entertainment. This system is intended to ensure that content which is determined as creative and innovative will succeed in the market. The entertainment industry is in constant validation, both internally and externally. When the industry loses touch with the audience, then the circle of validation is weak. Experts in the field must be knowledgeable in different ways, however, to come up with a solid feasibility analysis that will allow them to predict the success of a show and lower the financial risk of an investing company.

The model of creative validation has changed as a consequence of social media and the possibility individuals have to interact directly with an audience to

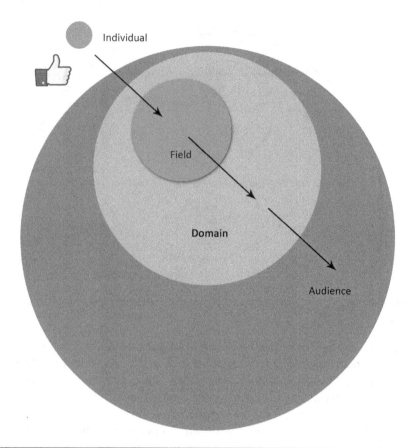

Figure 6-3. A variation of the adjusted sociocultural model illustrating the social media effect.

get early validation. As a consequence, a variation to the adjusted model is presented in Figure 6-3, which illustrates the creative individual interacting directly with the audience through social media.

Nowadays, creators of content are not necessarily in the sophisticated ranks of the field within the industry, e.g., as a contracted professional or an expert. These creators of content are everywhere and are part of an audience that is reached directly through social media. These creators of content receive validation in the form of Likes (Facebook), Retweets (Twitter), and Views (YouTube) and the industry takes notice.

To better understand the sociocultural model of validation in media, each of the components in Figure 6-3 will be explained: individuals, field, domain, and the audience.

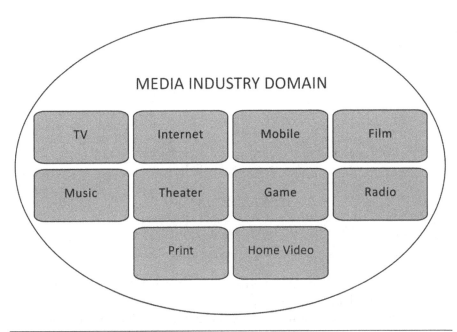

MEDIA INDUSTRY DOMAIN

| TV | Internet | Mobile | Film |

| Music | Theater | Game | Radio |

| Print | Home Video |

Figure 6-4. The media industry domain and its subdomains.

THE MEDIA INDUSTRY DOMAIN

A domain is the overall umbrella that defines the context of an industry. Art, science, economics—each is a domain and each consists of information, a set of rules, and procedures and instructions that define how to act within that domain. A domain is distinctive and not repetitive or overlapped with another domain. A domain changes over time and the changes determine what is obsolete and current—thus the need for a reference to determine what is new.

Subdomains within a domain can become domains themselves (Sawyer, 2006). To illustrate, we will focus on the media industry. Media is a subdomain of the arts. The media domain breaks down into several different subdomains (industries), each represented by specific media content. Figure 6-4 presents a breakdown of the media industry domain with each square representing a domain (or industry) of its own.

All of the different subdomains in the media industry domain represent an industry and a platform of exposition. Within each platform of exposition is well-defined content that is the ultimate source of exploitation for each platform or industry (music, TV shows, movies, etc.). Each platform of exposition through which we experience content has unique rules. For example, a film is made in

Domain	Content
Television	Animated TV Series
Film	*Spider Man 1*
	Spider Man 2
	Spider Man 3
Internet	Blogs
	Movie Trailers
	Webisodes
	Facebook Page
	Offical Website
Games	Video Games for PSP, Wii, XBOX
Music	Soundtrack of Theater Play
Theater	Broadway Play, *Turn Off the Dark*
Mobile	Twitter
	Mobisode

Each type of content must follow the rules of the specific domain in which the content exists.

Figure 6-5. Full breakdown of *Spider Man* content in multiple domains/platforms.

a specific way, following the patterns of screenwriting and film production. A television series follows specific rules for the medium, channel, time slot, and duration of an episode. Each internet element has a specific way of presentation. Similar requirements apply to games, music, theater plays, and mobile applications. Each domain has predetermined specifications that creative minds must consider when entering that domain.

Single content can coexist in different platforms of exposition even though the content of these platforms is not necessarily related. This type of content is called *multiplatform content*. To better illustrate multiplatform content, let's see what can happen with a single well-known content. *Spider Man* exists in many different platforms of exposition, including an animated series on TV, a film, a theater play, video games, and a music soundtrack. Figure 6-5 illustrates a full breakdown of the *Spider Man* brand into various platforms of exposition.

A variation of multiplatform content is when the *same exact content* (same characters, storyline, etc.) coexists *simultaneously* in more than one platform of exposition. This variation is known as *transmedia* content. Transmedia content is also prepared according to the specific rules of each platform of exposition—in other words, following the rules of the particular domain in which the content appears. Transmedia content coexists through simultaneous:

- Broadcasting or showcasing of a program via TV
- Streaming of an episode via the internet, a series website, web-supporting stories, episodic blogs, social networks, and widget applications
- Applications and webisodes via a mobile spectrum (smartphones, tablets, etc.)

A good example of a show coexisting on three different platforms is the U.S. version of *The Office*, a comedy series created by British actor and comedian Ricky Gervais. Creators of the *The Office* prepare a half hour series that airs weekly on TV. They also prepare B-story videos featuring the same characters in situations never shown on TV. Likewise, mobisodes, apps, and other mobile applications are developed around the show, not to mention the social network activities around an episode via Facebook. Like multiplatform content, all transmedia content follows specific rules and patterns to embrace an audience.

The multiplatform breakdown of any creative property helps creative individuals to project the potential a property they create can have if the property becomes a multiplatform phenomenon. Consequently, understanding how a creative property breaks down according to the domains of exploitation helps a creative individual to understand the potential intellectual property (IP) rights to better negotiate with networks, producers, or a corporation interested in the property rights. For example, a creative individual might want to negotiate the rights for TV exploitation, but keep the rights for the internet, theater, and movies, which could then be later negotiated at prices that depend on the success of the show on TV, helping generate more revenue from the same property.

As discussed earlier, each domain has very specific rules. Let's look at the TV domain in detail to better understand these rules.

THE TV DOMAIN

As seen in Figure 6-6, TV is part of the media industry content domain. The TV domain consists of all created TV shows, media, and genres and the successful ways of aural/visual narrative expression that have been produced and accepted by experts and audiences.

Subdomains

As an industry, the TV domain breaks down into four subdomains: technology, content creation, business, and marketing.

Technology. The technology subdomain has to do with the equipment used to collect and process the content: cameras, lightning, audio, video monitors, editing equipment, postproduction equipment, transmission, etc.

Content creation. As shown in Figure 6-6, the content creation domain is further divided into two subdomains: fiction and non-fiction. Each of these subdomains has specific sets of rules and conventions that must be learned by creative

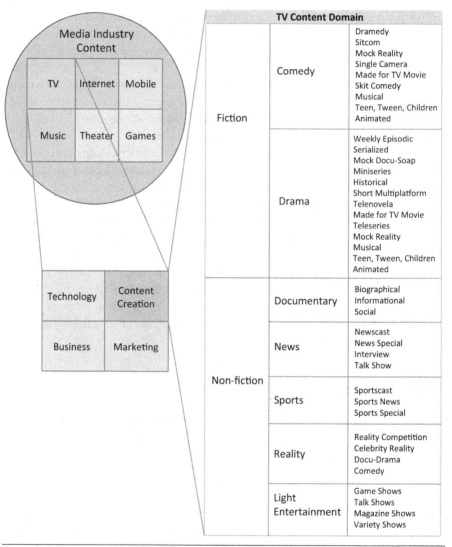

Figure 6-6. The TV content domain and its subdomains.

individuals to succeed and obtain acceptance from the experts that will decide if the concept is worth consideration.

Business. The business domain has subdomains determined by whether the TV signal is free or subscriber-based and by the type of negotiations and transactions used to generate revenue.

Marketing. The marketing domain is primarily determined by the nature of the contact the promotion has with an audience, either off-air or on-air.

This same type of breakdown can be done for each of the other media industry content domains illustrated in Figure 6-6 (internet, mobile, music, theater, games), which gives an overview of the different opportunities media content can present. Creative individuals who want to belong to a specific domain should learn everything possible about that domain—knowing how a specific domain breaks down is crucial for mapping a career plan and focusing on a specific type of content creation.

Domain Rules

In TV, content domains and subdomains are also called *genres* or *subgenres*. Every time a new TV show comes along, it becomes part of the domain. If the new TV show is considered a breakthrough or content that has never been seen before, then a new set of rules will be adopted. For example, when the first comedy shows came on the air in the 1950s, a new way of presenting comedy on TV was brought into existence. As a result, a new domain within the TV content spectrum was formed: the situation comedy or sitcom. After that, the sitcom genre, with a specific set of rules, began to evolve, resulting in the sitcoms of recent years, e.g., *Two and Half Men, Seinfeld,* and *The Big Bang Theory.* The same was experienced in drama, news, reality, sports, light entertainment, and documentaries. Once the first show that defined a genre appeared, a new set of rules evolved to define the formulas and constraints required to make shows of the same kind. Subsequently these new rules and constraints became part of that content creation domain. This new set of rules defined the formulas and constraints to do the shows. Constraints are also called *parameters.* Parameters define what is suitable and useful and may vary depending on what is more important for the industry regarding novelty or suitability.

The set of rules in any given domain is different and each has its own criteria for selection, restrictions, and validation. For example, in the TV fiction domain, rules refer to:

- Writing: Conceptual and narrative structural formulas to build scripts, storylines, and characters
- Production: Shooting styles and methods (multi- or single-camera, in studio or on location or both, 5 days per episode or cross-boarding episodes, etc.)
- Aesthetics: Editing, lighting, sound, camera framing, and visualization

- Budget: References in the industry or a specific region concerning production costs
- Network profile: The channel's brand, communication, and content purpose (the type of programming and audience that describes the channel)
- Geographic elements: Language- and country-specific
- Programming: References and strategies concerning time slots, genres featured, audience taste research, audience age target, demographic elements, and censorship
- Trends in the market and history: What is in vogue and has worked in the past
- Type of service: The model of exposition of a TV channel (pay TV; free TV; video on demand, VOD; Internet Protocol TV, IPTV; over the top TV, OTT; and mobile apps)

All of these rules are taken into consideration when content is presented to the industry and set to be produced. For example, the budget for a sitcom might be $1 million to make in Hollywood, but in The Netherlands the standard might be $250,000. This difference in the costs standard is covered in the set of rules that a producer needs to take into consideration when attempting to materialize his vision for a TV show.

Rules are made to be followed but also to be broken. In order to break the rules and still maintain relevance within the media industry, a creative individual must first master the rules and constraints of a domain. When mastery is achieved, then a creative individual, executive, or company is better prepared to break the rules of the domain and create a new set of rules.

THE FIELD AND VALIDATION

The so-called "gatekeepers" of the domain or industry are represented by the *field*. These gatekeepers are critics who validate the work of artists. These critics are members of groups composed of eclectic teams of individuals who are able to assess the potential of an idea from their own perspectives, all within the parameters of what is valuable in a domain. The TV content field is composed of creative individuals (writers and producers), creative executives (marketing, development, and programming), and specialized journalists who evaluate a product based on parameters determined by their backgrounds. For example, a development executive looks at the breakthrough potential of a concept, the strengths of the story, the characters, and the style. A programming executive evaluates the show to see if it has a "fit" in the programming grid this executive handles. A producer evaluates the feasibility of the concept. Each person in the field has criteria for measuring novelty and suitability. If the approval is generated based on all of these criteria combined, then the concept could be considered as validated by the field. In actuality, concepts are not necessarily evaluated from all possible perspectives by the members of the field. Sometimes a concept is evaluated by only one or few, causing the process to not be standardized—in other words, to be biased, flawed, and risky. In some cases, however, the state of an industry might cause that industry to be on the lookout for absolute breakthroughs and to give less emphasis to improved versions of existing ideas, and the exact opposite might occur. Emphasis in an industry therefore depends on the context that experts in a specific field choose to establish for filtering ideas.

TV networks define their own contexts for locating content that is fresh and suitable. A leading TV network might be very conservative and sometimes "formulate," with little experimentation made on novel products, in terms of the shows the network picks every season. CBS, for example, is characterized as looking for procedural or investigative crime dramas, regular studio-based sitcoms, and established reality shows. Another network struggling in terms of audience might be trying to "break the mold," expecting a massive breakthrough. In 2004, for example, NBC launched a series of nonconventional sitcoms looking for novelty (*30 Rock* and *The Office*). NBC took a risk and *30 Rock* and *The Office* became successful differentiated brands even though they were not massive hits. Evidently, the executives at NBC were set on looking for this type of programming. Soon *Community*, another single-camera comedy, and *Parks and Recreation*, a mock-reality comedy, came along. With these selections, NBC was obviously not looking for traditional sitcoms that defined their criteria of validating and selecting content. HBO has a different approach that is defined by the nature of their audience and type of service. One could infer from that approach that HBO's rule is to bring a product to the audience that surprises, stands out, brings value to paying viewers, and that is different from the programs viewers can see on free TV. HBO strives more for high-budget, risky, original, edgy content. HBO's set of constraints is different from those in network television: fewer episodes; a different act structure; and character-driven, unique, and unformulated concepts, etc. Examples of HBO's defining content include *The Sopranos*, *Six Feet Under*, *Veep*, *Curb Your Enthusiasm*, *Looking*, *Girls*, *Rome*, *Game of Thrones*, and *Sex and the City*.

THE FIELD EXPERT AND VALIDATION

The possibilities for field validation are quite large—there is no single center or place to validate all ideas. Instead, even though most companies in the same country share common ground rules and production criteria in terms of content selection, the selection process is intrinsic and different for each company. In other words, each company is a source of validation. For example, if a creative executive in Company X says a concept is valuable and worth exploring or developing, then that concept will be added to the domain; otherwise the concept will be ignored and dismissed. Even at this early stage, a concept could be added to the domain to become part of the history of the domain. If the concept is dismissed, it might go to another company and be considered there. The more consideration and praise a concept receives from critics in the field, the more possibility the concept has of entering the development and production stages. This is how a concept starts gaining value and becomes an asset to the domain—hence the importance of validation by qualified individuals in the industry to create value.

According to Sawyer (2006), an inconsistent or weak group of experts leads to inconsistent ratings and evaluations, causing the validation system to have poor judgment criteria. Absolutely key for people who have a career track and experience is to understand well the conventions in the domain that form the field. Evaluation by the field must be consistent. For that to occur, the group evaluating a product must be experts.

Expert members of a field are professionals who have been trained and who have gathered sufficient experience and expertise about a domain. These experts can also be creators who bring to the field experience that they have gathered while writing and producing content. They are influential individuals who not only decide what concept will be produced or advance in the process of creation, but they also decide which concept will receive the financial support that could lead to possible recognition in the form of awards. High-profile members in the field can speed up the green-light process to develop or produce a TV show and skyrocket the success of a show by endorsing it. For example, the film *Paranormal* came to movie theaters in 2010 after receiving Steven Spielberg's support. In 2011 Julia Roberts publicly endorsed the quality of Javier Bardem's performance in the movie *Biutiful*. Bardem ended up earning an academy award nomination despite little exposure of the movie in the United States. Spielberg and Roberts therefore became part of the validating process of those movies.

The degree of expertise within the field may vary. Junior executives may be analyzing scripts and ideas in a first round of evaluations, with more trained individuals reading second and consecutive rounds as the final decision-making stage to green-light the concept for development is reached.

All concepts validated in the process become part of the references and information in the domain. This information then allows the gatekeepers to have a framework of reference to make comparisons or to extrapolate ideas that could become a breakthrough.

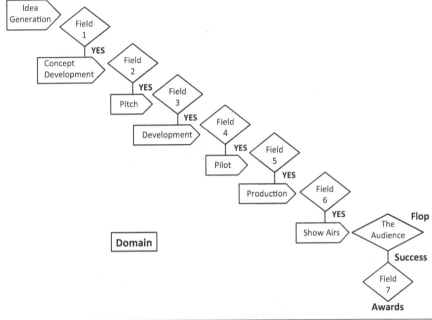

Figure 6-7. The validation process by experts in the field of the TV domain.

TV AND FIELD VALIDATION

The process of validation in TV follows the progression of an idea from its inception and determines if the concept is good enough to advance toward final exposition to an audience. Throughout the process of evolution and exposition, the concept is validated in seven different instances in the TV validation field. Figure 6-7 illustrates an idea generated by an individual as it enters the field and starts the process of validation:

- Field 1: Development executives and readers, after the inception process (idea generation), do first readings of the creative material that includes a series description, a synopsis, or episode 0. If acceptable, they then give the green light for the idea to enter the concept development stage. (To enter the concept development stage, an individual negotiates the rights of the property or idea with the creative corporation that wants to develop the concept.)
- Field 2: Development executives and readers reject or accept the concept. If the concept is accepted, the development executives and readers decide when they will be ready to enter the pitch stage. During this

stage, marketing becomes involved to prepare the material that will be pitched.

- Field 3: Network development executives reject or accept the pitch for the concept to enter the development stage (i.e., tailored to the network's needs). If accepted, the development stage gives form, structure, and adequacy to the concept that has been pitched and approved. During this process, creative network executives define the premises for writing and production.

- Field 4: Network development executives approve the script to enter the pilot stage. During the pilot stage, the first episode of the series is produced. Most of the time the pilot is not for audience exposure but for viewing and evaluation by network executives and decision makers.

- Field 5: Development executives, marketing, and programming alert studio executives if the pilot show is good. Revision of pilot episodes is then carried out and if approved, the show will be given a time slot, presented in the upfront, and enter the production stage.

- Field 6: Critics review episodes before they air. During the week of release, episodes are presented to the press (or experts in the field) to alert the audience if the show is strong or weak. Sometimes prizes and recognition are part of this stage, mainly from festivals that showcase the episodes or concepts before they are available to the public. (*Note*: Showcasing episodes applies more to film, however, nowadays transmedia concepts are first gaining traction on the internet before reaching the TV airwaves. As a result, the internet audience's reaction is key.)

- Field 7: After release, critics and members of academies or guilds offer a public analysis of the show and also provide feedback in the form of awards and prizes. For example, the Academy of Arts and Sciences is composed of professionals in the TV industry who validate the work presented by their peers to provide recognition in the form of an award which improves the value of a property.

The validation of each field yields a result that will become part of the domain memory, either as a finished product or as a reference for what happened to the idea. This memory is also part of the set of rules in the industry. For example, if the pilot was not picked up, and something similar comes up in the near future, the experts will bring that history up and might not approve the idea.

To be fair, the media industry field, as in any other industry, is composed of human beings. As a result, their experiences, knowledge, actions, and decisions can be imperfect. The process also goes through a constant process of checks and balances and the individuals validating content change. So individuals in the process come and go, the market changes, culture changes, and opportunities to be validated positively are not predictable. A good concept should always get through, but sometimes conditions in the process of validation by field experts do not open the possibility for brilliance. The key takeaway here is to be aware of the difficulties and the different stages of validation that a concept or idea goes through in the media industry. Understand and learn how to ride out this process, how to get ready for an elevator pitch, and how to get the best out the moment you have to convey the necessary impression needed to help you advance to the next stage.

VALIDATION OF THE CREATIVE INDIVIDUAL

The remaining level of the sociocultural model of creativity to be discussed is represented by the individual (the creative individual described in Chapter 2, *Defining Who You Are: Creative Individual or Creative Executive*). This individual is a writer, performer, producer, or an artist who creates a concept that could eventually make an impact on an audience.

This individual, in pure essence, writes and creates. The more successful a writer is, the bigger the entourage of individuals around the writer will grow: agents, managers, and publicists. Agents, managers, and publicists work to promote and sell a writer's strengths to always keep the writer working. Always working is the dream of every creative individual. Most writers struggle to find the right path while combining low-income jobs with the dream of becoming a high-earning creative individual. The value of a creative individual, however, grows according to how strategic the individual is and the validation received from the field in the industry.

Some artists are called "one-hit wonders." These artists have only a single successful project and then they disappear. Other artists are successful and consistent and work continuously. Many aspects in play favor continuous work. For example, a creative individual might be validated by the field for their creative work and also for their intellectual and emotional resources (see Chapter 4, *Assessing What You Have*). Conversely, if creative executives do not want to work with a certain artist, they might reject a project completely or pick the concept, but ban the artist from running or writing their own creation. All information about an individual forms part of the background experts in the field keep and later use to make decisions. Background information is stored in the archives of a domain.

A creative individual must believe in what they create and be strategic by being aware of the context they inhabit. They need to find sources of information that will tell them what the market wants, what could be different out there, and if what they have is just one of a thousand clones of a type of show or a potential gem. A creative individual needs to learn how to find differentiating factors and elements to succeed and to know that they are in the curve or at least at the edge of the curve.

An individual creates content based on what they believe to be true, but they also need to be aware of the forces of interaction and dependence between the experts in the field and the information in the domain. For example, when a writer presents a script as being unique, the writer must be certain that nothing like it has been done before. The writer must be aware of what is on TV and what has aired in the past and collect references of what has been pitched in the industry. Experts usually know these things and in a meeting could bring up the existence of something similar, killing the pitch. The creator of *Lost*, J.J. Abrams, broke into the TV industry with a cinematic mysterious event that defied the laws of narrative and budgets and became a reference in the industry that no one has yet been able to tap. Gatekeepers in the field validated Abrams' concept. Because there was nothing like it in the domain, his concept became a potential reference of novelty. The audience then gave *Lost* positive validation and the show became innovative. The field then created the need for more content of this same nature and as a result, from 2005 until this writing (2015), encouraged the proliferation of shows based on supernatural and mysterious events (*Revolution, Walking Dead, The Dome*, etc.).

Like creativity, an individual on their own cannot decide if a concept is a breakthrough or not. The validation received is what gives breakthrough status to a project. Some artists do not want to share their work because they consider their work to not merit commercial consumption, but if an artist does not want to share their work, what is the real purpose of creating it? Exposure can lead to validation. Validation starts with friends or random individuals who are exposed to a story or concept. Their positive reactions will permit an artist to get a feeling of the potential success that the show might have. This feedback can be also used to raise the profile of a concept. An artist also needs to find individuals who will not necessarily be "keen" to whatever the individual does but who will be honest in their reactions. For example, the father who created the cartoon series *Pinky Dinky Doo* did so to present the concept to his 4-year-old daughter and friends—who validated the idea immediately! These are some of the initial stages of validation to assess if you have something with potential in your hands.

Hiding material is not beneficial. Early validation will give you confidence as an individual and help you to get ready for the moment when you present an idea to the industry. An interesting aspect of getting early validation is that as a writer you do not necessarily get early validation with experts in the field but only with potential viewers to measure their initial reactions. In the past, these reactions were meaningless unless you had a possibility to certify them, but today you can get validation in the form of Likes or Retweets, which do have public value.

Validation by the digital world. Today, digital media platforms have become new sources of validation, with viewers taking a mainstream seat in the acceptance of a concept without intermediaries between them and an artist. An example of an artist who found validation and became relevant is Lucas Cruikshank, creator of *Fred* (Fred Figglehorn, an obnoxious teen character). Lucas Cruikshank, through a series of self-produced web episodes that provided him with audience recognition and leverage, reached stardom through millions of visits to his adventure clips, was invited and then featured on Nickelodeon's comedy series *ICarly*, and then got his own show. Another noticeable example is Justin Bieber, who grew such a fan base through the internet that the industry could not contain but embrace him. On the film side, *District 9* went on to become a major film after Peter Jackson saw the short that inspired the movie on the internet. The short became a viral sensation that caught Jackson's attention. Jackson then approached creator and director Neill Blomkamp to turn his original take on alien refugees into a film that ended up earning Academy Award nominations including Best Picture. Blomkamp received direct validation by the audience, among them Peter Jackson. Blomkamp did not go to the industry firsthand but to the audience via social media platforms. New media platforms have become the giant elephant in the room for executives defining industry constraints. To find content and what is relevant for the audiences "out there," the filtering process is balancing the criteria with a shift toward the multiplatform environment to determine what will become part of the domain. This shift toward a multiplatform environment favors creative individuals who now can receive direct validation from an audience without passing through the field and the domain. As can be seen in the adjusted model of sociocultural validation (Figure 6-3), in the new digital-social world, an individual is no longer within the field but is in direct contact with the audience. If social media validation occurs and the content becomes notorious, e.g., as happened with *District 9*, then the content enters the field and the domain and later goes back to the audience transformed into something mainstream. Even well-known actors and filmmakers are turning to the internet to unleash their creative selves, bringing content directly to the audience. They just do it and the audience reacts. Actors doing this in the United States include Will Farrell, Jimmy Fallon, and Andy Samberg.

Creative individuals in the TV domain. As in any other domain, TV is a constraints industry with sets of rules and parameters that creative individuals must follow to be contextually relevant. Nevertheless, there is a difference in creating content within the media industry versus independent creation. Creating content within the media industry is tied to the constraints the industry imposes (such as a budget) and established formulas to create and accept content. Independent creation occurs on the periphery of the media industry and could lead to more novelty. As a result, according to Gluck, Ernst & Unger (2002), there are two types of individuals in the creative industry:

- Free artists
- Constraints artists

A free artist is considered to be independent with no ties to companies in the industry. Free artists develop, produce, and release content without the support of major film, TV, or digital multimedia conglomerates. They even consider themselves to be detached from the industry. Free artists work with few resources and form what is known as the independent world of media making. The possibilities of succeeding as a free artist are related to the resources an artist has: economic, intellectual, and emotional. Economic resources, for example, will determine the free artist's ability to move certain projects forward. Some free artists, however, earn recognition in the field and the industry and become part of the system. These free artists manage to gain enough relevance and economic power through their independent films or TV divisions to receive support from media conglomerates. Private investors support their personal quests and provide economic resources for a free artist's next project. Some free artists are so notable that they will get a "yes" for any idea they come up with. Some critics, however, are of the opinion that when these free artists become part of the system, and start sailing through the seas of corporate safety, they will put aside risky projects and become proponents of the constraint system. (*Note:* Some free artists have succeeded independently and will continue to receive support to make their proven art.) Free artists must be strategic to assess and find opportunities to succeed. Key are understanding the context and the new ways people communicate and consume content. Facebook, Twitter, Instagram, and Sound Cloud are examples of existing social media platforms that have become reachable vehicles for showcasing independent products. Other sites are dedicated to providing artists with platforms to expose their work and seek funding. For example, Kickstarter, the world's largest crowdfunding platform for creative projects, bypasses traditional investment methods and allows artists to obtain funding through pledges from investors to produce a pilot, a movie, or a digital series. Investors in Kickstarter projects are offered some type of tangible reward in exchange for their pledges. A constraint artist is an artist who very clearly understands the creative formulas necessary to make content in the industry and takes advantage of that skill. A constraint artist is part of a corporation. Constraint artists deliver the product requested within the constraints established. For example, a writer knows how sitcoms are structured so the writer follows a formula to comply with industry expectations.

This writer works for a media corporation in two instances—writing, producing, and creating content on a work-for-hire basis or through *development/production* deals that guarantee the media corporation the content needed. *Work for hire* means that the company owns all the intellectual property the creative individual creates, whereas development/production deals might allow the creative individual to share some economic gains with the corporation. Knowing the rules of the game will keep you playing more. Later on, from gaining leverage based on repeated successes, you will be allowed to experiment but with more support from the industry. Important to understand is that being a constraint artist is OK. The good news is that a constraint artist is not uncreative or less creative. On the contrary, a constraint artist is an individual who is able to master the idea of a formula and creativity and become a vital participant in the generation of constant incremental innovations that the media industry needs every year. (*Note:* Free artists usually come up with more original products, whereas constraint artists come up with more functional ones that fit a purpose and the constraints.)

No matter if a free or constraint artist, creative individuals need breaks from projects to be exposed to the environment, new trends, people, and stories. Creative individuals need to feel and analyze what audiences are looking at, enjoying, and rejecting and evolve from there. The best creative individuals are the ones who are constantly in discovery mode and who understand and connect with their audience and environment.

THE AUDIENCE: THE ULTIMATE VALIDATION OF CREATIVITY

The field used to be the first source of validation to define what will be part of a domain, but now it is the audience who anticipates or determines if the field was "right" and if a concept produced a hit. The audience has therefore become the ultimate frontier in the system of validation—the audience ultimately decides what within a domain will become a sure reference of success in the future. Concepts that are not validated by any audience will never be a reference within the field but instead will be a rarity or an unknown gem within a domain (i.e., projects that were rejected and not made). The audience validates a concept by consuming the content, which then is measured by the quality of the feedback, attendance, TV ratings, clicks, views, or downloads.

But who is the audience? Is the audience a homogeneous group of people who are consuming content all at once? Of utmost importance is to understand the composition of an audience and how the different aspects play a role, such as demographics and psychographics, educational level, occupation, knowledge, interests, and income. To make the way content is promoted or brought to an audience (time slot, TV channel, platform of viewing, etc.) more efficient and successful, and to better understand market behavior, anticipate success, and improve a product, research professionals in the entertainment industry constantly cross-reference information between shows and the type of audience that would better respond to certain products. Nowadays, digital social networks allow the compilation of more precise data beyond samples of small groups of people watching TV.

The audience defines the ultimate relevance of a show, thus reaffirming the social aspect of creativity in media. The audience response is determined by the power of the promotional campaign and its viral effect (the social media strategy and impact). If a show is not promoted, an audience will not know about it and will not watch it. The show will irremediably go away.

When a new story comes out that earns the trust and support of an audience, the product is considered innovative and successful. Audience response therefore becomes key information for members of the field. The members of the field incorporate the background information about the audience into their evaluation process to improve the possibility of choosing the best possible product for that market, not just the best product that critics will love.

Different dimensions for audience validation exist outside the field and a domain. According to Sawyer (2006), these dimensions depend on the level of sophistication of the individuals being exposed to the product. The audience is therefore broken down into connoisseurs, amateurs, and the general public.

Connoisseurs. Individuals who are well informed about the different aspects of the field are known as connoisseurs. They read publications and books and are quite knowledgeable. They are the sophisticated fans who gather important details about a specific concept, project, or product. Other people usually listen to connoisseurs and look to them for references and advice. In the world of social media and bloggers, many people form communities around certain connoisseurs and follow their analyses and recommendations before making their own decisions. These connoisseurs are the most influential individuals in the audience. Connoisseurs think they are pretty close to being experts, but they will never be able to call themselves experts because they have not developed a career in a specific domain that would enable them to become part of the field. Examples of connoisseurs are architects with a strong knowledge about a TV drama series, doctors who have specialist roles for *ER* or *House*, etc. They study, read books, and understand the process, and, yes, they may eventually cross over to become part of the professional domain. For example, the producers of the drama series *ER* hired actual doctors as consultants for the show. Some of these doctors became front-row connoisseurs of the drama series production process and became so actively involved in the production that they ended up being directors or writers. Connoisseurs are also hard-core fans. These connoisseurs also play an important role in the creative process and become the closest way for an artist to connect with the audience (Sawyer, 2006). A writer being able to read the chats of connoisseurs about a TV show allows the writer to understand what people like or do not like about the characters, the story, etc. in a deeper way than just receiving "I don't like it!" or "It sucks!" from a regular angry viewer. Connoisseurs provide a more insightful analysis. Connoisseurs can also bring bias that builds a destructive matrix of opinion. For that reason alone, always beneficial is to balance out different opinions and points of view.

Amateurs. An amateur is an individual who has been exposed to a domain at some point, but has never developed the knowledge required to become a professional in the domain. Amateurs do not necessarily stay current with new events but instead are more connected with their inner desire to be an artist (TV director, filmmaker, musician, or actor). These individuals engage throughout their lives in activities that "keep the flame alive" but do not go any further. Amateurs could be individuals who play the guitar or the piano (not professionally), tape documentaries, or put together family movies. Amateurs are seen as being a niche rather than a driving force within the audience spectrum (Sawyer, 2006).

General public. The general public is the mass that ultimately consumes a product (watches, listens, attends, downloads, shares, pins, tweets). The general public does not have any influence in the decision-making process to procure the creation and green-light a show, but it does have the ultimate power to define and seal the success of a show by tuning into the broadcasting channel at the expected time or by accessing a specific platform to stream or download the show. The more audience registered (the more eyeballs), the higher rating levels will be and thus the possibility of attracting more advertisers and making the TV network more profitable. A ratings success show will then become a reference within the domain (Sawyer, 2006). Individuals in the general public are called upon to participate in focus groups because amateurs and connoisseurs can bias the output of a study. A show could be critically acclaimed (by the field) but not validated by the audience (no ratings). A critically acclaimed show might not have a big audience, only a niche audience (low ratings), ensuring an unfortunate cancellation if the show airs on a free TV network. *Critically acclaimed* does not mean an audience embraced the show. The combination of the two—critically acclaimed and validation by the audience—is the ideal situation. The shows *Seinfeld, Everybody Loves Raymond, CSI,* and *Who Wants to Be a Millionaire?* were critically acclaimed and ratings success stories. In this case, commercial met quality. The comedy series *Arrested Development* was critically acclaimed but had low audience acceptance. *Arrested Development* was cancelled in 2006—the same year the show was awarded an Emmy as Best Comedy Series. Seven years later, Netflix pleased fans when it decided to revive the show. On occasion, the general public will accept a product, turning it into a commercial success, even though the show was considered to be low quality by the field. As a result of commercial successes, the industry sets up premises and establishes antecedents that lead to more development of the same type of shows, despite what the critics say. A revision in the field happens to create acceptance and an understanding of the type of content people like. This kind of understanding is crucial because not all "good" films or TV shows are critically acclaimed. The content must please the audience. If the audience says "yes," then the content is worthwhile and the need for more like it is activated. Always keep in mind that good commercial content pleases the majority of the audience. *Sharknado* (2013, a made-for-television satirical disaster film) is an extreme example of fans supporting a poorly made film. The audience almost played a prank on the industry and turned this film onto a B-rated sci-fi cult film. The reaction via social media was so unexpectedly high that the show became one of the most-watched films in the history of the Syfy network in the United States. As a result, a sequel was made.

The media industry is a highly commercially driven industry. *Commercial* can mean something most people will be entertained by and easily understand. People do not want to be bored or confused. That's a reality. Outlets exist to expose all sorts of media. Highly commercial content definitely prevails in most massive platforms of exposition. *Highly commercial*, however, does not mean bad, simple, or poorly made. Successful film franchises such as *Harry Potter* and *Star Wars* were highly commercial and had appeal that transcended expectations, enchanting millions of viewers. These films were superbly crafted. Audiences appreciated the effort.

The audience then has a passive-aggressive role because they can choose what to watch and by doing so keep content alive or kill it. From a collective standpoint, the audience plays a powerful role in the final stage of the process of creative validation. The audience seals the fate of a show, both economically and in terms of its life cycle. In recent years, the audience has been key in saving TV series such as *Fringe* in 2011 and *Veronica Mars* in 2007 that were at the edge of cancellation.

Try this activity:

- Define an ideal path of validation to help a concept you have in mind gain value, momentum, and recognition in the field.
- Draw an example of the path of validation for a webisode series you have seen. Why do you think the webisode made it through the validation path? Who approved the idea?

Web
Added
Value™

PART III: INNOVATION

7

UNDERSTANDING INNOVATION

After learning the basis of strategy and creativity in content creation, innovation is the third concept to master. As stated in the *Introduction*, there is no innovation without strategy and creativity. The three concepts are interdependent:

- Strategy provides context,
- Creativity sets the background for what makes something creative, and
- Innovation is the application of these two—strategy *and* creativity—in a utilitarian, philosophical way.

Innovation gives creativity a purpose because of strategic thinking.

DEFINITON OF INNOVATION

The entertainment industry works around the idea of innovating every time. Players in the industry want to be trendsetters—to come up with never-before-seen forms of visual expression, storytelling, aesthetics, and entertainment in general—yet the entertainment industry does not necessarily follow the processes of innovation as other industries do. According to Aris & Bughin (2005), a study conducted by a global consulting firm (McKinsey & Company) revealed that media companies in Europe ranked innovation as their top priority (more than 66% of respondents), but less than 15% considered themselves as being "good" at innovation. These results clearly indicate the need in the media industry to understand what innovation means and how to implement the principles of innovation at the core of its processes.

The word *innovation* comes from the Latin word *innovare* which means "to make something new" (Del Zotto & Kranenburg, 2008). Its Latin root *nova* clearly indicates that *new* defines the essence of this concept. Something new without a purpose, however, fades away and creates no value for its creator and users. Purpose comes from strategy *and* creativity.

An innovation is *an original, valued, new product, service, or process that breaks through, providing users with a novel, utilitarian experience.* The utilitarian aspect refers to the fact that the new product provides value, fulfills a need, and creates new sources of revenue.

Innovations are also opportunistic, taking on needs people do not even know they have and becoming new practices, new standards, and new references (dal Zotto & Kranenburg, 2008). Innovations break old rules and respond to a creative process in the search to establish new rules. Innovations bring new meaning to existing products by improving their features and utilitarian sense. Innovators take on past experiences and create new ones, empathetically extrapolating the needs of a specific audience, and in "a stroke of genius" come up with something revolutionary and new. An innovation could be a feature, a combination of existing products, or a breakthrough. An innovation creates a new market and brings with it new processes to produce or achieve. An innovation, however, cannot succeed if the process to produce it is not affordable, efficient, and revolutionary in itself.

Sometimes a product is created with one intention, but innovative creative minds turn the product into something unexpectedly necessary for a totally different group and market. An example of such an innovation is the iPod. The iPod was initially conceived as a music player, but it evolved into a mobile multimedia entertainment device to watch videos, communicate with others, and search the internet. The iPod then turned into a phone, the iPhone, and grew in size to become a tablet, the iPad. A new market then opened up with more than 300 million devices sold to date (Edwards, 2011). Other examples of innovation include:

- 3M's Post-it®: The adhesive was initially prepared for a heavy-duty purpose, but after failing, it was accidentally used to stick a bookmark in a hymnbook.
- Fast food: The fast food restaurant concept was merged the speed of the supermarket with the notion of having ready-to-eat food from a restaurant.
- Carry-on bags: Years passed before wheels were added to suitcases.

All of these innovations changed our lives by providing valuable experiences and creating new business and markets. Innovations make us feel better. They provide us with the notion that we have just solved a problem, received value, or fulfilled a need.

INNOVATION IN ENTERTAINMENT

The entertainment industry has delivered innovation in different shapes and forms, using very specific ways to look for new products and to develop content and ultimately produce it. Some entertainment corporations take greater risk than others and use a more intuitive approach to content creation, while others are more analytical, preferring to rely on the past (sometimes most of the established big media corporations). Everyone wants to accurately predict the future and ensure success, yet breakthroughs occur even when the outcome is not easy to predict, surprising the market in a very positive way.

Sitcoms were created as an evolution of theater plays and radio comedy experiences to fit into a format suitable for a new medium called TV, following the time standards established by sponsors and advertisers at the time (Perebinossoff, Gross & Gross, 2005; Brooks & Marsh, 2007). As a result of this revolutionary approach, sitcoms had a structure that differed from theater plays and radio shows and a unique duration and pace—a half hour. *Pinwright's Progress*, a great example of innovation in media content creation, was the first regular half-hour televised sitcom created and produced by the BBC in the United Kingdom in 1946. *Pinwright's Progress* defined not only the narrative of this particular genre, but also its aesthetics and the three-camera shooting style (Lewisohn, 2003). This revolutionary sitcom approach was innovation—an excellent example of how to take an existing product or experience and turn it into a different one by making the experience relevant for a different, broader market (in this case, a TV audience). The rest is history. More than 400 prime-time sitcoms have been produced in the United States alone, including *I Love Lucy*, one of the most notable sitcoms of all times, and other titles such as *Adventures of Ozzie and Harriet, Father Knows Best*, and *Leave It to Beaver* that created a legion of memorable characters who became the best friends of many families throughout the decades (Edgerton & Rose, 2005; Brooks & Marsh, 2007).

Other examples of innovation in media content include MTV's reality show *The Real World* (1992) and the reality game shows *Survivor* (1997) and *Big Brother* (1999), which captured real reactions and events in a group of people who were secluded in a closed or remote precarious environment. When these reality shows were broadcast in the 1990s, they definitely broke the mold of storytelling and brought viewers the possibility of witnessing how real people interacted and overcame the obstacles and problems imposed by the show. The reality game shows *Survivor* and *Big Brother* took lessons learned from *The Real World* and, relying on the power of voyeurism, brought to life a new type of competition that spread quickly all over the world, generating a new business model, new production processes, and new formulas to exploit them through lucrative and efficient replicas (the format business).

Other examples of innovation in media content creation are the introduction of the docu-camera style for directing and writing a comedy series (*The Office*) and the innovative directing style of handheld camera framing and movement by MTV in the late 1980s (and then adopted in 1-hour drama series such as *The Shield* or *ER*). These innovative styles opened up new ways to tell stories, present situations, and entertain the masses. (The different drivers of innovation in media content will be discussed in Chapter 9, *Drivers of Content Innovation.*) Before we get into the process of creating innovations, let's review where innovations come from.

FORMULA VERSUS INNOVATION

As Roger Martin (2009) established, innovation comes from a combination of analytical and intuitive thinking. *Analytical* has to do with the utilization of existing data and results to predict the future. (As we reviewed in the model of social cultural validation, experts in the field tend to rely on the past—information in the domain—to make decisions.) Intuition, on the other hand, is mysterious and risky, opening opportunities for unknown, never-seen products. *Intuition* is related to feelings, emotions, and "guts." Although innovation emerges in more risky environments, always important is to consider analytical information, manage it, and make the best out of it to further assess the opportunity at hand. If the numbers or the facts are adverse, always revisit why something similar did not work and understand why the new approach brings something new that might make the opportunity better and cause it to work this time. The idea is to collect knowledge and to use that information to your advantage, even when pitching a show, to ensure that everyone understands why you believe the program or the show will be better this time.

Figure 7-1 is a graphic representation of the relationship between the number of shows produced versus the degree of analytics and intuition, which defines formula content and innovation/risk. The left side of the graph starts with one innovation that then becomes a new formula that is replicated, forming the area of formula content which is based on analytics in terms of successful experiences and data with which the industry feels comfortable. The number of shows increases when the formula is first established because many shows of the same type start being produced. The formula is intrinsically related with genre. Examples include sitcoms, 1-hour procedural dramas, game shows, and talk shows. On the other hand, more innovative propositions are lower in number and occur within the area of intuition/risk, the right side of the graph. At the lowest part of the area of risk is a new innovation, which then becomes a new formula and the whole process starts all over again. Recommended is staying within the highlighted

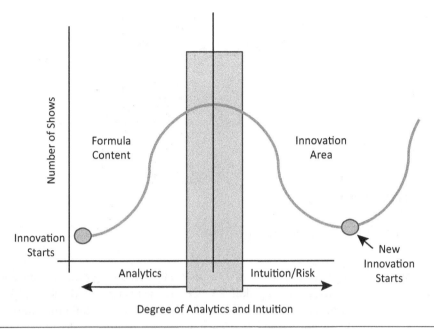

Figure 7-1. Number of shows versus degree of analytics and intuition.

area between analytics and intuition/risk so that you can take the best from the formula and apply variations that will add value to the production of new shows that will stand out and be better than the formulas and safe bets of the past. The highlighted area represents the evolution of the formula. If we continue to transit the right side of the graph, we will enter an area of thinking and creation that is more intuitive, aiming for ideas that have not been seen or proven before. Notice how the number of shows decreases on the right side of the graph. That is because those shows are the ones that are more difficult to get done—not everyone is willing to take high risks when creating content. As can be seen, the higher the degree of risk, the higher the possibility is to produce breakthroughs.

WHERE DOES INNOVATION COME FROM?

Innovation is the result of the creative processes or what is called *creativity*. Innovation comes from opportunistic ideas. As seen in Figure 7-2 (based on Figure 5-2 in Chapter 5, *Understanding Creativity*), ideas are the result of a process that combines expertise, knowledge, and intelligence, which are gathered in the context of creation. The context is defined by the industry or domain where the creative process happens. Within this context, creative individuals identify an

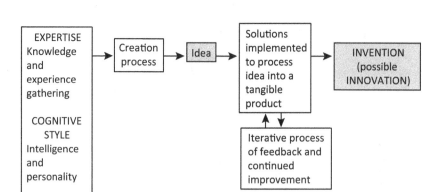

Figure 7-2. The process of creativity.

opportunity that later is transformed into an *idea* by combining a set of knowledge and experience (such as writing skills). Once the idea is perfected and built into a product, it becomes an *invention*, which is in essence a potential innovation.

Expertise, knowledge, and experience gathering are the results of research, exploration, real-life experiences, and academic formation. These three aspects combined with cognitive style, intelligence, personality, motivation, and the environmental context are of utmost importance to guarantee the generation of innovations (see the section on *Resources for Creativity* in Chapter 5).

Experience is connected to the events in an individual's life experiences. *Knowledge* is represented by a particular set of skills (intellectual, procedural, and technical) and years of experience in the work field. *Intelligence* is related to the capacity to solve problems *and* the information gathered over time. In one way or another, the combination of experience, knowledge, and intelligence influences identifying opportunities for coming up with an idea that could potentially turn into a product that would fulfill an unknown need in the market.

Expertise fuels the generation of valuable ideas. As discussed in Chapter 5, a 10-year rule represents the time individuals spend preparing before they accomplish true excellence expert status. After 10 years of dedication and preparing in a particular field, an individual might be ready to create an invention that could eventually become an innovation (Hayes, 1989). This 10-year rule corresponds to the notion that an individual has possibly mastered a skill set and now understands this set of skills in the context of its surroundings in such way as to ignite a spark that leads to a new product. As Bilton (2007) stated, "For an idea to be innovative in business or in art it must derive from the historically established norms and conventions, not just from our own personal history." Those "norms and conventions" are *knowledge*.

Some agree to disagree with the 10-year rule, and they may be right, but the truth of the matter is that whoever invents something does it after going through a process of realization in which their knowledge takes center stage—it does not matter that this knowledge started being collected at the age of 8. Remember that Steven Spielberg and his breakthrough in the film industry at an early age was a result of his early exposure to cinematic experiences. Taylor Swift is another example of a very young innovator. Taylor Swift started to experiment with music when she was a child and then wrote her first song at the age of 12. By the time she was 16, Taylor Swift was a major music sensation. We could even say that we might not have seen the best of Taylor Swift yet. At the time of the writing of this book, she was 24 and had sold millions of records. Taylor Swift has mastered her artistic sense and continues to evolve and innovate.

Let's review a hypothetical situation. A young woman decides to enroll in medical school to become a doctor. After 4 years in the medical program, during her internship, she decides to drop out of school to follow her true passion—to become a film/TV writer. She then spends the next years of her life mastering the skills and developing a career as a writer, also taking time to gather information about others like herself who have dropped out of medical school to pursue other interests. She starts collecting information she finds in newspapers and specialized journals and hears in conversations. The process just described is nothing else than the process of intelligence generation and experience and skills gathering illustrated in Figure 7-3. In our hypothetical situation, when the young woman embarked on the process of creation, she had an insight and noticed that people might be interested in knowing about the experiences of doctors. She then embarked on the idea of developing a TV show about medical school grad student dropouts. This idea was the result of the process of creation led by the spark she had to combine her writing skills with her failed medical experience. She then turned the idea into a tangible product and put together a concept and a treatment called *Not Quite MD*. This material or new product was then an invention.

Creativity thus plays a critical role in this process of innovation. As we have seen, creativity sparks the initial idea and helps improve it as the idea moves forward in the process of creation (Harvard Business Essentials, 2003) until obtaining a tangible initial product called an invention. But what happens from the moment an invention is fabricated? How does it turn into innovation?

THE EVOLUTION OF INNOVATION

Ideas must go through stages until finding their real utilitarian purpose and becoming innovations. Ideas evolve over time like larvae or tadpoles that go through different stages in a process of metamorphosis until becoming butterflies

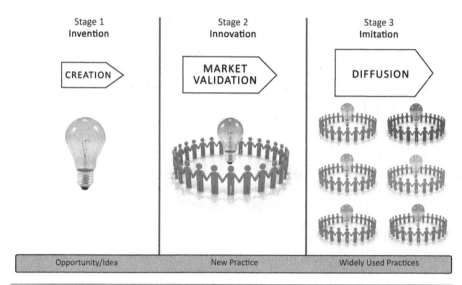

Figure 7-3. The evolution of an innovation.

and frogs. Following this analogy, an innovation starts as an invention, which is the initial result of the process of creativity (Figure 7-3).

As illustrated in Figure 7-3, this evolution occurs in three stages: invention, innovation, and imitation. Evolution starts with identification of an opportunity to improve something; an idea is then created which materializes in the form of an *invention* (Stage 1), which is then validated by a market that embraces the new practice (or product), turning the invention into an *innovation* (Stage 2). Once the market has accepted the innovation and the conditions for a new entrant are in place, the diffusion of the innovation starts and the practice is widely applied and used, yielding *imitations* (Stage 3). (Del Zotto, 2008). An invention can be in a drawer for years until being discovered by an entity (a corporation or an individual) that is enthusiastic about the invention's potential and willing to pour the necessary resources into taking the invention to the market for ultimate validation. If validated and embraced by an audience, the invention becomes an innovation.

From previous discussions, we know that innovation and invention are different terms and that they are sources of imitation. Proper definitions are:

- Invention: A product with no proven utilitarian purpose; a product with potential, but still not with the assurance of being relevant for a specific audience
- Innovation: A new product that serves a purpose, possesses commercial value, and generates a new market

- Imitation: The evolution of an innovation; serves to grow markets and generate variations of an existing innovation

The market embraces content innovation when its utility becomes evident. When people see value and the invention provides an experience worth paying for or spending time to enjoy, then the product succeeds and the invention becomes an innovation. The main differences between an invention and an innovation rely on its utility, the economic process to produce it, the commercial power, and the market value.

Innovation in media, as in any other industry, is about people working within a creative environment that fosters the generation of ideas, the exchange of insights, and the acknowledgment of new possibilities to bring to audiences the "next big thing." Innovation is the result of the creative process and might be either the result of one person's creative work or the work of a team. If this creative work produces a utilitarian experience and adds value to the end consumer, then it is considered to be an innovation. If the work is just imaginative, with no real purpose or application, then the work is merely inventive and not innovative.

In the context of the media industry, innovations are called *intellectual properties* (IPs). The economic value of an IP increases as an idea advances through the process of innovation. The validation that the idea receives throughout increases its value. Once the IP makes it to the TV screen, its value is exercised. Although value is pre-negotiated, when the idea is recognized as having potential in the market, its initial value is tapped. This value is determined by a negotiating entity, which could be an individual (producer, director, etc.) or a corporation (a studio, production company, TV network, on-line platform, or media conglomerate). In media content, a media content innovation is a new IP that:

- Provides a new utilitarian experience for an audience,
- Creates a new business model,
- Opens a new market, and
- Increases the value and profit generation of a media firm.

Because of the potential value of successful IPs, highly skilled jobs are created and the industry fosters the dissemination of innovative ideas and knowledge with applications in different media platforms and scenarios (Bilton, 2007). Innovative ideas come in different forms, and different industries participate in a major success. Engineers, managers, lawyers, etc. all become supporting industry functional areas in the materialization of a big idea into a TV show (or any other form of content) for audiences to experience.

Now, let's revisit the sitcom example to see how the sitcom evolved from an idea to a widely produced form of entertainment. When the idea for the sitcom *Pinwright's Progress* was produced in the United Kingdom in 1946, this idea became an inventive solution for bringing theater and radio-type entertainment to the new medium of TV. Then, when the idea went on the air and people accepted it, validation occurred immediately. With viewers accepting the idea, an innovative solution was born, the sitcom.

Creative TV professionals in the United Kingdom and the United States soon embraced this new formula for entertainment and collaborated to write and produce more sitcoms, causing diffusion of the genre. In 1947 the first sitcom aired in the United States. *Mary Kay and Johnny* aired on the now-extinct DuMont Television Network and became the spark for a proliferation of the genre in the United States. In the mid 1950, *I Love Lucy*, *The Honeymooners*, and *The Goldbergs* became solid hits and went on to be on the list of pioneer sitcoms made in the United States (Perebinossoff, Gross, & Gross, 2005; Brooks & Marsh, 2007). The process has been the same for other TV genres, which have gained air time and become new practices generating thousands of TV shows.

Another example of innovation diffusion occurred in 1953 when ABC's founder Leonard Goldenson envisioned TV as a medium that was different from radio and decided to create exclusively produced fictional content that could be inspired by the Hollywood cinematic experiences only featured in film in theaters. That is how, through an alliance with Warner Bros. Entertainment Inc. (commonly called Warner Bros.), ABC produced the first hour-long prime-time western *Cheyenne* in 1955. The idea proved successful and the innovative model of content creation in Hollywood diffused in the industry, which by 1959 had produced and aired more than 28 westerns (Perebinossoff, Gross & Gross, 2005).

An interesting example of innovation evolution occurred when the drama series *Lost* aired on ABC in 2004. *Lost* became a major breakthrough in terms of grandiloquence, story, cinematic, aesthetics, direction, and narrative strategy. Thanks to ABC, mystery and sci-fi made it to the air when no other channel had anything similar on network TV. Soon after *Lost* aired, other shows tried to follow. Series such as *Surface* (2005) and *Invasion* (2005) promptly appeared, but unfortunately none of them succeeded. Years later, the trend continued and networks gambled by producing more shows such as *Revolution* (2012–2014) from the creator of *Lost* that had doses of mystery in a post-apocalyptic world. In the international TV market, the imitation process sparked similar shows. For example, in Spain a show was made called *El Barco* (*The Ship*) in 2011. The *El Barco* series presented how 20 people onboard a ship realized that they were the lone survivors of a major event that had disintegrated the rest of the planet. The only thing left was the ocean and the ship they were on. The series was a major sensation in Spain and soon after was remade in other countries such as Russia. Do not be surprised if *El Barco* comes to a U.S. network at some point.

Mad Men (2007–2015), the U.S. TV drama series, was the trigger for other series such as *Magic City* (2012), the short-lived *Playboy Club* (2011) and *Panam*

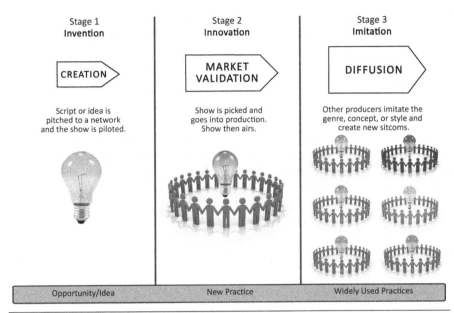

Figure 7-4. How a script turns into an innovation.

(2011), and more recently *Masters of Sex* (2013). The single-camera sitcom *The Office* (2001) in the United Kingdom triggered the diffusion of a new genre that mixed reality aesthetics with comedy. In the United States, *Arrested Development* (2003–2013) and *The Office* (2005–2013) followed the path of diffusion set by *The Office* in the United Kingdom and became innovations on their own, which opened the door for other series such as *Parks and Recreation* and *Modern Family* in 2009.

Pop *Idol* (2001) in England sparked a wave of singing reality competitions. The *X Factor* (2004, United Kingdom; 2011, United States), *Got Talent* (2005, United Kingdom; 2006, United States), and *The Voice* (2011, United States; 2012, United Kingdom) appeared as a response. In 1997, *Big Brother* from The Netherlands was key for the proliferation of reality shows with isolated contestants in a locked space. As a result, around the world, other shows aired, such as *Survivor* (United States), *Protagonistas* (Latin America), *Celebrity Big Brother* (United Kingdom), *Captive* (New Zealand), and *Operacion Triunfo* (Spain).

When we look at the process of a new innovative TV series being picked up by a TV network, we see how an innovation evolves from an invention to an imitation. As illustrated in Figure 7-4, Stage 1 is the presentation of an idea in the form of a script or treatment. When the script is validated and approved by the network, the idea becomes an invention waiting to be tested as a pilot. If the pilot is produced, the pilot becomes an invention waiting to be exposed to different layers of validation, such as the executives inside the TV network (and ultimately the audience). These executives decide if the show makes it to Stage 2 and exposure to the audience. If the show is a hit, then the invention becomes an innovation. If the show is a breakthrough, then you can bet that many other shows of the same type will follow in the process, with diffusion (imitation) coming right after, as described in the previous examples.

An initial innovation may break through the market (market validation) and be diffused in the form of different shows of the same type (imitation). This process of breakthrough and diffusion defines the two different types of innovation that will be discussed in depth in the next chapter.

8

CLASSIFICATION OF MEDIA CONTENT INNOVATION ACCORDING TO DEGREE OF NOVELTY

Creative individuals such as producers, writers, and directors prepare their next big content proposition in an attempt to get ultimate validation from the industry and the audience and "break the mold." When the field and the audience validate the work of a creative individual, they identify the nature of the artist's style and qualify it as something absolutely new or something within existing parameters but new on its own terms. In the pursuit of that validation and ultimate success, creative individuals spend their time experimenting with a particular style to define themselves as artists and put emphasis on the differentiating aspects of their artistic proposals that make them unique. Throughout the years, creative individuals have been responsible for bringing to life novel ideas that have defined the industry and made it evolve. These novel ideas are, of course, innovations.

In Chapter 7 (*Understanding Innovation*), the concept of media innovation and how an innovation evolves through the three different stages of invention, innovation, and imitation were explained. Formula and intuition were also discussed. Exemplified was how an idea or invention in the media industry, after being validated and accepted by the audience, becomes an innovation and starts diffusing in the industry in the form of imitations. Then throughout this process of evolution, the degree of novelty changes and determines the different types of innovation.

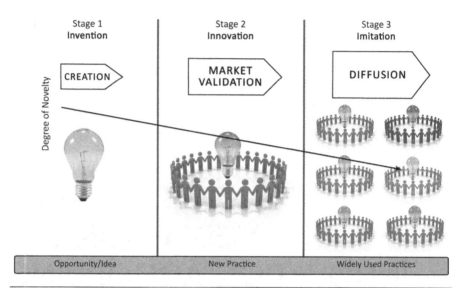

Figure 8-1. Degree of novelty versus evolution of innovation.

The degree of novelty for a validating audience depends on the stage a show is in—in the sense that the idea presented in the invention phase was the newest form with the highest degree of novelty and that imitations have the least degree of novelty (Figure 8-1). The degree of novelty therefore becomes the key aspect for determining the classification of innovation into two groups: radical and incremental. Because the new idea has not proved its utilitarian sense during the invention phase (Stage 1), radical innovation occurs in the second phase (Stage 2), once the market accepts the idea. Incremental innovation is then related to the process of imitation and diffusion (Stage 3).

Figure 8-2 helps visualize how incremental and radical innovations occur based on how analytics and intuition play out in the process. As we can see, incremental innovations start when the formula content is altered positively and brings new groundbreaking utilitarian experiences to viewers.

The highest numbers of innovations are a result of incremental improvements, which occur in the center of the curve. The more risk and intuition in the process, the more innovative a show will be. When we increase the degree of intuition and risk, innovations tend to be more radical and fewer in number.

RADICAL INNOVATION

A radical innovation is essentially a breakthrough—a new concept, program, service, or process—that redefines an industry and goes beyond that which exists

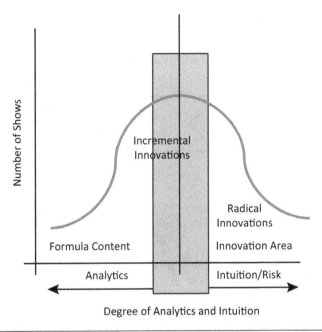

Figure 8-2. Degree of innovation versus analytics and intuition.

(Harvard Business Essentials, 2003). A radical innovation is something new to the world that creates a new spectrum of operation, a new industry and business models, and a new field within the entertainment domain. In Figure 8-3, an evolution diagram for innovations, Stage 2 is defined by radical innovations. A radical innovation is the result of an invention being validated in the market. Many radical innovations in the media have potential to displace established programs and ways to produce a source for new bursts of creative thinking.

Most radical innovations appear as the result of an unexpected combination of the existing forms of consumption serving a new purpose. At the World Innovation Forum in 2011, Dr. Paddy Miller urged attendees to look at the past to define the future. The past is where innovations are dormant, waiting to be discovered. These innovations are within a big puzzle that defines a context waiting to be noticed. The example used by Dr. Miller at the forum was the carry-on bag. A carry-in bag combines two existing products, a suitcase and wheels, created millions of years apart. The act of putting them together is what turned these unconnected products into an innovative and highly utilitarian product.

That is exactly what happened when TV was created. The advent of TV paved the way for a new industry in which creative professionals could adapt radio content, theater plays, and newspapers into TV shows. For example, newspaper

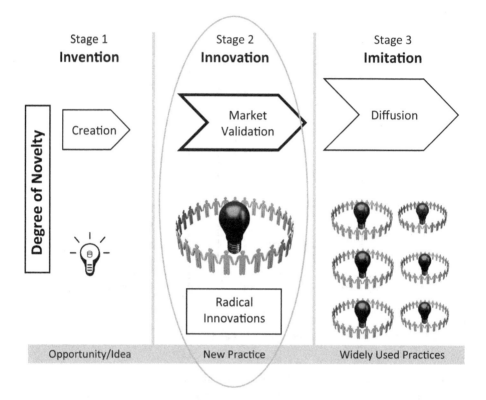

Figure 8-3. Radical innovation in the process of evolution.

and radio news now appeared on TV in the form of "revolutionary" newscasts. What was revolutionary? It was the printed page of a newspaper and a voice on the radio that now had a "face." The same thing happened with theater and fiction programming on radio. TV could now spread the dramatic and comedic world of possibilities through a box that let the audience travel beyond the stage or airwaves to witness stories and events as if they were really happening. That is how the TV fiction genre was born, and it was revolutionary! The merge of the new TV medium with existing platforms of entertainment created a list of radical innovations that defined TV content in the twentieth century. Most early TV developments in fiction during the 1930s and 1940s were adaptations of other forms of entertainment.

The development of a new slate of shows that filled TV screens in the 1940s had a radical consequence on the TV industry, which grew as a result. Each genre in development (fiction and non-fiction) began to demand specialized individuals from theater and radio to lead these productions. TV networks created news departments and scripted divisions and hired professionals to become variety and entertainment show producers, writers, and directors and hired teams of professionals to develop and produce the best possible content. The industry turned into a very competitive ground, which grew through new business models, processes, and careers. Universities now needed to create programs to prepare professionals for the new TV world as radio, print, and film professionals transitioned to it. The advent of these new forms of content and exposition enabled a new burst of creativity among film artists, TV producers, dance choreographers, sportscasters, documentary producers, newscasters, engineers, and directors.

The first shows (or platforms of exposition) created are examples of radical innovations in media content:

- The first drama series: *The Queen's Messenger* (shot in the United Kingdom in 1928 and broadcast on W2XB/WGY/WRGB in Schenectady, NY)
- The first crime investigative series: BBC's *Telecrime* (written especially for the new TV medium in 1938)
- The first game show: BBC's *Spelling Bee* (1938)
- The first U.S. celebrity game show: DuMont Television Network's *Play the Game* (1946)
- The first sports program: NBC's *Gillete Cavalcade of Sports* (1946)
- The first talent show: DuMont Television Network's *Doorway to Fame* (1947)
- The first cop shows: ABC's *Stand By for Crime* and DuMont Television Network's *Chicagoland Mystery Players* (1949)
- The first U.S. variety/comedy show: ABC's *On the Corner* (1948)
- The first soap opera: CBS's Procter & Gamble's *The First Hundred Years* (1950)
- The first medical drama series: CBS's *City Hospital* (1951)
- The first subscriber-pay channel: HBO (1972)
- The first dramedy: CBS's *MASH* (1972)
- The first reality show: PBS's *An American Family* (1973)
- The first thematic channel: ESPN, a sports-dedicated channel (1979)
- The first news-dedicated channel: CNN (1980)
- The first music-dedicated channel: MTV (1981)

As TV evolved and a new world of multiplatform opportunities continued on an ascending curve of sophistication, improvements and new ways to enjoy content proliferated. New platforms now redefined the way stories were told and obliged producers to offer more content and more information through them. A very interesting example of radical innovation in content is the drama series *Lost*

(2004). *Lost* used different platforms of entertainment such as TV, the internet, print media, and mobile devices to allow an audience to submerge itself in a world of events that J.J. Abrams presented week after week. The audience was able to see adventures of castaways in the background through a series of webisodes. The audience also had access to the website of a fake company featured in the show to learn more about it. The website posted job offers and held online interviews for roles. The minds behind this multiplatform experience even created a book that was supposedly written by one of the passengers on the plane that crashed and became the centerpiece of the whole story. Creative content is "spreadable" (Jenkins, 2013). The dimension that J.J. Abrams gave to his show *Lost* is the radical innovation of our times that caused all TV networks to look for the "next" *Lost* (see Table 8-7).

Radical innovations occur over time. They define periods and eras. Radical innovations are now just "signs of the times" and set the basis for what is next.

HOW RADICAL CONTENT INNOVATION SPREADS ACROSS THE WORLD

Radical innovations in content occur within a particular sociocultural context, meaning a country or a regional sociocultural environment. A regional sociocultural environment can entice a country, several countries, continents, and even the whole world. Depending on the context in which the content is first exposed, radical innovations can therefore be global or local. The origin of radical innovations defines the rollout of a specific work throughout the world. Radical innovations in media can be found in three forms:

- Global: Fiction (movies and TV series), music, and special events that either happen live, air simultaneously across the world via TV or the internet, or are rolled out according to patterns of media distribution across the world
- Formats: Radical innovations that start as a local phenomenon in a country and are replicated in a major diffusion effort in the form of formats ("recipes" that allow producers in other territories to replicate a successful show in another territory that generate a local innovation)
- Genres: Radical innovations that become new formulas, with their diffusion igniting new genres with specific methodologies that can be learned and implemented to tell all sorts of stories across the world

Radical Innovation with Global Impact

The first form of radical innovation, innovation with global impact, concerns events that transcend frontiers and languages. Examples include:

- Movies such as *The Matrix* and *The Harry Potter* franchise
- Pop singers such as *Madonna* and *Lady Gaga*
- A drama series such as *CSI*
- The *MTV Video Music Awards* and *The Olympics Opening Ceremony* (events of big magnitude which are costly and watched worldwide by audiences despite language or culture)

Radical innovations (also called blockbusters) have universal appeal, are unique, and cannot be easily replicated. They encourage research and development for more events of the same type. Live events airing across the world are called multicultural global phenomena. They showcase high-end technological advances or performances that the world watches in awe. A man landing in the moon in 1969 was one of the first global multicultural TV phenomena. Live news coverage of the Gulf War in 1990, the first televised World Cup, and the Olympic Games also fit the criteria. These types of events have long-lasting life cycles of exploitation (Aris & Bughin, 2005).

In recent years, the internet ignited the global rollout of content. With the advent of social media sites such as YouTube and Facebook, media content started spreading quickly and simultaneously in many countries, launching the careers of unexpected performers such as the Korean pop star Psy. The internet also became the home for user-generated content that could be seen by audiences around the globe. This process differed from prior years when innovations occurred in one country and only many years later made it to another country. Nowadays, everything happens much faster.

Other radical innovations with global impact are fiction shows that travel as finished products. In that sense, Hollywood studios are the leading force behind global entertainment and the distribution of media content worldwide. The world follows closely what the United States generates in content. The global distribution operations of studios, record labels, and communication companies know how to turn these events into worldwide phenomena. Examples of successful innovations in the form of finished products are the U.S. prime-time series *Law and Order* and *24*. These series became major successes worldwide thanks to the translated versions of the shows that originally aired in the United States.

Using Formats to Roll Out Radical Innovation

Realization by the TV industry that a show produced in one country did not need to stay in just that country and that a show could travel everywhere, not as a ready-to-air product but by being remade with a local flavor, led to the birth of the format industry. In the 1990s, the format industry became an industry and grew exponentially, creating new worldwide business opportunities for companies that created content.

A format is a *recipe* for making a particular type of show so that people in a country different from the country of origin can also produce the show. The initial breakthrough show therefore becomes the source of a local breakthrough show if the same concept or genre is breaking into another market for the first time. The format industry is a way to turn global innovations into local innovations. This type of disruptive process can happen many times for the same product. For example, *Big Brother* is one of the most successful formats ever (produced by Endemol, a Dutch-based company that produces and distributes multiplatform entertainment content with operations in over 30 countries). *Big Brother* was produced and aired successfully in The Netherlands in 1997 where it became a major sensation. Endemol then decided to replicate the show in different territories and soon Spain launched *Gran Hermano* in 2000. The concept spread around the globe as a phenomenon, becoming a revolutionary new competition format in more than 80 countries. Every time *Big Brother* was produced as the first reality show in a country, the show became a radical innovation in that country. If another similar format (not necessarily a copycat) was produced first in other countries, then that format would be the radical innovation in those territories.

Note: In a global context, the first show is the radical innovation, but in a country, the "first mover" is the one that counts. In The Netherlands and in Spain, *Big Brother* became a breakthrough, but *Survivor*, a format coming from Sweden called *Expedition Robinson*, produced in 1997, was the first to air in the United States (in May 2000; *Big Brother* aired in July 2000), becoming the first reality game show in the United States (as of this writing renewed through 2015). The mainstream aspect of *Survivor*, together with a powerful story, events, competition, and a $1-million prize, hit the jackpot of reality and became the biggest reference in the U.S. market (most successful show and the show to beat).

Many TV shows that U.S. audiences think originated in the United States actually come from the United Kingdom, The Netherlands, or other countries, but because the original shows had not been previously exposed in the United States, the U.S. versions became breakthroughs in the U.S. market. Likewise, many innovative concepts such as game shows and fiction that originated in the United States have been replicated around the world.

In the 1980s, TV formats were usually non-fiction programs, such as the game shows *Wheel of Fortune*, *Pyramid*, and *The Newlyweds Game*, but with the advent of reality competitions, the format industry grew and started experimenting with the fiction genre. A key player in the rollout of fiction formats worldwide was the major studio Sony Pictures. Sony Pictures established a breakthrough business model that other studios such as Disney, Fox, and Warner Bros. followed, together with production companies and distributors of content in Europe, Asia, and Latin America. As a result, the fiction format industry evolved and a very healthy creative exchange of fiction content started occurring internationally. Examples of fiction shows that originated in the United States and were exported as formats include *Married with Children, The Nanny, Grey's Anatomy, Gossip Girl, ER,* and *The OC.* U.S. TV series such as *Ugly Betty, Elementary, Jane the Virgin, Devious Maids,* and *The Mysteries of Laura* are remakes of formats, respectively, from Colombia (*Yo soy Betty, la fea*), the United Kingdom (*Sherlock*), Venezuela (*Juana la virgen*), Mexico (*Ellas son la alegría del hogar*), and Spain (*Los misterios de Laura*).

So, a radical innovation starts at a point of local relevance and is replicated in territories where the show might be a hit. Local context also defines the nature of novelty and helps to identify a product as a breakthrough or not. If the original version has been seen in a country, then the impact of a remake will be less, whereas if the show is totally fresh for the audience, the show might become a local breakthrough.

Using Genre as a Vehicle to Diffuse Radical Innovation

Radical innovations establish a new practice, and people start experimenting with the new practice to come up with new products of the same kind. The diffusion of a radical innovation forms a cluster of shows that are ultimately made under the same formula, which is now the formula of the new genre. Genres such as telenovelas, sitcoms, game shows, and reality shows bring attached to them a methodology that people learn and then start applying to bring new stories to life. Different from formats, in which the same story is told in different languages and with a local cast, in a newly created genre, new original stories are told within the parameters of the new genre.

For example, soap operas began airing in the 1950s in the United States and aired a few years later in Latin America. Even though American soap operas were first, Latin American audiences did not know about them until they saw the first Latin American versions. For South American audiences, the breakthrough was a soap opera in Spanish, not one in English. In this case, Latin Americans did not remake a U.S. soap opera but took the essence of the genre and made their own stories with a beginning and an end.

Another example is *Pinwright's Progress,* the first sitcom (see Chapter 7, *Understanding Innovation*). Even though *Pinwright's Progress* was produced in the United Kingdom in 1946, the first sitcom for U.S. audiences was *Mary Kay and Johnny* in 1947. These two, however, defined the genre. Both paved the way for the sitcoms we see aired today. Their structure, the three-film camera shooting

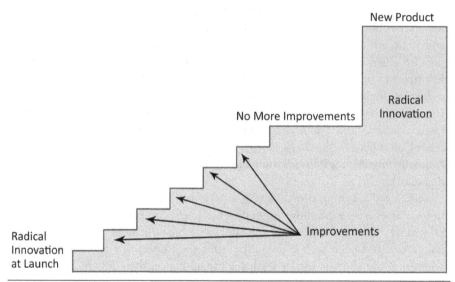

Figure 8-4. Incremental innovation.

strategy in the studio, the writing style, and the acting were all new implementations effectively made for television.

INCREMENTAL INNOVATION

Incremental innovation occurs during the diffusion phase, represents improvements to existing products, and eventually leads to another breakthrough that creates a new status quo in the industry. Improvements to radical innovations also occur over time. The new concepts then air to allow audiences to experience new events and new emotions, all within the same genre.

To visualize incremental innovations, imagine a staircase (Figure 8-4). Each step represents a product in status quo. The vertical lines represent the improvements that elevate the product to another level (or another step) (Harvard Business Essentials, 2003). At some point there is no more room to continue improving or moving up, causing the product to stall. At this point, the product opens up opportunities for a breakthrough product (program), which is a departure from what exists, creating a new formula, genre, market, and industry. Figure 8-4 can be smoothed out and converted into what is called the *S-curve of innovation* (Figure 8-5).

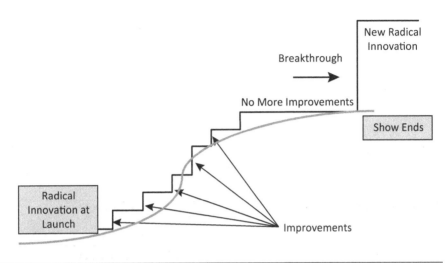

Figure 8-5. The S-curve of innovation.

From Figures 8-4 and 8-5, we can see that a show is launched and evolves over time. If the show becomes a hit at launch, people embrace the show, igniting the need for producers to infuse a series of improvements to guarantee that performance always ascends (measured in ratings, likes, buzz, awards, etc.). Nevertheless, the show will reach a point at which it cannot be improved anymore. At this point, the life cycle of the show on the air either comes to an end or stays, pretty much with no change, until cancelled or a new program breaks through and takes over with a new innovative proposition (indicated in Figure 8-5 as a new radical innovation program) (Harvard Business Essentials, 2003). This process then repeats itself over and over. Figure 8-6 presents how the S-curve of an established program crosses with that of a new rival, which then starts its own process of improvement.

Note: Radical innovations pave the way for creating new competitive marketplaces for audiences to experience a certain type of entertainment. Incremental innovations can also follow radical innovations (Harvard Business Essentials, 2003), so generally understood is that incremental innovations benefit from existing radical innovation products or forms of content (Figure 8-7). Incremental innovations are therefore also a part of the process of diffusion of radical innovations. They add value to the competitive environment that is formed thanks to the fertile ground that is created by the original show.

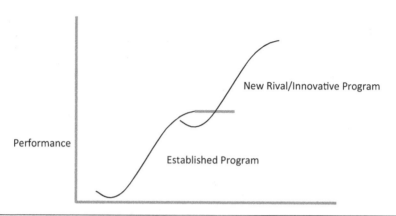

Figure 8-6. The S-curve of an established program and a new breakthrough/rival.

Radical Innovation	Incremental Innovation
Lost (2004): storytelling, cinematographic experience	*The 4400* (2004), *The Walking Dead* (2010), *Falling Skies* (2011), *Revolution* (2012), *Under The Dome* (2013)
The Office (2001, UK): directing, documentary, reality style	*Arrested Development* (2003), *The Office* (2005, US), *Parks and Recreation* (2009), *Modern Family* (2009)
Expedition Robinson (1997), *Big Brother* (1997)	*I'm a Celebrity … Get Me Outta Here!* (2002, UK; 2003, US), *Big Brother VIP* (2003), *Celebrity Survivor* (2006), *Glass House* (2012)
Curb Your Enthusiasm (1999)	Radical innovation that has not been imitated
21 (Twenty One) (1956)	*Who Wants To Be A Millionaire?* (1998, UK; 1999, US)
Pinwright's Progress (1946)	Sitcoms in the 1950s, 1970s, 1980s, 1990s, 2000s (family, young, teenage audiences)
Hannah Montana (2006, The 360 Disney experience)	*I Carly* (2007), *Wizards of Waverly Place* (2007), *Ant Farm* (2007), *Jonas* (2009), *Sunny With A Chance* (2009)
Lost In Space (1965)	*Star Trek* (1966), *Battlestar Gallactica* (1978)
Stand By For Crime (1949), *Chicagoland Mystery Players* (1949)	*Dragnet* (1951) (all police procedural dramas)
Doorway To Fame (1947)	*Gong Show* (1976), *American Idol* (2002), *The X Factor* (2004, UK; 2011, US), *Got Talent* (2005, UK; 2006, US)

Figure 8-7. Examples of radical innovations and their incremental innovations.

INCREMENTAL CONTENT INNOVATION

A creative professional either develops an improved version based on content that already exists or reconfigures existing content to serve some other purpose. Competition then flourishes, creating the ecosystem necessary for producers and writers to start improving an initial program and to create new programs so that audiences can enjoy an initial program more. This reasoning leads us to a discussion of the two types of incremental innovation in media content generation:

- Incremental innovation intrinsic to a show and
- Incremental innovation intrinsic to a genre and a competitive environment.

Incremental Innovation Intrinsic to a Show

Incremental innovation intrinsic to a show moves a concept forward in a new direction or along its current path of success (Sternberg, Kaufman, & Pretz, 2002). This process includes:

- Taking existing content and refueling it from season to season or within a season
- Evolving a show because of technological or pop culture changes
- Milking a concept through spin-offs of an original idea
- Keeping a show alive by shifting the target market

Taking existing content and refueling it from season to season or within a season. TV shows can have a finite run (telenovelas), an infinite run (soap operas, game shows, and newscasts), or runs in seasons (series and prime-time reality competitions). In all of these cases, producers and writers must pen a story so a show moves forward in such a way that it always grasps the audience's attention, maintains interest, surprises the audience, and ultimately sustains the success of the show. In other words, the show has to be in constant improvement until it is over. Incremental innovation can occur within a show and could be in the form of a new storyline, a new character, or a new plot in the case of fiction or a new set design; a new way to eliminate contestants; or a new host in the case of non-fiction shows. Examples of innovations intrinsic to a show include:

- *Big Brother* (UK) (1999 –) and *Big Brother VIP* (2002 –): *Big Brother* was initially created to have ordinary people as contestants in reality competitions. These contestants had to survive the pressure of being confined under surveillance 24 × 7 in a house filled with cameras. After several seasons of *Big Brother* being on the air, show creators in the United Kingdom decided to spice things up by bringing in real celebrities to experience the show and created the *Big Brother VIP*. The move propelled *Big Brother* to success again, just when its ratings were showing symptoms of decline. The improvement was adopted across the world, and the reality *VIP* concept was born. *Big Brother* has continued improving its offerings and has brought previous winners or popular contestants back to the house, igniting new interest to watch the show.

- *Scandal* (2012 –): *Scandal* is a soap-style political drama thriller created by Shonda Rhimes, depicting the story of Olivia Pope, the leader of a crisis management firm that handles all sorts of scandals involving key political figures in Washington, DC. The key irony of the show's plot is that Olivia Pope is the protagonist of the ultimate scandal due to a secret affair she is having with the president of the United States. On top of that, the relationship is interracial, defying orthodoxies and conservative points of view. The series has proven successful, edgy, and unconventional and is characterized by its twists, turns, suspense, revelations, and constant surprises, which have maintained an audience wanting more.

- *American Idol* (2002 –): Talent competition on *American Idol* has improved gradually season after season. Improvements have been applied based on audience reaction to specific phases of the show. Surprises have been incorporated year after year to keep the show interesting. For example, the casting sessions were rather short in the first season. Reaction to the casting sessions was so positive, however, that the casting phase was extended and showed more detail in every city the judges visited. (The same reaction occurred with the second phase of the show *Hollywood Week*, which brought to the show the drama and reality components that the audience usually does not see in a talent competition.) *American Idol* contestants had a chance to perform live in the third phase of the show (which also experienced different variations after 14 seasons on the air). Although judges on the show have changed several times, *American Idol* has remained relevant for American audiences.

- *Doctor Who* (BBC, 1963 –): This U.K. sci-fi series is perhaps the best representation of how to keep a fiction series relevant for over 50 years. The show implemented within its formula the possibility of replacing the main characters of the show in an organic believable way. The Doctor, the Time Lord, is a humanoid alien. Usually after several seasons, the Doctor departs from the human body that contains him and comes back personified in a different body, opening a new era represented by a different actor (12 doctors since inception of the show). Not only does Doctor Who change but so does his sidekick, who is replaced organically keeping the show interesting, surprising, and truthful to its premise of Doctor Who traveling through time and space to fight his enemies and solve all sorts of problems taking place in the entire universe.

Evolving a show because of technological or pop culture changes. Other incremental innovations within a show can be tied to trends, improvements in the production process, and the incorporation of new technologies to adapt and expand the show within the realm of the platforms now used by the audience. These incremental innovations are a direct consequence of audience behavioral changes, pop culture evolution, and the proliferation of new technologies. TV shows maintain relevancy when they offer an audience what it wants and how it wants it. Nowadays, audiences watch TV shows through different devices and enjoy the multidimensional informational aspect that entertainment can now offer. In other words, a TV show now needs to have a mobile application, an online site, and a multiplatform narrative that are able to offer more information and greater access to the show beyond the regular TV experience. In 2014, the *MTV Video Music Awards* offered viewers the possibility to access an online platform created for the show which showed never-seen-before live footage of what was going on backstage and in the green room, makeup room, and dressing rooms. Viewers could also gain access via social media platforms and comment on the information they were being provided. The TV show *American Idol* (2002) unleashed an entire multiplatform voting system to take advantage of all connected devices. Fiction series have also taken advantage of this trend. *The Walking Dead* (2010) also launched extended online content with the purpose of adding value and incremental improvements to the experience. New technologies also allow the incorporation of technical resources that make processes more efficient and devices such as digital cameras instead of film cameras, digital editing systems, storage systems, lighting devices, and 3D capabilities among others.

Milking a concept through spin-offs of an original idea. Spin-offs, prequels, and sequels are also examples of original concepts that have been moved forward in a new direction. An original series may be over, but a new realm of opportunities is now open to be embraced by the audience. Examples include:

- *Little Monk*, a web series ordered by USA Network that aired during the final season of the series *Monk* in 2009, was a ten-episode online series that was a prequel depicting the adventures of a 10-year-old Monk during his elementary school days.
- *Footballers Wives*, a British series, was so successful that producers came up with extensions of the content that aired between seasons

entitled *Footballers Wives: Overtime* and *Footballers Wives: Extra Time.*

- *Being Human*, a supernatural drama series in the United Kingdom, had a healthy run on BBC 3, but after its last episode a new online take on the series called *Becoming Human* was released and posted on BBC.co.uk.
- *Frasier* (1993 – 2004), a notable example in the United States, is a comedy series that was a sequel and a spin-off of the comedy series *Cheers* (1982 – 1993). Dr. Frasier Crane first appeared on *Cheers* in 1984, but once *Cheers* was over, Frasier Crane reappeared with his own TV series and stayed on the air for 10 more years (until 2004). Overall, *Frasier* was a fixture in prime-time television for almost two decades.
- *Boy Meets World* (1993 – 2000), a recent example, is the sequel to an ABC sitcom, which after 14 years was revived by the Disney Channel as *Girl Meets World* (2014). The new family sitcom is a continuation of the original series, set 14 years later, centering on the life of a girl who is the daughter of the beloved protagonists of the initial comedy program.

Keeping a show alive by shifting the target market. This concept applies to a show that has reached a plateau in a specific market but still has potential to create more business opportunities in a different market. Ways to achieve a shift of the target market include repurposing the show to:

- A different time schedule
- A different platform

Repurposing from one time schedule to another is the concept of shifting the target market related to changing the broadcast time of the program and therefore targeting a different audience and generating a new era for the show while it is still on the air. Application of this concept usually occurs with game shows. For example, a game show may have had a successful run in a prime-time slot, but after several years, the show starts losing its competitive edge, urging programming executives to replace it with another show. If the show is good, instead of replacing it, executives might decide to repurpose the show to a daytime or prime access time slot and run it daily. The show then is revamped for the time schedule and starts a new run, now targeting a more niche type of audience. Examples of this type of change include *Jeopardy* and *Who Wants to Be a Millionaire?*

- *Jeopardy* aired for the first time in 1964 as a weekday daytime game show. In 1975 *Jeopardy* was also shown as a prime-time syndicated version through various stations in the United States. Then a special version of *Jeopardy* appeared on prime time in the summer of 1990 on ABC featuring previous winners of the daytime regular series, which was a surprising twist to the usual contestants featured in the show. In 2003 the regular syndicated show changed its long-time rule of a winner leaving the show after five consecutive wins, so that a winner could stay as long as he or she could. *Jeopardy* is still on the air and besides being aired in different time slots, the show has been adapted for other channels such as VH1, when in 1998 a special edition called *Rock and Roll Jeopardy* aired. (Brooks & March, 2007).

- *Who Wants to Be a Millionaire?* is a $1-million-prize show that aired in the United States on ABC from 1999 to 2002. The quiz show was highly successful and went from airing 1 day a week to up to 5 nights a week. Some critics stated that the show lost its momentum due to overexposure but then got a second chance when a daily syndicated version of the program started running on different stations in the United States, either in the afternoon or in prime access time slots. In 2014, the show was still airing in the United States (Brooks & March, 2007).

Repurposing from one platform to another is a concept of shifting the target market related to a show that starts on a channel and is cancelled but then resurges on a different channel or platform to end its life cycle. Notable cases include:

- *Damages* is a drama series starring Glenn Close that started airing in 2007 on the cable channel FX, but was cancelled in 2009 after three seasons. *Damages* found life after cancellation in 2010 on the DirecTV channel Audience Network. The show ran for two more seasons.
- *Arrested Development* ran for three seasons (2003 – 2006) on the Fox Network. *Arrested Development* was critically acclaimed but never attracted a wide audience, leading to its cancellation in 2006. The show subsequently generated a cult following and continued appearing in publications as one of the funniest shows of all time. In 2011, the show found an unprecedented new home when Netflix, a video rental and streaming service provider, commissioned new episodes of the series as part of its strategy to develop and produce original exclusive content for its platform. The show then bounced back in 2013.
- *Veronica Mars* is a drama series that aired on network TV (UPN and CW) in the United States from 2004 to 2007, was cancelled, and then 7 years later in 2014 reappeared in theaters as the movie *Veronica Mars* to provide an ending for the TV series fan base.

- *Sex and the City* (1998 – 2004) came to movie theaters in 2008 as an extension of its successful run on HBO.

Incremental Innovation Intrinsic to Genre and the Competitive Environment

The process of creation of incremental innovations intrinsic to genre is also called the *derivative process of innovation in media.* This process consists of learning well the different attributes of a TV show and, based on that, coming up with a new idea or a better way to produce the show. When a TV show is released, it becomes part of the entertainment domain, which represents the creative competitive field. If the show is a breakthrough, the show then paves the way for a new genre or sub-genre, leading to a new formula, which is then learned by writers and producers who try to create new shows that could potentially attract viewers who liked the original show. Each new show created within the process of diffusion tries to bring a novel experience that is better than the original experience. New stories are written; new characters are developed; and new game shows are launched as derivatives of the first successful shows. As we can see, innovations intrinsic to competitive environments are basically related to genre because a radical innovation ignites the creation of new shows following the formula of the genre that the new show has brought to the field and the domain.

To illustrate this concept, let's look at the talent competition genre. All shows within this genre have a common element that defines the framework of creation—competitors who are showcasing their talent for a prize. The writers and producers creating new talent competitions make a special effort to come up with unique dynamics, which will be seen as enhancements to the original. For example, *Pop Idol* appeared in 2001 in the United Kingdom. We could say that *Pop Idol* was a derivative of DuMont Television Network's *Doorway to Fame* (1947) or the classic *Ted Mack's Original Amateur Hour* which first aired in 1948 (Keller, 2008). *Pop Idol's* signature feature was a celebrity panel of three judges. Celebrity panels were then seen on *X Factor* (2004), *Got Talent* (2006), and *Dancing with the Stars* (2004). Each of these shows had different dynamics in the competition, ranging from the variety of talent showcased (singers, dancers, celebrities, and ordinary people, etc.) to the different ways of critiquing, evaluating, coaching, and eliminating participants. The genre has enjoyed success, and more shows continue to appear on TV. *The Voice* is an example of one of the latest incremental innovations. In *The Voice* (2010), creators added a very exciting twist to the casting process by not permitting judges to see a contestant performing, instructing the judges to turn their chairs around only if they liked a contestant's voice. The show differentiated itself from the others and became a major sensation worldwide. *The Voice* has become one of the most successful derivative talent shows ever.

Incremental innovations come from looking at what is successfully on the air or has aired in the past. For example, shows that did not succeed such as *Viva Laughlin* (2007) might have been the genesis for other more successful musical series such as *Glee* in 2009. The Disney channel's *High School Musical* TV movie trilogy (2006 – 2008) also created an audience that was ready to embrace musicals. So Ryan Murphy might have capitalized on the *High School Musical* fans who grew to become the core audience for *Glee* (2009).

Try this activity:

- Make a list of radical innovations with incremental innovations.
- Take a success from the past and think of incremental improvements to make it relevant today.
- Make a list of shows that have benefited from technological changes and how. Make a specific list of the multiplatform aspects of technological changes. Describe the various elements and platforms.
- Think of a show today and how its life cycle could be extended through spin-offs, sequels, prequels, or shifting the target audience.
- Think of a show in decline today (check ratings listings and historic performance to justify your selection) and propose a series of improvements to keep the show alive. Propose a strategy.
- Do you have an idea for a radical innovation in content? If so, write it down.

9

DRIVERS OF
CONTENT INNOVATION

Innovation in the context of the creation of content is tied to aspects that are either intrinsic to the process of generation of a product or program, such as the story, characters, and aesthetics, or are a consequence of changes in the cultural and industry context tied to audience habits and behavior, technology, and business. All of these aspects are *drivers* that ignite the generation of radical content or *modifications* that improve such content. The key drivers of content innovation are therefore classified in the following aspects:

- Innovation driven by the product (a program)
- Innovation driven by technology and services
- Innovation driven by business

INNOVATION DRIVEN BY THE PRODUCT

In media, the product is a program or the content: a story or an event packaged in specific lengths for audiences to experience in any platform of visualization. Content can be either fiction or non-fiction, with fiction being the representation of a story through vivid characters that are able to express and communicate actions following a script, whereas non-fiction is the presentation of real events as they happen. The elements of content include:

- Concept
- Genre
- Story

- Narrative and scriptwriting
- Characters
- Aesthetics
- Production value

The mix of all of these elements constitutes the attributes of a program that we can watch on TV, online, or on a mobile device. A program could be innovative as a consequence of a revolutionary genre, because the art design is a notable radical proposition for a televised event or just because a character is mesmerizing. Each of these aspects causes a product to be innovative and each by itself represents a driver of content innovation.

Concept-Driven Innovation

"Concept means premise, basic idea, or central dilemma" (Cooper, 1997, p. 53). Conceptual innovation is related to premise originality, which refers to a never-seen-before way of packaging stories, characters, situations, actions, environments, dynamics, and participants. Being original is at its core the fundamental reason for artists and creative minds to exist. Writers and creators of content want to express their talents in ways we have not experienced before. They want to break through, to be impactful, and to change the game. When a show is original and becomes a hit, the show is called *innovative*—a game changer. Every hit show is automatically an innovation, validated by an audience which praises what is new, surprising, and a turning point in their experiences of being entertained. An innovative concept catches viewer's attention and grows with it.

Cooper (1997) identified two types of concepts: high and soft. *High concepts* easily convey meaning to viewers about what they will experience. The term high concept by itself drives your interest when you first hear about it. *Soft concepts* are those that demand more explanation. Soft concepts are intriguing for an audience who will not know what to expect until they see it. Either concept can be successful, but high concepts are more commercial and hence are the concepts that TV outlets are more willing to invest in. Despite how commercial or not a concept is, as long as the concept surprises and stands out from the rest, it has a clear chance to succeed.

An original concept that is validated by the market becomes the starting point for diffusion. For example, the first newscast with a face became an innovative concept with the advent of TV. After that breakthrough, other newscasts proliferated. All of the concepts for TV shows that first aired at any given time schedule served as the genesis for all of the TV shows we see today. The successful ideas were innovations driven by a concept. The concept then became a framework for content. If the framework was successful, producers and writers embraced the framework and made more and more of the same concept. This concept framework generated a formula and a cluster of shows that together formed what we know as a *genre*. Shows worth mentioning as conceptual game-changers include:

- *Spelling Bee* (1938): The first quiz show on BBC TV (to find the most intelligent individual on TV)
- The first newscast on NBC (1944): A person reading news in front of a TV camera without any video support or reports (the origin for the news genre)
- *The Kraft Television Theater* (1947): The anthology series show concept that brought different stories to TV every week (In 1959, Rod Sterling, one of *The Kraft Television Theater* writers, created *The Twilight Zone*, which became one of the most successful anthology series of all time by combining mystery, terror, sci-fi, and inexplicable events under the same umbrella.)
- *Candid Camera* (1948): The first TV show (created by Allen Funt) in which real people were caught in front of cameras reacting candidly to unusual situations
- *American Bandstand* (1952): A show created to showcase music talent that evolved into a program showcasing ordinary teenagers engaged in dance competitions or just dancing in front of the camera
- Cooking shows: The first time a recipe was prepared on TV (possibly *Fanny's Kitchen* on BBC in 1955), in front of cameras, giving a new utilitarian purpose to TV, besides being entertaining and informing
- *American Family* (1973): A 12-part documentary show that aired on PBS and followed a middle class family in Santa Barbara, CA over 7 months; considered to be the genesis of reality shows (Lim, 2011)
- *Saturday Night Live* (1975): A live variety show that had a special renowned guest and combined music and comedy
- *Top Gear* (1977): A factual entertainment show on BBC about cars made in the United Kingdom, revamped in 2002, that has become the most-watched show around the world in its genre
- *MTV Unplugged* (1989): A TV show with an intimate setting created to showcase rock and pop acts performing only with acoustic instruments
- *The Real World* (1992): The first soap opera-style reality show (MTV) that allowed audiences to follow the drama that sparked between six strangers who auditioned to live in the same house with cameras recording their relationships (in a setting that moved to a different city each season)

- *Crocodile Hunter* (1997): A personality-driven factual reality show that showcased Steve Irwin's unorthodox approach to wildlife and conservationism
- *Extreme Makeover* (2003): A life-enhancing show in which a taskforce of home-improvement specialists turned a house upside down and then remodeled the house completely for a person in need
- *YouTube Awards* (2007): A show that brought the chaotic essence of the YouTube video site to celebrate web sensations and music stars who were invited to participate in live music video performances as if they were uploading the videos to an internet site

Genre-Driven Innovation

A genre is the direct consequence of a concept that becomes a success or a breakthrough that propels the proliferation of other shows with the same formula or theme, creating a cluster of TV shows. This cluster forms a genre.

Fiction and non-fiction are the two main genres, the roots and the source of all content. Everything falls into one of these two categories. As indicated in Chapter 6 (*The Sociocultural Model of Creative Validation in Media*; see also Figure 6-6), these two genres define the entire TV content domain of the entertainment industry (Figure 9-1). Within each of these categories, new sub-genres proliferate, combine, or evolve, nurturing the domain and creating new experts in the field who are capable and ready to write and produce content under the rules and characteristics (the formula) established for the particular genre.

Genre can occur as a consequence of a totally original concept (e.g., a story, character, or aesthetics) or as a result of the combination of two (or various) genres with other external elements to form a new sub-genre. Content then mutates into other forms, leading to innovative formulas and ideas.

The fiction genre (also called scripted) started with the Greeks and their first representations of events in life through actors using a script, thus creating the theater and the first approach to representing fiction to an audience. This event was a breakthrough. Within this genre, several sub-genres appeared, evolving through time into new and more sophisticated forms of representation.

Comedy Fiction

The chart in Figure 9-2 presents examples of how the comedy genre mutates into other forms. The first genre in the chart is variety (1), which is a consequence of mixing comedy with music and skits. *The Milton Berle Show* in 1948, also known as the *Texaco Star Theatre* hosted by Milton Berle (1948–1956), is the first variety show (Brooks & Marsh, 2007). With a new sponsor, *The Texaco Star Theatre* became The *Buick-Berle Show* in 1953 and finally *The Milton Berle Show* from

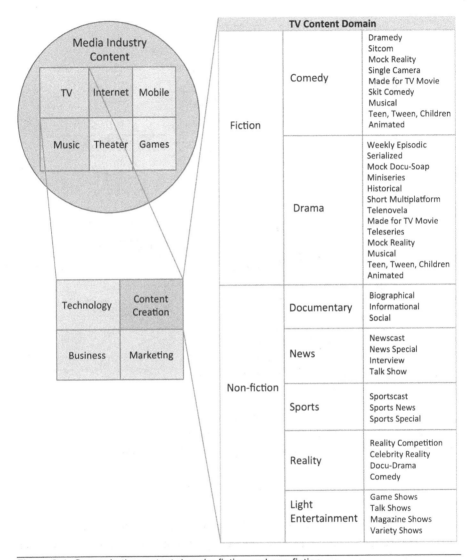

Figure 9-1. Genres in the content domain: fiction and non-fiction.

(1955–1956.) Comedy mixed with a half-hour duration, radio comedy plots, three cameras in a studio, and a sponsor gave rise to the sitcom (2). When a sitcom was taken on location and shot in a single-camera style, the single-camera sitcom (3) was generated. The single-camera situation comedy genre was then mixed with the documentary and reality genres and the mock-reality single-camera sitcom (4) appeared in the spectrum of comedy sub-genres. Hour-long dramedies (5) came from mixing single-camera situation comedy with a 1-hour weekly drama

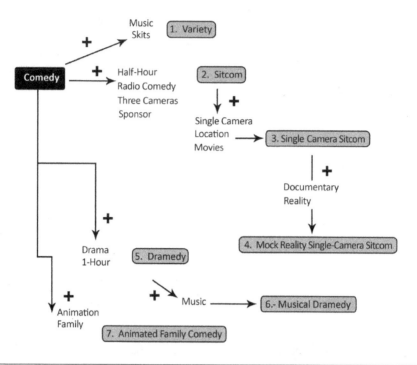

Figure 9-2. The comedy genre: evolution and mutation.

series. The dramedy genre was then mixed with musicals to produce 1-hour musical dramedy series (6) (*Glee* in 2009). Mixing comedy with animation and family comedy led to animated family comedy series (7) (*The Flintstones* in 1960 and *The Simpsons* in 1989).

Drama Fiction

Figure 9-3 presents examples of how the drama genre has also permuted to produce other subgenres (seen in shaded rectangles). With the advent of TV, creators of content took romantic ongoing storylines usually heard in radio dramas or seen in the theater and produced them for TV, with the support of the soap brands' serial dramatic series. These productions were called soap operas (1). Latin American producers took the essence of these soap operas but gave the stories a beginning and an end, producing what has been one of the most popular genres across the world—telenovelas (2) that usually entail between 80 to 120 episodes. Real-life events and institutions (police, legal, private investigation firms, and government), theater drama plays, and literature also became sources for a new realm of stories that began to be told in an episodic fashion in the form of weekly

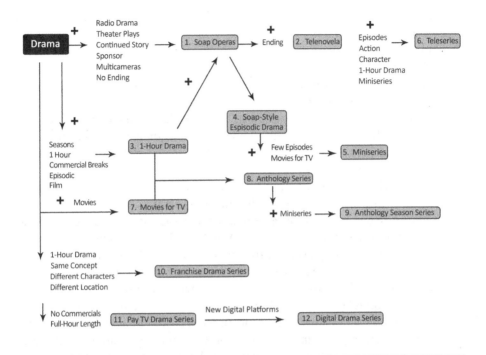

Figure 9-3. The drama genre: evolution and mutation.

drama series (1-hour dramas, 3). Weekly series are presented in seasons and contain from 13 to 26 episodes.

The weekly drama series (3) genre merged with soap operas, leading to soap opera-style drama series (4). Soap opera-style dramas, through continued storylines on a weekly and seasonal basis, presented the evolution of a crime, a political tale, or a family-driven story (*Dallas, Revenge, Once Upon a Time, Parenthood, Brothers and Sisters*, and *Scandal*).

Soap-style episodic drama merged with movies and used three-act stories that could not be told in 2 hours but required 7 or 8 hours, paving the way for miniseries (5). The telenovela genre also merged with weekly series dramas and miniseries to form what is known in Latin America as a teleseries (6), which is the format of choice to tell continued stories differently from the romantic tales of telenovelas. Teleseries move at a faster pace in seasons of 40 to 60 episodes. Themes include drug cartels, anti-heroin character-driven stories, action, mystery, murder, and crime-related or adaptations of U.S. drama series (*Breaking Bad* and *Grey's Anatomy*).

Movies came to TV as made-for-TV movies (7), which became a new TV genre in itself. Made-for-TV movies implied telling stand-alone stories in 2 hours.

Creators saw an opportunity to create umbrella concepts, under which different stories could be told in a self-contained episode, and came up with a mix of movies and weekly series now known as an anthology series (8), with a season having 13 to 24 episodes, each one presenting a stand-alone story with a different cast. One of the most recognized anthology series is *The Twilight Zone*. This umbrella concept grew even more when, instead of each episode, each season of the series was presented as a miniseries with a beginning, middle, and end, overall related under the umbrella theme, a genre known as an anthology season series (9). Two great examples of this genre are *American Horror Story* (FX, 2011) and *True Detective* (HBO, 2014).

The franchise drama series (10) genre is a consequence of duplicating a successful series in another location, with different characters, in the same country, for the same channel. Franchise genre means that a show diffuses under the same umbrella within the same country. Producer Jerry Bruckenheimer first brought this concept to TV through the *CSI* franchises. The first *CSI* was set in Las Vegas. Later, a new series with the same name and premise, but with different characters and locale, was made in Miami as *CSI: Miami*; then a third series was set in New York City as *CSI: NYC*. For several seasons, all of the *CSIs* aired on the same TV network without cannibalizing one another. On few occasions, creators did some cross-programming stunts in which some of the characters in different *CSIs* met in one episode. The franchise strategy has revolutionized procedural and investigative shows because the strategy opened up the possibility for one producer to do different shows, derived from the same concept, that otherwise would have been done by other creators in the process of diffusion and imitation. In the franchise genre, diffusion occurs within the same umbrella or brand and its own creators imitate the show. *NCIS* and *Law and Order* did the same with *NCIS: Los Angeles*, *NCIS: New Orleans*, *Law and Order: Special Victims Unit*, and *Law and Order: Criminal Intent*.

Pay TV drama series (11) are a consequence of HBO original series, which rescued the TV miniseries concept and defied the regular structure (two or four acts) for full 1-hour and half-hour episodes because a show did not have commercials. The audience pays to access these series, which usually contain unique characters and strong edgy stories together with extraordinary production value. The immediate evolution of this genre came with the advent of Netflix and Amazon producing exclusive digital drama series (12) for their subscribers (Netflix's *House of Cards* in 2013).

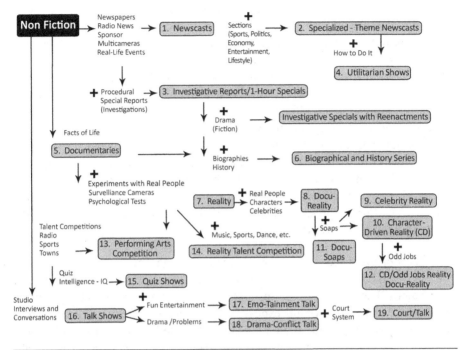

Figure 9-4. The non-fiction genre: evolution and mutation.

Non-Fiction

Figure 9-4 presents an exercise I conducted exploring four sources of content—newspapers, facts of life, talent competitions, and talk shows—in the evolution of the non-fiction genre.

Newspapers. Newspapers were the first medium to provide real stories about events happening in the world in print. In 1944, NBC used the newspaper as a basis for informing audiences by having a person read the news in front of the cameras (Brooks & Marsh, 2007). As a result, newscasts (1) came into existence. Their utilitarian sense was immediately recognized—audiences realized that they did not need to buy a newspaper or read the news if TV was doing all that for free. The genre evolved into more sophisticated forms of reporting the events of the world, leading to the proliferation of long-form newscasts and special reports. The different sections in a newspaper became the sections of the newscast, which soon evolved into specialized thematic newscasts (2) about entertainment and economic, political, and current affairs. News specials also took center stage through the medium of investigative 1-hour programs that showcased special reports (3). Today TV newscasts have become a 360 multiplatform experience in which not only TV but also social media and internet sites are linked, complementing each other with more aural/visual information. Newscasts then opened the door for print magazines, which in essence had a more utilitarian sense to become the source for TV shows that primarily targeted women at home. Magazine shows contain different sections and applications to help people learn and stay informed. Magazine shows did to print magazines what newscasts had done to newspapers. The how-to-do-it state of mind set the basis for utilitarian TV shows (4) to teach people how to cook, decorate, shop, and solve any kind of domestic home improvement-related situation. Programs such as *Today* and *Good Morning America* are examples of magazine shows. Thematic specialized channels also have TV shows dedicated to home improvement, travel, health, cooking, beauty, science, etc.

Facts of life. Facts of life were captured through documentaries (5), which derived from biographical and historical/factual TV series (6). In the 1990s, reality shows (7) took the best from documentaries and sociological experiments to produce shows that would expose ordinary people "bursting forth" in front of TV cameras to provide drama. Reality TV started with real people but soon incorporated celebrities to create celebrity reality shows (9). More recently, cable channels such as Discovery, A&E, Bravo, and MTV are giving special emphasis to finding larger-than-life individuals to attract audiences who want to see how these individuals live. These shows comprise the character-driven reality genre (10, 11, 12). Examples include *Jersey Shore, Pawn Stars*, and *The Real Housewives*. Character-driven reality shows also helped to franchise the reality genre, allowing creation of different reality shows under the same umbrella. Franchised programming has become one of the most efficient and powerful content innovations in reality TV. Several shows could be created under the same title but with different casts, in different cities, that could even air simultaneously without cannibalizing one another.

Talent competitions. Talent searches, the third source of inspiration for content, and its combination with sports competitions, radio contests, and local festivals pushed the creation of a series of competitions to showcase any type of artistic ability or skill to become a TV star (13). This genre later mixed with reality shows to form reality-talent show competitions such as *The Amazing Race* and *American Idol* (14). These TV competitions not only sought artistic talent, but they also looked for the smartest, most intelligent individuals in the form of quiz shows (15). These game shows and competitions gave viewers the opportunity to participate in shows and to be in front of the camera to win a prize, either monetary or some other type.

Talk shows. The talk show genre (16) was the result of radio studio interviews and the possibilities the new medium of TV provided for seeing people talk about almost any topic. In essence, these conversations were either fun (*Ellen*) or more dramatic because they dealt with people's problems (*The Dr. Phil Show*). Dramatic talk shows emphasize giving troubled people a chance to solve a problem. These shows are highly emotional and have derived into emo-tainment talk shows (17) (*Oprah*) and other deviations (*The Jerry Springer Show* and *The Ricki Lake Show*). The host of each of these shows acts as a mediator to help people to find solutions. Soon, talk show creators introduced the court system as a framework of interaction and resolution and created court talk shows (19).

The list of different sub-genres in fiction and non-fiction is long. The idea here is to understand that the crossing and mixing of genres opens up opportunities for the creation of differentiated content. The combination of fiction and non-fiction also offers the possibility of creating a risky blend that could yield very unique shows. For example, the show *Outnumbered* (2007) from the United Kingdom is a sitcom that combines scripted dialogues and scenes with the non-scripted, ad-lib, spontaneous reactions of the characters. In *Outnumbered*, a married couple with four children has to face the pains of day-to-day family matters. In this comedy, all dialogue from the parents is scripted, whereas the children react in a spontaneous non-scripted way.

The combination of the two main genres, fiction and non-fiction, has been a game changer, and when applied properly, the technique ignites a new breed of subgenres such as docu-comedies and docu-dramas. Among them the teen soap reality hit *The Hills* (2006) is an example of using reality techniques to capture events and also using the essence of screenwriting to create lives filled with conflict and drama. Show producers act as writers on the fly, using and igniting situations that the characters (real people) face and then react to, creating the desired moment. *Curb Your Enthusiasm* (2000) is another example of content driven by this hybrid approach to genre. The actors improvise according to the storyline created by Larry David, the leading creative force of the show. The actors participate in the show using their real names and professions and act ad-lib, following stories created by Larry David.

As we can see, a combination of genres or the modification of existing genres leads to new forms of content. Always important to keep in mind is that the creation of a new form of content is not about choosing two genres to merge but about a concept and a story that would benefit if told through new approaches that leads to new genres.

Story-Driven Innovation

The story is the heart of a fiction show. A good story is the reason why we turn on a TV or download an episode. The story is what makes formula shows innovative. The story, the sequence of events that a character goes though, defines a journey that the audience follows week after week, episode after episode. Sitcoms and procedural dramas are examples of formula TV shows.

Among procedural dramas, criminal investigative shows such as *CSI*, *Bones*, *The Closer*, and *Without a Trace* present a well-defined writing framework that even though their stories are a formula, the stories are plagued with momentum and originality that makes them stand out and be relevant for the viewers.

An innovative storyline surprises audiences with risky scenarios that have not yet been shown on TV. For example, when Shonda Rhimes introduced the story of a high-profile politico, a Washington, DC fixer, whose job was assisting important personalities with getting out of scandalous, career-threatening public situations, while being the protagonist of the ultimate scandal of all, the mistress of the president of the United States, the show quickly became an obsession with viewers because of its surprising plot, edginess, and risky hypothesis of being set in Washington's powerful stratosphere.

Innovative stories have to be intriguing and surprising. They necessarily need to open the door to a new, unsuspecting, or never-exposed world to viewers. Innovative stories must present situations that audiences have never seen or ever imagined they would see on TV. Great stories present a unique journey that a character, who could be an ordinary person, goes through when life is altered by an event. As pointed out by McKee (1997), a story event creates meaningful change in the life of a character, either positive or negative, that is achieved through conflict. The elements that compose the story determine an arc and the reason for an audience to follow every episode until the end. The elements are:

- Structure: A sequence of events
- Events: In the form of scenes
- Setting: Referring to period, duration, place, and level of conflict
- Characters' decisions
- Irreversible change at the end

If the story is innovative, the momentum or level of anticipation to see what is next propels the audience's interest and the need to watch night after night, turning the show into a success (Cooper, 1997). Examples of innovative stories are found in:

- *Modern Family* (2009, ABC): A hilarious look at families today through the lives of the Pritchett-Dunphy-Tucker clan

- *Downtown Abbey* (2010, BBC): The lives of the wealthy Crawley family and their servants in early twentieth-century Britain
- *American Horror Story* (2011, FX): Different horrifying tales each season presented in a miniseries style
- *La Reina del Sur* (2011, Telemundo): The quest of Teresa Mendoza, a Mexican who becomes the most powerful drug dealer in Southern Spain
- *The Americans* (2013, FX): The lives of Russian spies in the United States during the cold war era of the 1980s
- *Orphan Black* (2013, BBC): A street-smart hustler dragged into a compelling clone conspiracy that generates an undefined number of women who look exactly like the hustler

Another interesting example of an innovative story is presented in *Masters of Sex* (2007, Showtime), set in the 1950s. Initially many viewers likely saw the resemblance with *Mad Men* (2007, AMC), but the *Masters of Sex* story is so unique, based on real facts about a doctor (Dr. William Masters) experimenting and studying in depth human sexuality and orgasm, that the show quickly managed to establish itself as an innovative tale despite being set in the same context as *Mad Men*.

Storytelling-, Narrative-, Scriptwriting-, and Show Dynamics-Driven Innovation

TV shows stand out for their cleverness, unique characters, and original edge while staying faithful to established narrative structures in film. Quentin Tarantino, Spike Jonze, Christopher Nolan, and Charlie Kauffman have succeeded by experimenting with narrative structure and storytelling in film. A good writer first needs to master the formula and then break it. Innovations in storytelling occur when a writer breaks down a commonly used formula to structure a story and then comes up with a new, understandable way to present it to the viewers, surprising them.

TV has been a highly formulated medium, but the crossing over of film writers to TV and the proliferation of outlets of exposition (the digital multiplatform) have led to the exploration of nonconventional forms of storytelling. Cross-over writers from other industries (advertising, independent filmmaking, experimental video production, short-form digital video, and transmedia) bring fresh insights to the writing process overall. Likewise, other media platforms infuse the possibility of exploring new unconventional techniques.

TV is considered by some critics to be a formula—in form and writing structure—because TV scripts usually follow a structure formed by acts. The 1-hour four-act structure and the sitcom 30-minute two-act structure are derivatives of the three-act story.

Network TV sitcoms have two acts with a teaser and a tag, whereas drama series have a four-act structure with a teaser and tag. A teaser is a technique for jumping directly into a show at the beginning. A tag is a short mini-act of 1 to 5 minutes at the end of a show or episode, but before (sometimes during) the end credits, that is used to show the effects or aftermath of the episode. Each act has a purpose within the storytelling process. Writers need to clearly understand the purpose so that they can concentrate on story and character development. This structure was an innovation when it was first applied in the 1940s. The methodology used in the early days evolved, and writers learned how to efficiently and creatively use this convention.

Writers have continued challenging established formulas to create new narrative forms. Among the shows that have broken established formulas and presented a unique way to experience weekly series are *Law and Order* (1990), *24* (2001), *American Idol* (2002), and *Lost* (2004).

Law and Order (1990) combined the law, procedural courtroom, and cop-investigative aspects in a very innovative way (Webber, 2005). Half of an episode presented the investigative aspect of the case involving police officers and all of the action usually found in police departments; then, halfway through, the show became a procedural drama focusing on the sentencing of a criminal in the court system. The *Law and Order* series had a unique narrative structure in which four acts became the platform for merging two different sub-drama genres.

24 (2001) was the first TV show ever to present 24 hours of a chaotic, action-packed, hectic day in 24 episodes. The type of stories presented in *24* had been seen in movies over a lapse of 2 hours but never under the episodic, continued, real-time structure that *24* had. Thanks to this innovative real-time dynamic, *24* proved to be addictive, with a powerful hook to keep audiences glued to the TV screen week after week, until the final resolution. Not only did audiences watch the show week after week, but the unique structure of the show also caused people to download all of the episodes via Netflix or Amazon or keep them stored in DVRs so that they could watch the shows in a 24-hour-marathon fashion. This viewing response might have helped Netflix and other digital-on-demand pay-per-view home video services to release original series in full seasons so that viewers could sit down and watch all the episodes at one time (also known as binge viewing).

American Idol (2002) introduced a new narrative structure and altered the conventions of talent competitions when the writers built the season of a show in a 5-month three-act structure. The first act dealt with casting in actual locations across the country; the second act was a week in Hollywood to pick contestants who would go through the next phase; the third act focused on big-stage live competition. In the past, talent competitions happened only in a studio featuring a string of competitors, performing one after another and facing elimination until the winner of the night was chosen. Now competition lasts several weeks and showcases how the contestants progressively improve. Producers and creators of these narrative-structured shows concentrated on surprising the audience and the contestants through a series of twist and turns, which fueled the reality appeal of a show through viewers' real emotions and how the contestants were prepared, chosen, and evolved through the three-act narrative arc.

Lost (2004) was another show that defied all of the rules and forms of storytelling. *Lost* continued its way to the "TV drama hall of fame," when the writers introduced the use of flash forwards, combined with flashbacks and situations occurring in parallel time dimensions in the form of flash sideways, to give viewers enough information to understand why, how, and where the characters were at any given time. J.J. Abrams defied conventions in the four dimensions of a story's setting and clearly created his own period, time, location, and space and placed the hierarchy of human struggles to resolve conflict at a level that only existed in his *Lost* world with its own laws of probability (McKee, 1997).

Nowadays, the storytelling structure has evolved to a new level thanks to new viewer habits defined by the utilization of various devices to watch content and the impact of social media. This technological reality has determined a multidimensional way to tell a story. The episode on TV, the information on a website, a social media platform linked to the show, and even the utilization of traditional media to enhance the story (print, books, magazines, etc.) have opened new ways to engage viewers in a multidimensional way.

Character-Driven Innovation

Content revolves around the power of characters. Unique, multidimensional, attractive, surprising, interesting characters enlighten the screen and become the pillars that sustain audience interest for long periods of times.

The same as with the story, an innovative mix of characters makes formula TV shows relevant and unique. This notion applies to any type of show, fiction or non-fiction. The characters of the show are those who stand in front of the camera, conveying a message and giving viewers reasons to watch. If the characters are not likeable or endearing, the audience will find another show where they can find characters that are.

The two types of characters, depending on genre, are real people and actors. The non-fiction genre has real people as characters whereas the fiction genre has actors portraying other people. The casting department is the key functional area in the creation process of locating the characters.

Non-Fiction

Two groups compose the category of non-fiction characters: those conducting and hosting the show and those participating in the show. The first group, those conducting or hosting a show, includes on-camera professionals, informers, and entertainers.

On-camera professionals. On-camera professionals have the charisma, knowledge, and ability to lead newscasts, variety shows, sportscasts, lifestyle series, home improvement shows, documentaries, travel shows, magazine shows, talk shows, and court shows, among others. These non-fiction characters have the knowledge, credibility, and editorial approach to convey messages, provide points of view, and make solid conclusions or recommendations about a particular topic. They are either informers (news/information driven) or entertainers who know how to keep viewer attention. They know how to create empathy with some people and how to cause a reaction in others, either negative or positive, but always with a purpose.

Informers. Informers are influencers. They drive conversations and make us think, laugh, and cry. They generate controversy, help us discover the world, and try to teach us something that will make us feel better. Examples of key innovative figures belonging to this group include Anderson Cooper (CNN), Nancy Grace (HLN), Oprah Winfrey (OWN), Christianne Amanpour (CNN war correspondent), Bill O'Reilly (Fox), Barbara Walters (ABC), Peter Jennings (ABC), Phil McGraw (Syndication), Drew Pinsky (HLN), Martha Stewart (Syndication), Daisy Fuentes (MTV), and soccer commentator Andres Cantor (FDP).

Entertainers. The mission of entertainers is to keep us in suspense, awake, smiling, interested, and connected. Entertainers talk to participants, guide them, and even make them suffer or feel better. Entertainers convey the good and the bad news, making us laugh or helping us to discover a better world through their shows. The list of breakthrough entertainers includes Chef Gordon Ramsey (*Hell's Kitchen*), Donald Trump (*The Apprentice*), Steve Irwin (*Crocodile Hunter*), and Anthony Bourdain (*No Reservations*) as well as Rachel Ray, Joan Rivers, Bravo's Andy Cohen, Jimmy Fallon, Jay Leno, Conan O'Brien, Steven Colbert, John Stewart, Johnny Carson, Judy Sheindlin, the cast of *Queer Eye for a Straight Guy*, Howard Stern, Carol Burnett, Sony and Cher Bono, Neil Patrick Harris, Ellen DeGeneres, Billy Crystal, Johnny Knoxville, and Don Francisco.

The second group of non-fiction characters are the participants, the real people whose lives become the centerpiece for a show. Participants are found in documentaries, reality series, talent competitions, sports competitions, and game shows. Casting for participants is as important as the casting for a host, presenter, or journalist. Participants fill up most of the available space on a show. Their real traits and actions caught on camera are what make the show appealing and interesting. Participants in a show include competitors, contestants, regular ensembles, celebrity guests, and casual participants.

Competitors. Competitors can range from sports professionals to real people who are competing for a prize. Shows in this category include live sports and sports entertainment-related events: a controversial boxer, a baseball home run hitter about to beat an important record, a rookie coming of age in front of a worldwide TV audience, or a record set at the Olympics. All of these competitors make up the casts of sports events. Michael Phelps, Serena Williams, and John McEnroe are examples of innovative competitors, not only for their excellence and discipline of expertise, but also as individuals. They are vibrant, interesting, intriguing, and sometimes controversial, but they ignite our interest to follow what they do inside and outside of competition. Teams in a league and coaches are also in this group. Other competitors are unknown amateurs who appear in reality competitions driven by challenges that require physical strength of any type. Memorable contestants are in the casts of *The Amazing Race* and *Survivor*.

Contestants. Contestants are part of any show in which a winner is selected from a group. Contestants can be aspiring young women in a beauty pageant, singers waiting for a chance to be on *American Idol*, or even a nun. The nun who participated in *The Voice Italy* became a global sensation and won the show. Contestants in game shows are also in this group.

Regular ensembles. Regular ensembles come from a pool of participants who agree to be followed for a period of time without wanting the award of a final prize but instead to receive monetary remuneration. *The World According to Paris* (Paris Hilton) and *The Kardashians*; the casts of *Jersey Shore*, *The Real World*, *Big Brother*, *Duck Dynasty*, and *Here Comes Honey Boo Boo*; and the judges on *American Idol*, *The Voice*, *Dance Moms*, and *The Real Housewives* are examples of powerful regular ensembles. These ensembles have unveiled unbelievable personalities and real drivers of emotions, conflict, and polemic who have been able to keep audiences asking for more. This genre has been a game changer thanks to reality stars, receiving the name character-driven reality shows. Humans are not always the center of attraction in a regular ensemble-based show. An ensemble could be animals or even machines. To illustrate, some of the most groundbreaking ensembles seen were the meerkats in Animal Planet's *Meerkat Manor*. The show showcased multiple reasons to love meerkats. The meerkats took us to their shelters, we met their families, and most importantly we followed them in their quest to survive life in the wild.

Celebrity guests. Celebrity guests are participants who are invited to perform on TV shows to surprise, entertain, and provide a compelling experience for viewers. Producers of late-night shows, variety specials, concerts, awards shows, talk shows, and any show requiring a celebrity or an interesting guest emphasize finding characters who will make the show special, unique, and interesting to watch. MTV has focused on making its live events such as the *Video Music Awards* (VMAs) a major trending topic worldwide or the epicenter of controversy. MTV has created shockwaves with performances by Madonna kissing Britney Spears and Cristina Aguilera at the 2003 VMAs; Kanye West's memorable interruption of Taylor Swift's acceptance speech at the 2009 VMAs; and more recently the Miley Cyrus' performance at the 2013 VMAs. Other memorable performances include Michael Jackson's first moonwalk at the *25th Motown Anniversary Special* in 1983 and The Beatles on *The Ed Sullivan Show* in 1964. The unpredictability of these variety shows continues to grow thanks to candid reactions by guest stars that increase the anticipation of a surprise and the willingness of audiences to watch the event live.

Casual participants. Casual participants are the audience, people participating unintentionally, or participants at home. These participants can be a live audience in the studio or people on the street, the victims in hidden camera shows, and people being interviewed on newscasts.

Fiction

In the fiction genre, audiences expect memorable characters with traits and dimensions that make them real, believable, relatable, and capable of expressing emotions that provoke in viewers a sense of recognition (Cooper, 1997). Viewers want to relate to the characters—to cry, laugh, or enjoy their experiences. Leading and supporting characters generate innovation driven by the characters in a fiction story. If the mix of characters is not well structured, the story will not be compelling, and viewers will skip the show.

Characters who constitute the mix of people who will live the story need to have well-defined psychologies, objectives, motivations, and dimensions that lead to unique ways of reacting to different conflicts and situations. This mix of characters represents the elements of the story puzzle, with each element being different and having a function in the story arc. The relationship between the characters defines storylines and how the characters react to events, trigger responses among the other characters in a direct or indirect way, and move the story in different directions.

The character mix is built on the personality and set of experiences that constitute each character's persona. When put together, the writer sets the story in motion in an evolving path of actions, tensions, and emotions. Excellent character mixes are found in the casts of *Modern Family, Seinfeld, Married with Children, Brothers & Sisters, Parenthood, Silicon Valley,* and *Mad Men.*

As noted at the beginning of this section, each character should be memorable and relatable and have a clear reason to be in the story. Innovative characters in a memorable, breakthrough show could be heroes or protagonists, antiheroes (the unlikely protagonist), antagonists, supporting characters, live action or animated, or guest stars. No matter what their specific weight in the story is, each character needs to be relatable and memorable.

A memorable character is someone who we can relate to and care about. When we relate, we care; otherwise, nothing gets our attention and the character does not drive the story. To be innovative, a character must be surprising and refreshing and bring an abundance of new experiences to us. Surprise could come in the form of:

- Physical appearance: The shocking aspect of a physical impediment or the transformation in a character fighting the fight against all odds is always a compelling, wonderful way to relate to an underdog. Maura Pfefferman in *Transparent* and Arti Abrams in *Glee* are examples.
- An underdog: An underdog is an unlikely hero or person who we least expect to succeed in a dangerous or difficult scenario. Rocky Balboa is a well-structured underdog. A character in a drama or comedy series such as Betty Suarez in *Ugly Betty* also represents an underdog.
- A fish out of water: This element has to do with a person who has very unlikely characteristics to fit within a certain context. Lily Munster in *The Munsters* and Penny in *The Big Bang Theory* are examples of this type of character.
- Personality and way of thinking: This aspect entails whether a character is extroverted or introverted and also their set of beliefs. Joe MacMillan in *Halt and Catch Fire* and Norma Bates in *Bates Motel* have strong, intriguing, well-defined personalities that drive their respective shows.
- Knowledge and intelligence (and the opposite as well): A character with extraordinary intelligence and a different way of going through the world always makes a compelling and interesting character to watch. This type of character becomes even more interesting when they are taken out of their comfort zone. A lack of intelligence is also an interesting trait that allows surprising, unthinkable, natural, and honest reactions that audiences always love. Haley Dunphy and Alex

Dunphy in *Modern Family* play exactly those roles, one is dumb and innocent and the other clever and clumsy.

- Big personality: Characters in series such as *The Big Bang Theory, The Munsters, Modern Family,* and *Entourage* are examples of characters with very strong, identifiable personalities. Their bigger-than-life, unique visions of the world make them very compelling and intriguing. Gloria in *Modern Family* and Sheldon Cooper in *The Big Bang Theory* are solid examples of characters with strong, powerful personalities within their context and series character mix.

- Drive and capacity to respond to conflict and adversity: These characters are absolutely resourceful, intelligent, and willing to go the extra mile to achieve their objectives. Teresa Mendoza in *The Queen of the South,* Pablo Escobar in *Escobar, el patrón del mal,* and Carrie Mathison in *Homeland* are examples.

- Dialogue: The aspect of dialogue makes a character distinctive. The proper use of words can make a character compelling and relevant. Sawyer in *Lost* became an easy-to-relate-to antihero in the Lost series, not only for his mischievous traits but also for his razor-sharp pop-culture-reference punch lines that made him believable, relevant, and likeable. He was funny, dramatic, intriguing, and sensible. He was multidimensional. Dialogue played a very important part in this achievement. Francis Underwood's distinctive tone and carefully calculated conversations combined with his SMS (mobile short messages) interactions made him both down-to-earth and stratospheric as a person. Dr. Gregory House in *House* is another example.

- Inner drive exposition: Exposing someone's inner feelings and thoughts can unravel intriguing reasons to follow a character in a rather peculiar quest. What is behind the character's life? What is the internal drive that moves the character's actions forward? Once we figure that out, we have found a reason to follow the character's quest. When *Mad Men's* Don Draper started revealing his real identity in the show, his character grew in importance. The intrigue surrounding finding out what would be next in the world he created around himself turned the show into an obsession.

- Hero potential: Characters with the potential to bring evil characters to justice are another reason to care about a character. Heroism is the possibility a character has to solve a problem or a conflict and save others from harm or disgrace. This possibility gives us a reason to root for a character. Emily Thorne in *Revenge,* Olivia Pope in *Scandal,* Sarah Manning in *Orphan Black,* and Rick Grimes in *The Walking Dead* totally fit this criterion.

- Super hero: Characters with super powers can be surprising, depending on the context and realism with which their character is built. Clark Kent in *Smallville* is a powerful representation of this as well as all of the lead characters in the series *Heroes*.

- Divine antagonism: Within the character mix, antagonists are the main catalyst of a story. They become the target to beat and a good reason to support the hero. We do not mind watching this character do bad things because we know that all will come to an end at some point. The *how* is what drives the momentum of the story. Antagonists are always juicy characters who unleash their powerful evil actions to accomplish their personal goals, only spreading their questionable love to those who are on their side. Glenn Close in *Damages*, Victoria Grayson in *Revenge*, Wilhelmina Slater in *Ugly Betty*, Fiona Goode in *American Horror Story: Coven*, and Cookie Lyon in *Empire* are examples of this type of always likeable characters. We watch these characters do evil with the hope that in some distant time they will be brought to justice.

- The antihero: Antiheroes are lead characters dragged onto the wrong side but always with good benevolent reason behind their actions. Even though they are criminals or have a non-approvable façade, they are good on the inside and the audience roots for them. Examples are Walter White in *Breaking Bad* and Teresa Mendoza in *The Queen of the South*.

- Shock: The king of shock Ryan Murphy unleashes his imagination to create unexpected characters with unusual, taboo-type stories. *Nip/Tuck* was a series filled with this type of characters. *American Horror Story* has taken characterization to a new level of shock. An unexpected background, a unique trait, physical features, and unexpected interests and situations the character likes to get involved in are some of the sources that fuel shocking elements in the process of characterization.

- Luck: This aspect has to do with characters with incredible luck despite their own weaknesses. These characters lead us to ask questions such as: how did they make it here? How did that happen? Selina Ward and Francis Underwood are characters with these criteria. How did they become presidents of the United States? For some it is luck. For others, it is because they know how to play the role within the context and achieve unthinkable goals. Another example is the amazing luck of Jane Villanueva in *Jane the Virgin*, who by being in the right place at the wrong time changed her life forever. Obviously, the decisions these characters make beyond their crazy luck are what moves the story forward. Other peculiar characters facing incredible situations are Forrest Gump, Hannah Horvath in *Girls*, Dr. Mindy Lahiri in *The Mindy Project*, Carrie Bradshaw in *Sex and the City*, and Lucille Ball in *I Love Lucy*.

- In-your-face: These characters say what needs to be said in their own terms. They are outrageous, outspoken, and always enjoyable. Ja'mie in *Ja'mie: Private School Girl*, Sawyer in *Lost*, Morgan Tookers in *The Mindy Project*, Jonah Ryan in *Veep*, Fran Fine in *The Nanny*, and Ari Gold in *Entourage* are in this group,

- Comedic relief: Characters in comedic roles make us laugh with hilarious, critical, and cynical representations of our own lives. Skits on *Saturday Night Live* are filled with characters that reminds us of ourselves and people we see everywhere—on the streets, on TV, in the news, etc. (e.g., Tina Fey's impersonation of Sarah Palin). Comedic characters always surprise us when they "hit the right chord"—when we can relate and identify their actions with our own. Characters in *Veep*, *The Hangover* (the character trio), and *Modern Family* bring that good sense of humor that enchants and intrigues an audience.

- Dead and supernatural creatures: Zombies, ghosts, creatures, and other supernatural characters are always intriguing, pivotal elements in a story, elements that bring danger and surprise within the realm of possible actions. In addition to the zombies in *The Walking Dead*, Sookie Stackhouse in *True Blood* and the legion of vampires, shifters, witches, etc. that filled her unlikely world are also examples of up super-powerful, supernatural, always-surprising criteria.

- Realism: Representation of characters in a realistic fashion makes them attractive and believable. The combination of dialogue, experiences, and backgrounds and having these characters go through problems people can easily relate to makes them empathetic. When real people face extraordinary situations, magic happens. The reasons to watch what is next in their lives are powerful. Characters that represent this notion are Nancy Botwin in *Weeds* and the casts of *The Walking Dead*, *The Purge*, and *Lost*.

There is no formula to tell you how to build a character, but once you come up with one, test it according to the elements that distinguish how surprising the character might be. If your character has at least one of those features (and I am sure you can think of many more), then you are well on your way to constructing a character who is potentially innovative and one who we could care about.

Innovation led by characters relies on how surprising and memorable the characters are and comes from a combination of context and traits. What it is that causes characters to be unique is not only their identifiable different, sometimes never-seen-before traits, but also the decisions they make within the context of the situations they face. That is what helps bring to life interesting situations that help characters to evolve and show layers of depth— the same way as we do in real life.

Media Aesthetics- and Production Value-Driven Innovation

Innovation driven by media aesthetics is related to the application of the different elements used by directors and producers to clarify and intensify the message for viewers. This notion is related to art direction, production design, and media aesthetics elements such as lighting, color, camera framing, time, motion editing, and sound (Zettl, 2013). Examples of TV shows that have defied aesthetic conventions, exposing audiences to new and innovative ways to visually communicate the message, include:

- *The Shield*: De-saturation of image and chaotic camera movement to emphasize violence, drama, and the inner turmoil of the characters
- *MTV Unplugged*: Intimate set design with a very cozy array of lightning tailor-made for top groups or singers to showcase their talent without instruments plugged to any electric source
- *MTV VJ*: A handheld camera moving around the subjects that became the synonym of cool in the 1990s (The erratic camera framing, which also included correcting focus while shooting the scenes, added a sense of reality to these shows that had only been seen in news reports. The technique diffused not only in other non-fiction types of programming but also in fiction such as *ER* and *The Shield*.)
- *Lost, Heroes, Boardwalk Empire, Tudors, Game of Thrones, Mad Men, Homeland, and Masters of Sex*: Brought to TV the majestic cinematic experience of outstanding series, special effects, colorimetry, sound, editing, and production design
- *The Peep Show*: Subjective camera framing combined with the inner thoughts of characters that magnified "inner TV," allowing the discovery of a usually unknown side of the characters—what they were really thinking
- *Glee*: Incorporation of commercial music to intensify and clarify the drama, comedy, and storytelling

INNOVATION DRIVEN BY TECHNOLOGY AND SERVICES

Technological developments and services evolve constantly, allowing the implementation of sophisticated and powerful tools to:

- Improve the means and resources to make content
- Create new platforms of exposition
- Enable multiplatform digital content and narrative structures to reach audiences and build communication infrastructures and services to allow audiences to enjoy content wherever they are, whenever they want, and to share it
- Create multiplatform digital content and narrative structures
- Create new content

To Improve the Means and Resources to Make Content

The entertainment industry has always relied on technology to make better content. From black-and-white grainy images to full-color high-definition 3D capability, content quality has improved throughout the years. Equipment and resources have become more sophisticated, making possible the impossible. In general, television, film, and video makers have gained access to better cameras, storage solutions, editing systems, color correction hardware, lighting gear, sound and design tools, and software to generate more sophisticated content despite the platform. Filmmakers have switched to digital video equipment, taking advantage of cost and quality benefits, whereas TV and other platforms have incorporated formerly costly film processes, thanks to the digital alternatives now available.

Technology has not only had an impact on the quality of video produced but also on the efficiency and complexity of production processes. Writers have engaged in the utilization of software to facilitate the writing of scripts. Producers have adopted scheduling and budgeting tools to organize and track production plans and costs. Technology has positively impacted team communication, networking, and exchange of information, data, and video, providing more capacity to react and to speed up delivery. Using technology, processes have been simplified, opening up time to explore new paths and formulas to produce.

Reality TV is a good example of how technology has made possible the implementation of a complicated production process. Reality shows once required the incorporation of multiple cameras, large storage drives, and a complex editing/visualization array to make possible the capture of enormous amounts of video footage needed for the preparation of the episodes seen on the air. Now, professionals can use lower-cost devices with highly sophisticated features that allow more efficiency and quality and the possibility of capturing and processing images in a way that could not have been done few years ago.

Not only professional video makers have benefited from these technology advances—so has the general public. Professional tools formerly available at prohibitive prices for professionals (HD cameras, computers, editing software, special effects software, etc.) are now available to the general public at very low cost, allowing non-professionals to apply sophisticated effects in the creation of fun content to be shared with others.

Telephones have built-in cameras. Inexpensive mobile applications allow the editing of original content, not for commercial purposes but for social purposes. Nowadays an 8-year old child can grab a tablet, activate a video generation application, and put together a video that can then be shared with the world and receive thousands of views and recognition. This process was unthinkable 20 years ago. Social video production has become a new way to communicate and relate. People are no longer sending just emails; they can send self-made videos and pictures called *selfies*. A new generation of young content innovators has been awakened, with new organic and eclectic visual and narrative approaches.

Content also drives technology when creators push for new ways to accomplish their visions by engaging scientists, software developers, and technical experts in the creation or adaptation of current technologies to produce what they want to show on the screen. Filmmakers such as James Cameron, George Lucas, Steven Spielberg, the Wachowski brothers, and J.J. Abrams are known for pushing the limits of imagination and bringing new technological developments to the production of their movies, which then become fixtures in the industry. When Andy and Lana Wachowski produced *The Matrix* in 1999, they set the tone for a new way to portray action-driven scenes through visual effects techniques that had not been explored. The 360 circular slow-motion camera movement around Keanu Reeves in one of the movie's scenes became an iconic visual portrayal of speed and reaction and has been replicated in hundreds of action films.

Technology can also have a positive effect on content, animation, and live action series. In terms of a live action series, special effects offer video and filmmakers the possibility to materialize worlds, characters, features, and objects that do not exist or could not exist unless a visual artist created and then composed them in a very specific arrangement to tell a story: the sublime colorful world of *Pushing Daisies*, the cinematographic visual power of the series *Heroes*, the futuristic urban world of the drama series *Caprica*, the horrific special effects of *The Walking Death*, the cloning conspiracy of *Orphan Black*, and the vampires and shifters brought to life in the surreal world of *True Blood*. Animation is another direct consequence of content that has been driven by technology—since the early cinematic days, when short cartoons were put in motion, to the 2D and 3D children's programming of today that is filled with a variety of options that lets them enjoy a world of fun and imagination, every day and at all times. Content has also benefitted from technology. Storytellers have been able to bring to life contexts that otherwise would have stayed only on paper or in their minds. These creative individuals push technology, and technology enables them to create brave new content worlds.

To Create New Platforms of Exposition

The advent of the internet redefined the medium through which people could enjoy media. Initially TV and film were the two mediums of choice to enjoy aural/visual entertainment. The possibility of accessing content through internet or wireless networks was far from realization until conditions to support and deliver high-quality media content materialized at the end of the twentieth century. This new technological reality provoked a merging between the internet and traditional media, which added new patterns of communication and consumption of media, leading to the generation of new platforms of exposition and the proliferation of content adapted to the new possibilities people had to watch media through different devices. Examples of innovative platforms and services include smart TVs, HDTV, 3DTV, mobile devices (iPhone, iPod, and iPad), internet (online sites), internet-enabled consoles (PSPs, Blu-rays), over the top channels (OTT-IPTV), mobile TV, mobile applications, satellite TV, and digital cable.

Services such as Amazon, Netflix, cable video on demand, on-the-go/mobile access by pay TV channels and services, iTunes, digital video recorders, and free online video services (YouTube, Vimeo, Crackle, and the Cloud) make up the vast realm of possibilities we now have to access content. Communication services such as Short Message Service (SMS), email, and social media sites such as Facebook, Twitter, Instagram, Google+, and Pinterest, among others, have also become vehicles to spread content among groups of followers and friends.

All of the devices and platforms are part of our connected environment through internet availability networks (Wi-Fi) and blue-tooth capabilities that make possible the synchronization and pairing of devices with smart TVs to enable the visualization of internet content on a large TV screen. Video can be seen anywhere and played from any device.

Digital devices have given us not only the possibility of accessing hours of content but also the means to generate and share content with friends or communities with the same interest. Social media platforms are a direct consequence of the internet's capability to share information instantly. Content can be published and shared to the world with the click of a mouse. The entertainment industry has been cautious about how to take advantage of the new digital medium without generating the collapse of their media rights model. Nevertheless, the audience has spoken and shown the industry that the new medium offers the possibility to be in control and they want to be in control. Renowned cases such as the Napster situation in 1999 shook not only the music industry but also the entertainment industry overall when users started to download and share music for free using a new internet base site. (*Note*: Napster was co-founded by teenagers who initially saw it as an independent peer-to-peer file sharing service. Napster, using the nickname of Shawn Fanning, one of its founders, operated from 1999 until 2001 when it was shut down by court order.)

In 2005, when the social media video site YouTube made possible the uploading of homemade videos onto the internet for the world to watch, the reaction was massive acceptance. Once again made evident was that people were not only interested in what professional video makers, studios, or distributors had to offer them, but they were also interested in the content ordinary people in the real world were producing. The freedom of posting any video generated by a user turned YouTube into the biggest competitor traditional media could ever face. It was this low-cost user-generated content made from home videos with a camera that a computer had, and then shared through social media sites such as Facebook, that made the industry realize that people were ready for other types of platforms of aural/visual entertainment. People were spending time on their computers watching videos, reducing the time they spent in front of their TVs. People had taken an active position within the scheme of content generation, pushing the proliferation of innovative surprising content. The YouTube generation found a way to validate this content through a direct click on an icon called Like. As a consequence, new stars were discovered, and the YouTube sensation became ubiquitous.

This new context of YouTube gave creative individuals the possibility of producing content with any resources available and then sharing the project directly with the public without passing through the industry, generating a direct process of social validation (as discussed in Chapter 6, *The Sociocultural Model of Creative Validation in Media*). The internet had become the place to find video references, enjoy experimental videos, and to find talent, not just for on-camera but for jobs for producers, directors, and writers.

To Enable Multiplatform Digital Content and Narrative Structures

The 360 multiplatform environment of today entails online, mobile, and social media sites and traditional platforms. Multiplatform digital content uses all available platforms of exposition to convey a message. Depending on the application given by the creator, content can have different purposes:

- To expand an original experience (a TV show) and become shareable (social media links) by supporting and complementing traditional content in other platforms through web-based B-stories and viral content to create awareness and complement traditional content through second-screen capabilities such as voting, additional storylines, other points of view, and behind the scenes: The voting system in shows such as *Rising Star* (2014) is a direct second-screen application that gives people from home the ability to vote while a contestant is performing. Likewise, connecting live feeds from cameras posted in different places of a venue where a major live event is happening, such as the VMAs 2014, also enhance the experience.

- To integrate new communication habits such as email, SMS, WhatsAPP Messenger, Facebook, and Twitter into a narrative: In the twentieth century, we had letters, telephones, and telegraphs. Now our options are more immediate and diverse. These new tools to communicate have become part of how characters interact on a fiction show, how conflict flourishes, and how we engage viewers in game shows or talk shows to interact, vote, or participate. *House of Cards* (2013) is a good example of how to integrate SMS interaction within the narrative of a show. In this series, characters are presented in a frank dialogue. The conversation is interrupted but not stopped when one of the characters receives an SMS message. We see the message popping up on the screen while the conversation in the scene still goes on—just as it happens in real life: we live between two layers of communication, one is defined by our devices and the other is defined by the actual event we are in physically, and that needs to be reflected in content.

- To allow multiplatform storytelling: Creators of content have engaged in the creation of storylines that encompass all platforms of social interaction. For example *La Mina TV*, a multiplatform digital telenovela created for Univision, presents a story that happens daily online in a few minutes but which continues developing via SMS, Twitter, and Facebook throughout the day until the next online episode is shown. Producer Erick Foster created the scripting methodology, through which the events presented on the social media platforms were a continuation of the plot presented in full video online. To understand the story, fans needed to stay logged into the *La Mina TV* social platform.

No standard or rigid formulas are available for creating multiplatform content. As a matter of fact, the creative environment has become a very dynamic one where creators decide the best way to present a show based on the motivation behind its conception. The show could be an independent production, studio-supported content to complement a traditional series, or an initiative supported directly by a brand or a non-media-related corporation. Trends in high-profile multiplatform content include:

- Short length of 3 to 15 minutes
- Duration increasing up to a half hour and 1 hour
- Young target audience (children, tweens, teens, young adults, 18- to 34-year olds) or niche audiences targeting an established community
- Non-standardized numbers of episodes per season/run
- Interactive narratives through transmedia production (Data and video "collide" through blogs, chats, emails, videos, etc.)
- Video streaming, webcasts, mobilecasts, and appcasts through social media platforms
- Mid-high production value; improved and compelling stories
- Casts ranging from unknown actors, participants, or hosts to high-profile celebrities (Justin Timberlake in Audi's *The Next Big Thing* or Marion Cotillard in Dior's series *Lady Blue Shanghai* and *L.A. dy Dior*)
- Proven TV writers, producers, directors, and crew
- Strong product integration
- Multiple points of access (simultaneous and not)
- Windowing (some content repurposed to traditional media outlets after a run on the internet)
- Technology affecting intellectual property management as a consequence of the proliferation of multiple devices and many windows of exploitation

To Create New Content for New Platforms

Delivery services such as cable, smart TVs, OTT channels, online channels, VOD services, iTunes, Netflix, and Amazon are infusing a web of thematic and niche programming, generated by professionals, amateurs, and users:

- Cable series on premium thematic cable and digital channels such as AMC, HBO, and FX have embarked on the generation of innovative programs that differ from prime-time network series, primarily by not being cancelled easily and therefore enjoying longer runs. Seasons have fewer episodes (8 to 13). Cable has figured out a model to bring audiences to these shows. The series are more character driven and most of them are continued storylines (soap-style dramas). Examples include *Mad Men, Breaking Bad, The Shield, Damages,* and *Sons of Anarchy.*

- OTT channels on smart TVs and set-top boxes are internet-enabled channels that allow the exposition of premium content such as films and series, music videos, movie trailers, and news reports, as well as user-generated content. These OTT channels range from Amazon TV and Netflix applications now showcasing originally produced content for TV platforms, such as *Orange Is the New Black* and *House of Cards*, to low-cost, to highly thematic channels transmitting programs such as *Adventures of the Flying Dog* (amateur videos of dogs flying through the air).

- The notion of creating your own channel was fully realized when YouTube gave its users the ability to create a site to showcase the videos they had created. YouTube channels have launched the careers of online celebrities and content makers who have built communities of followers who enjoy what they produce. YouTube channels are set up by independent users and companies that have taken advantage of this direct-to-consumer video service. SA Waderga, a digital production company in Poland, has become notorious for prank videos, which are compiled on a YouTube channel with more than 2.5 million subscribers. A video prank about a dog dressed as a giant tarantula became a viral sensation in 2014 with over 15 million views in 2 days and became the most watched video of that year with over 150 million views.

- The *YouTube Awards*, launched in 2013, is an interesting example in which a new tactic for awards ceremonies took on the essence of the spontaneity that allows users to post videos online. Spike Jonze, a film director, used this tactic and created an event, ad lib, as chaotic as the YouTube site suggests—anything can happen—with no scripts and top-notch acts performing a music video live on tape. Jonze was given the opportunity to create an event that broke all conventional molds—and he delivered.

The New Competitive Landscape Enabled by Technology

The way technology is blossoming is a hint of what is coming. The idea of watching TV has evolved into a different concept, but attention continues to be centered on the content, not the device. The device is just a means to watch the content. For example, my pre-teen son and younger daughter no longer watch television according to schedules or TV guides. They use TV as any other device to access, get, and watch the content they want, whenever they want it. The same as my children, a new generation is emerging with the same habits. The challenge then is to let these viewers know about the existence of content, be it a TV show, a

YouTube video, a video game, or a film, so they can go and get it. This new generation of viewers is no longer a slave of the TV medium because they control it. For that reason, content relevance is key—with awareness being the most difficult challenge producers of content now have in this prolific and competitive world of entertainers and multiple platforms of exposition.

Content is ubiquitous and continues to be king! People will always need a good story to relate to, an entertaining show to watch, a game to play, a sports event to witness, or a trustful source for getting the latest news. The merge of technologies and platforms is inevitable. New gadgets will continue to be out there to watch content on the go, on demand, in the car, in your bed, and on your couch. Yes, the couch will still be there and the big super TV set will also be there for us couch potatoes. It does not matter what capability the TV has—3D, 4D, internet-enabled, socially networked, 3G, 5G, holographic, interactive, or shape shifter, maybe even as a convertible, foldable 10- to 100-inch ultrathin screen that you can carry in your backpack—just as movie theaters and TV sets have proven unbeatable over time, a screen will always be in front of us to experience content. The challenge is to make that content good, relevant, and noticeable.

Overall, what this all means is that opportunities will continue blossoming for content generators. Content is in super-high demand and the many ways to experience content are generating more and more needs, outlets, and ways to create and produce it.

INNOVATION DRIVEN BY BUSINESS MODELS

Business opportunities and needs are a third aspect that propels innovation. Corporations trigger insight for the creation of content initiatives thanks to new business models and market strategies that ensure a positive effect on the bottom line of a business. These strategies urge creative executives, individuals, and executives from different functional areas to work together to come up with ideas and creative solutions that match the criteria.

Branded Content Initiatives

Business models triggering innovation include the direct support of brands and the direct involvement of these brands in the process of content generation. Brands include commercial products and media platforms, such as radio, theater, and print, crossing over to video production via their online and mobile sites. *USA Today* and *The New York Times* are multimedia platforms that feature full video reports in combination with text and pictures. These multimedia platforms also have TV programming featured in airplanes and hotels throughout the United States.

Using the branded content model, commercial brands develop, produce, and deliver content directly to their target consumers. For example, Coca Cola and Red Bull have created their own platforms of exposition, Coca Cola TV and Red Bull TV, to showcase content that projects the identity of the brand and allows a community of followers to be entertained by the content the brand offers directly. Brands usually rely on the power of the content that other media platforms generate, and they measure affinity to the brand in order to invest in it. Advertising brands can now develop and produce their own content, securing brand affinity with audiences from the get go. Brands also invest in marketing strategies to promote their own TV brand and to ensure that consumers learn about the content the brands have prepared exclusively for them. Another model has brands supporting and sponsoring stand-alone online and mobile platforms that showcase content with strong affinity. For example, Alloy Entertainment, a company and website dedicated to packaging books and producing content for teenagers and young adult girls, started adapting books packaged as web series that were supported by key sponsors such as Procter & Gamble. Some of the shows created for the site became TV series. Alloy Entertainment (now owned by Warner Bros.) has generated series such as *Private, Gossip Girl*, and *Pretty Little Liars*.

Product integration, a brand embedding their products in the story in an organic way, is another way for brands to get closer to the inside of a show. Product integration has led to very creative initiatives in which short-form content (miniseries) have been made available through social media and other mobile platforms. Brands creating content with strong product integration include LG, Phillips, Axe (Unilever), Audi, Dior, and Procter & Gamble.

The 360 Model of Exploitation

360 Models of exploitation, through the activation of several platforms of exposition to showcase a product, trigger new monetization and revenue opportunities. Examples of the 360 model include the activation of an online platform related to a TV show from which people can download music, episodes, extra footage, B-story episodes, behind-the-scenes interviews with the cast, and relevant information about the show. Likewise, concerts, merchandising, and other ancillary initiatives can be activated. Creation of a show becomes complex because its creation has to include all of the initiatives that could be undertaken in a coherent and connected fashion.

International Co-Productions

A business model that triggers powerful content is international co-productions through which several countries join forces to create content with global relevance. For example, the four-part miniseries about the *Titanic* (2012) was a costly endeavor that was produced under the auspices of ABC in the United States, ITV in the United Kingdom, and the Global Television Network in Canada and Hungary (iMDb, 2012). International co-productions ensure that funding comes from the different countries that share the same interests in the product. This collaborative effort, needed for the creation of powerful content with global relevance, makes possible an almost impossible quest by a single country—production of a TV show that is so expensive that without funding from several countries, the show would never be made.

TV Formats and Distribution

TV formats also spark generation of content that could potentially be replicated in different countries, monetizing the concept over and over again through a format fee payment per episode produced. Examples include *The Pyramid Game* and *The Voice* and fiction formats such as *Married with Children* and *Ugly Betty*. Producers are now not envisioning the success of a show only in its country of origin but are creating shows with universal appeal that could be reproduced everywhere.

The universal aspect of finished content has become the rule in U.S. studios so that worldwide distribution is guaranteed. The United States does not make content for only local markets but for the world. In fact, part of the financing for shows originally made in the United States comes from international sales divisions. Locally driven content shows do not sell overseas, but high-concept action-driven, procedural, soap-style shows are hits in the international market.

Try the following activities:

- Conceptualize a new way to present a fiction series or a non-fiction show to an audience.
- Think of an idea that would derive from the merging of two or various genres. Be specific in terms of the genres being used.
- Think of a book or a story that you know that no one has told on a TV, film, or any other platform you know. Do some research to sustain your notion.
- Name and analyze a show that has been driven by a mesmerizing character. Why was this element the main driver of innovation?

- Pick a show you find innovative and break down the different elements that drive its innovative nature (concept, character, story, technology, etc.). Remember: One show can be the result of one or more drivers.
- Write a short story and then break it down into a unique narrative sequence or add layers of storytelling platforms to tell the story. Does it make sense? Would you tell the story that way?
- Do some research and come up with four productions that have been done as the result of an international co-production or endeavor.

STEP 2
CREATE THE CONDITIONS FOR INNOVATION TO OCCUR

Chapter 10. Implementing the Process of Innovation

10

IMPLEMENTING THE
PROCESS OF INNOVATION

We have discussed the importance of strategy and what creativity in the media industry means and have reviewed the concept of innovation and the key drivers of innovation. After gathering intelligence on strategy, creativity, and innovation, creative leaders must activate the next phase—the process of implementation, which is setting up the right environment to innovate (Figure 10-1). This chapter concentrates on how creative individuals, professionals, and companies set up a proper environment for innovation by making a solid commitment in terms of the organization and its human resources.

CREATING THE RIGHT ENVIRONMENT

The process of innovation relies on individuals to create the conditions necessary for innovation to happen. Strategy and planning skills play essential roles in finding out what these conditions are. Who you are, where you are, and what you have define the identity, the playground, and the resources for embarking on the process of finding the next big idea. Once you have answers to these questions you must convey them to and address them with those who join your quest to create so that you can synchronize all the thoughts and efforts. In other words, you must ensure that everyone aims at the same goal.

Aiming at the same goal—understanding the goals—also helps create an environment where people believe that ideas are welcome, that feedback is necessary, and that a diversity of opinions is essential to shape up a concept toward

Understand	Set	Discover	Deliver
Strategy	Strategic Goals		
Creativity	Environment		
Innovation	Conditions		

Figure 10-1. The process of innovation.

its realization. This notion is key in the entertainment industry. If ideas are not welcome and people are not informed, innovations will not happen.

The recommendations in this chapter are based on the findings of dal Zotto & Kranenburg (2008), Skarzynsky & Gibson (2008), Dyer, Gregersen & Christiansen (2011), Trias de Bes & Kotler (2011), Lehrer (2012), and Meister & Willyerd (2010). The precision of their recommendations and the effectiveness of their implementation processes are well defined. The precision of their recommendations and the effectiveness of their implementation processes are well defined. These authors are key references for understanding the methodology, processes, and concepts behind innovation and have become drivers in the implementation of processes throughout my career. By reading their works, I discovered the essence behind the right environment, why companies succeed, what makes a good leader innovative, and what constitutes a proper innovative environment. Their findings led me to a moment of insight in which I visualized the need I had to project this information into the entertainment industry, specifically to be applied to the process of innovative media content creation. To structure the proper innovative environment, their findings have been adapted and blended with my own experiences to address considerations in two groups:

- The organization
- The people

THE ORGANIZATION

Considerations in the organization entail compromise, leadership, communication, time, and space. These five aspects work in conjunction, not in isolation. An innovative organization is committed to ensuring the right conditions to those working there so that can they spend their time and efforts creating superb content. If these conditions are not in place, people start looking for another way to help them realize their potential.

Support Compromise

As an innovator, of utmost importance is creating an atmosphere of compromise through the adoption of an innovation-oriented environment, which must vigorously be on the constant lookout for the next big hit. Innovators working in an atmosphere of compromise not only have a great sense of creativity and discovery but also an outstanding notion of delivery (Dyer, Gregersen & Christensen 2011). A key problem in organizations and creative teams today occurs when a business is not oriented to innovate but to just deliver a service or a product. For example, a creative team could develop extraordinary expertise in executing a very specific type of show and become the go-to company for delivery of this type of project. Continued success in making the same kind of shows might lead these producers to rely on a winning but fixed formula that allows little to no room for experimenting or developing something new (Dyer, Gregersen & Christensen 2011).

Unfortunately, current organizational cultures are mostly delivery oriented, which is accentuated by the size of the firms. The bigger, more established, and successful a company is, the more the need is to find ways to sustain success through formula approaches, focusing on incremental innovations of what worked in the past and leaving little room for breakthroughs. On the other hand, the smaller and more entrepreneurial a firm is, the more innovative it can be because that type of firm is more willing to take chances and incur risk (Dyer, Gregersen & Christensen 2011). The key message here is not to stay small but to keep thinking big like small entrepreneurial firms do. No matter the size of the company, producers and creative teams need to keep dreaming about the new. Companies need to take risks to innovate and that means compromise. For example, big companies willing to work with smaller firms to create content demonstrates a willingness and commitment to always be creating something new.

Compromise also requires a willingness to find new solutions to old problems or situations. Important for creative teams is to anticipate when a formula is "running out of steam" and then to prepare to make internal changes and find new ways to continue surprising audiences. A company committed to deliver innovation, change, and shake up the status quo avoids creative freezing and ensures an openness to new practices, criteria, and thoughts.

Compromise, of course, comes from the top of an organization and permeates throughout thanks to the leaders. Leaders and followers need to share the same sense of commitment. Leaders know how to spread goals and create teams that look for innovation and deliver results.

Have Entrepreneurial Leadership

Entrepreneurial leadership is the second consideration in pursuing an innovative organization. Innovative leaders must be entrepreneurial in essence—individuals who think outside the box and try to change and evolve all of the time. Innovative leaders acknowledge formulas and the importance of incremental innovations, but they never stop finding, testing, and exposing audiences to a new idea or a concept that could potentially be a breakthrough.

Strong leaders do not let the discovery process stall by concentrating only on execution. Instead, they nurture and encourage the process of finding ways to surprise an audience. Dyer, Gregersen & Christensen (2011) analyzed the characteristics of innovative organizations and individuals and found that companies with the highest growth and success rates were those that kept discovery activated and knew how to deliver all the time. Their recommendation is to reach a balance. The perfect innovative leader for an organization or a team knows how to discover *and* deliver. Remember: Innovation does not end with the idea. It ends with people enjoying the TV program. So an innovative leader discovers *and* delivers.

Leaders also have to communicate the purpose and nature of an operation. They must be able to put into place the best organizational infrastructure possible and then empower teams to make decisions (dal Zotto & Kranenburg, 2008). A great leader motivates and also gives autonomy to teams so that team members can become the guardians of new ideas and new approaches to a breakthrough.

A great innovative leader nurtures collaboration, agility, and openness. A great innovative leader shares know-how but also learns from others, understands the importance of having knowledgeable team members, and realizes that the best leaders do not need to know it all but to keep open the opportunities for everyone to share their knowledge and experiences to better collaborate and develop new content.

Understanding *open* innovation is essential for a leader who wants to create inquisitive assertive environments that find new ideas. A great innovative leader appreciates feedback and encourages team members to look for ideas outside their comfort zones. A great innovative leader also understands that all solutions are not in-house and that all ideas are not within a team. Experimentation with individuals with or without a track record is of essence in looking for a brilliant concept. Interaction with the outside is essential.

Nurture Learning, Communication, and Collaboration

Essential for creative organizations is to implement perceptive channels of communication and to nurture the concept of learning throughout the organization. Creative individuals need to have the space and time to learn and experience new things. They have to be in touch with the outside world and get close to the different innovations and creative trends that proliferate in the industry. Exposure to innovations and creative trends provides background and knowledge and constitutes the basics of creative thinking to come up with new ideas and concepts.

Communication, of course, is essential in the learning process. Information, findings, trends, feedback, premises, and goals are a few of the elements that need to permeate throughout a group or a creative company. Leadership needs to ensure that communication infiltrates all different departments and that information does not stay at the top, in the middle, or at the bottom of the management chain. If information does not permeate, there is no gain. If people do not receive information, they disconnect from the core of the business. Communication engages and enhances the feelings of belonging that provide autonomy and brand identity from within. Nothing is better than having a team of creative individuals who are fueled by the power of the brand they represent. Communication brings connection and conversation, which according to Skarzynski & Gibson (2008) is the combinational chemistry that serves as a breeding ground for creative collision that yields breakthrough ideas.

Technology today plays a crucial role in implementing communication, learning, and collaborative environments. Social network solutions ensure that communication reaches out to all levels. Through these platforms, people can share ideas and find out about the progress of the projects of other teams, even providing the possibility of solving a crisis if necessary. Creative leaders must use social media to attract, motivate, connect, engage, develop, retain, and listen to team members (Meister & Willyerd, 2010, p. 4). Meister & Willyerd also add that the social media revolution is not about technology but rather about creative communities of people.

Provide Time and Space

Innovative companies or teams must create the time and the space for people to innovate and even daydream (Lehrer, 2012). The same as with communication, if people do not have the time and space to bring up new ideas, they will shut down, disconnect from the company, and focus on nurturing independent efforts during their free time and for their own purposes (Skarzynski, 2008; Lehrer, 2012).

When I talk about time and space, I do not mean to just activate a confined or separate area where people can gather and think about an innovation for an hour or so. Instead, I am referring to letting them set up a space or to go to a place where solutions might be. Encourage them to explore other environments, to talk to people at the right locations, and to observe things with their own eyes to share and process findings. Giving creative individuals the opportunity (the space) to participate in other projects or activities outside their daily routines creates the time. These other projects could be from outsiders, third parties, fellow work colleagues in the company, or even from a creative individual's project. New projects developed within the time provided could grow as a tangible opportunity. The individual in charge could end up leading or participating in the project until completed. Having space and time provides autonomy, trust, and appreciation and empowers individuals, making them feel that they have a voice and that their voice counts.

Some companies such as Google allocate 20% of the available time during the week for work on special projects. Often, however, leaders in key management positions do not want to distract their teams with out-of-the-box projects because they fear this type of distraction will cause a loss in productivity, but contrary to that, out-of-the-box projects actually increase motivation and make people feel more committed to deliver their work so they can participate on another project. The 3M Company was first to implement a policy called "flexible attention." This flexible attention policy allowed members of a research team to use 15% of their time to think about speculative ideas, with the condition that they share the ideas with their peers. Many think that Google came up with this concept, but actually Google imitated, the same as other firms have, the innovative concept of time and space utilization (Lehrer, 2012).

Outside of a corporation, independent creative individuals can also set aside time and space to create innovative projects. For example, a writer who is concentrating on one project or specific projects commissioned by a client could devote 20% of their time to writing up another project that the writer believes in. This suggestion might sound obvious, but sometimes setting aside time and space is difficult for individuals who do independent work.

THE PEOPLE

The people relates to team diversity, skills sets, and assigning the right roles to achieve the proper mix of human resources.

Diverse Teams

The importance of team diversity relies on the power of collective differences to solve problems and to come up with unexpected solutions. On occasion, companies or creative leaders tend to bring together people with similar profiles, thus creating a group of clones who thinks and acts similarly and forms a rather homogeneous team that does not see solutions away from their comfort zones or radius of acceptance and tolerance. People who differ in points of view always clash—and that is exactly the point because conflict creates a need for consensus, thus solutions. People with different experiences, knowledge, and visions of the world add different ingredients to the mix of possibilities and help discover a market's unmet needs and ideas that are worth exploring. Page (2007) conducted experiments at the California Institute of Technology and concluded that diverse groups always outperform combinations of the best and the brightest.

Skarzynski (2008) made an extraordinary recommendation on how to ensure team diversity. He established that important is not just composing a team with different genders, races, cultures, and ethnicities but to also have different capabilities and perspectives. The combination of all of these aspects creates the diverse thinking that leads to innovation insights and new opportunities. To ensure diversity on a team, Skarzynsky proposed the following groups:

- Convergent and divergent thinkers: Convergent thinkers tend to see things through the same perspective when trying to reach conclusions. Divergent thinkers look at problems from totally different points of view and tend to generate a positive clash of visions. Working together, divergent and convergent thinkers find disruptive solutions, breaking the status quo and conventional ways of thinking.
- Analytical and intuitive individuals: Analytical people rely on numbers and the past and tend to make decisions based on what has worked best. Intuitive people are willing to take chances and go for the untried. They believe in gut instincts. A combination of both brings the balance that makes analytical and innovative visions co-exist well (Martin, 2009). The past brings reference, and the future brings uncertainty, but data helps alleviate the uncertainty and speeds up the decision-making process. Having teams with analytical and intuitive characteristics helps to create an environment not only willing to take chances but to also understand what is at risk. (*Note*: Ensure that you also include individuals who concentrate on audience behavior, such as marketing and programming professionals, with the individuals who are behind the creative process.)
- Above-the-line management and below-the-line workers: Great teams share visions, information, and concerns. When above-the-line (top) management shares information with below-the-line workers, a company starts acting as a whole. Everyone searches for the same goal. Again, people feel empowered when they are included in the strategy.
- Younger and older individuals: Take advantage of a generational mix, a clash of generations. Baby Boomers, Traditionalists, Gen Xs, and Gen Ys (Millennials) are all part of the current workforce spectrum (Meister & Willerd, 2010). Have all of them interact in different ways to mix perspectives and generational points of view. A generational mix is the perfect way to explore the past with glasses of the future. The right generational mix could turn an old approach into something revolutionary, current, and relevant.

- Experienced individuals and others with a lot of imagination: Young people without experience can bring fresh and out-of-the-box ideas that more experienced individuals might not even consider. Experienced people are experts in the field. They have clear information on what might work or might not. The vision of an experienced individual can help define the path for bringing forward a new and revolutionary idea. For example, *Big Brother* needed more than 50 cameras located all over a locked studio house to capture independently all of the events happening inside the house. Experienced producers and technical gurus made that process happen without altering the fresh vision of John de Mol who created the show.
- Technology-driven and emotion/people-driven individuals: Young people now have a special capability to handle, manage, and figure out new technological applications. Some with no work experience might have had extensive exposure to new technologies from a consumer standpoint or from creating content on their own for social platforms. They can bring a fresh take on content creation that, together with the insights of professionals who are people- and emotion-driven, might help create something surprising.
- Individuals from inside and outside the company: Embrace people from inside the firm as well as people from the outside (the networks; the open innovation approach). Even bring international talent into the mix! Be open to having a diverse, multigenerational, global world. Also ensure the involvement of new in-house voices, such as newcomers to the company and people from other functional areas (the doers) in the organization. Mix everyone up with outside-content providers and idea generators and doers.
- Creators and executers: Put dreamers and doers together so that they can imagine and get a show done in a complementary fashion.
- Weird or different individuals: Include people as team members who might cause you to feel uncomfortable, such as overly socially responsible, serious, or formal individuals.

The Right Skill Sets

Identifying the different individuals needed to achieve team diversity must be accompanied by an assessment of the key skill sets needed and the capability of the team members to shape, manage, participate, and optimize a collaborative process of ideation, creation, and execution. Each skill set has a different utilitarian advantage, depending on the individual's background and experience. What is important is that each individual brings relevancy to the team. For example, wanting to include a "different" individual does not mean incorporating a person who has nothing to add to the process at hand. An eccentric writer on a team with mechanic engineers could be different but necessary *if* he writes a mechanical development (a robotic application for a film, for example). In this instance, the writer and the engineers complement each other and collaborate to develop the best possible solution. Members of an innovation team need to have the following skill sets to some degree:

- Intelligence: Intelligence is a collection of information that allows an individual to create solutions. Intelligent individuals are resourceful and have valid references and information.
- Curiosity and an attitude to learn: The willingness of individual to explore, find, and increase their knowledge is a must-have trait for innovative team members. The willingness to apply new techniques, methodologies, or visions enhances the possibility of breaking the status quo and developing something new.
- Know-how: Having know-how in a specific skill set needed to execute a task makes some individuals specialists in certain professions. Examples include the writer, director, producer, and art director.
- Imagination: Imagination is the capacity to come up with ideas and to visualize things and solutions.
- Assertiveness and execution capability: Individuals on a team need to be able to accomplish things. No matter what functional area they are in, assertiveness is a strength team members need to have to move a creative process forward. Otherwise, the process stalls.
- Entrepreneurial instinct: Successful creative individuals are mostly entrepreneurs in spirit. After entrepreneurs create an innovation, they want to move on to a different one. Entrepreneurial people are more intuitive, take risks, and are constantly looking for innovative ways to grow a business or to improve an existing product.

Defined Roles

Once the members of an innovation team have been identified (based on having the right skill sets), next is defining the roles that these individuals will have throughout the process. These roles are not related to a specific task or functional area. They have to more do with the traits, characteristics, and capabilities of the team members, as professionals or individuals, to accomplish tasks (Trias de Bes & Kotler, 2011). These roles depend on the nature or characteristics of each individual. Leaders and recruiting management must be able to define the real nature of each individual and the role they might play within a creative team.

Trias de Bes & Kotler (2011) identified six types of roles that are necessary to ensure innovation. These roles are the basis of what Trias de Bes & Kotler call the "A to F Model" to produce innovations (explained in detail in their book). In this fascinating model, Trias de Bes & Kotler say that people and their roles come first and that the process is the result of interaction among the two. As a result, Trias de Bes & Kotler propose the following roles based on an individual's capabilities and strengths:

- Activators: Activators initiate processes, resources, and goals. An activator understands the strategy of a group or company clearly and sets a framework to create and operate. As a result, an activator ensures that everyone understands the framework so that the team will generate content that meets particular criteria. An activator does not create limitations; instead an activator keeps creativity grounded. For example, an activator for CNN would keep the news and information framework in full force. If a producer wanted to do a celeb-reality show or a drama series, either show, of course, would not fit the framework of operation and the idea would be dismissed.
- Browsers: Browsers search for information. They do not produce new concepts or ideas. Browsers just compile relevant information for other participants in the process. Browsers are crucial for strategic research activities and competition analysis.
- Creators: Creators produce ideas, ideate concepts, find new solutions, and locate possibilities throughout the process. Writers are creators.
- Developers: Developers turn ideas into programs. They provide structure and make the idea tangible. Developers work based on the idea provided. Writers and creative producers are developers.
- Executors: Executors implement and deliver the show that will be exposed to the market. Production teams led by an executive producer are executors in the process of content creation.
- Facilitators: Facilitators approve investments and resources to ensure that the innovation process moves forward. They prevent a process from getting stuck and find solutions to keep the ball rolling. Facilitators could be in charge of many projects at the same time. They multitask in essence and are able to combine resources between projects and find synergies to make things happen. Facilitators work very well with activators. Facilitators include general managers, project leaders, executive producers, the head of a studio, chief executive officers, chief financial officers, and chief operation officers.

According to Trias de Bes & Kotler (2011), the rationale is that, based on these roles, the order in which these individuals interact does not correspond to a linear pre-established process, but instead to a process that might differ according to the task at hand. Each show to be made therefore represents the problem at hand, and every activity to be completed needs people working in proper roles to move the activity forward. The team essentially interacts and finds the best way to come up with a solution to the problem.

People need to understand what their role is. Nothing is worse than having a team that is confused in terms of their roles and responsibilities. Although finding professional individuals who demonstrate a combination of the roles expressed above is possible, each individual must still have a role that identifies that individual first hand. For example, a facilitator or an activator might be a creator, but the main responsibility of this individual in the process depends on the time they can actually put into a specific role or task.

Mindy Kailing and Ryan Murphy, executive producers and show runners of content, are examples of being an activator, a facilitator, a creator, and an executor. Their combination of these roles allows them to oversee and manage the entire process. Their dedication to the process of creation and execution, however, is possibly less than those who focus on certain activities 100% of their time. Executive producers such as Mindy Kailing and Ryan Murphy rely on other people to move the process forward. They execute through management that provides direction. Leaders and managers usually have a combination of traits, but they concentrate on the activity that fuels the process ahead.

In Chapter 2 (*Defining Who You Are: Creative Individual or Creative Executive*), you were encouraged to answer the question: who are you—a creative individual or a creative executive? To complete your identity profile, you are now encouraged to complement your answer by selecting a trait that better identifies you as a professional.

Now that the people are in place and the organization is committed to allocating the time, space, and conditions to innovate, we are ready to start implementing the processes of discovery and delivery.

STEP 3
ADOPT DISCOVERY
AS YOUR CORE

11

THE DISCOVERY CIRCLE

Innovators concentrate on the discovery of ideas and opportunities. As we discussed in Chapter 5 (*Understanding Creativity*), innovators evaluate and validate ideas and opportunities before entering a stage of delivery and diffusion. Discovery and delivery are the two umbrella activities that, once implemented, distinguish an innovator or an innovative organization or a team from mere idea generators or executors (Skarzynski & Gibson, 2011). The difficulty here is not only to discover the idea but to also achieve the end result *and* deliver the innovation—to do both.

Discovery is the main component of the entire innovation process. Discovery is also called the core, the heart, or the DNA (Skarzynsky & Gibson, 2011). Discovery has to be embedded in all of the activities dedicated to content creation. In other words, discovery is mandatory. Discovery responds to understanding the what, where, and how to look for ideas—not an easy quest—but understanding how it works helps creative individuals to be alert to the hints that life places everywhere to be grabbed and turned into a fantastic story, a character, a game, a format, or precious audiovisual content.

Many experts in the content field dedicate their professional efforts to understanding and mastering the rules of the game, while others take chances and innovate. Some concentrate on learning how to deliver while others concentrate on experimenting and coming up with new concepts. Those who experiment, and think beyond the day-to-day processes they are embedded in, are the ones who are actually discovering and realizing new ways to execute things. But innovation should not be assigned to or expected from just few individuals. Innovation must exist throughout a process, with the entire creative team and the organization participating. Everyone should always try their best—because anyone can. The

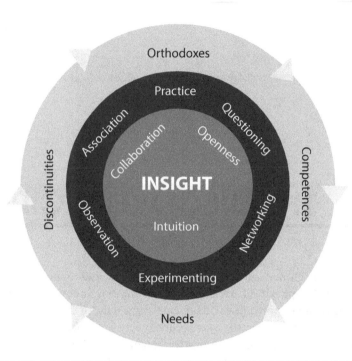

Figure 11-1. The discovery circle.

more people who engage in the discovery process, the better (Dyer, Gregersen & Christiansen, 2011). Engagement must keep pumping like the heart.

The discovery process relies on organization, group intelligence, and insight. To provide a methodology for implementing discovery in the process of innovation, the findings of Dyer, Gregersen & Christiansen (2011), who explored the fundamental actions disruptive innovators must undertake, will be used and ideas from Skarzynski & Gibson (2008), who introduced masterfully what they called "the lenses of innovation," will be extrapolated as a guide to discovering breakthrough ideas and opportunities. Both models will be mixed with my personal views to create a framework I call the *circle of discovery*. This circle is the heart of the process of innovation and becomes a summary tool to help keep a creative team aware of the different notions and activities that compose the discovery process. The circle of discovery must be active all of the time. Everyone in a company or on a creative production team must embrace this circle to create insight.

As presented in Figure 11-1, the discovery circle is formed by three layers and a nucleus composed of a combination of the skills, traits, and actions necessary to always pursue innovation in content. Without discovery, there is no creativity and innovation. Discovery responds to strategy and prevails throughout a process to successfully deliver insights.

INSIGHT

Insight is the nucleolus of the discovery circle. The nucleolus, a small spot in the nucleus or, in this case, in the center of the discovery circle, is that precious moment in which we visualize the solution to a problem in a clear, obvious way—what is called an eureka moment. This eureka moment happens when the brain "connects the dots" and we realize a solution after going through a period of mental blocks that prevented finding a solution that would allow us solve a problem (Lehrer (2012).

Creative individuals and professionals within a company or group are always solving problems that are activated from the moment a strategy is set. To illustrate this better, let's suppose the company (or a group) decides that it wants to develop the best comedy series ever, for example, a breakthrough reality program, or in a broader sense to find that piece of content that will differentiate the company from all the competition in a specific genre. As a result, the team starts making their best efforts to find a solution and concentrate on locating that gem that will "motorize" and energize actions and goals in the company.

According to Lehrer (2012), however, "Trying to force an insight can actually prevent the insight." Forcing a solution can make a creative individual or team fixate on the wrong answers. When we try to force a solution, we engage in a mentally focused state of mind that actually blocks the search for solutions that are outside the possibilities we already have in front of us. We might think that increased focus is always better, but actually it is not. That is why taking a break from a dedicated situation and engaging in another activity to let the brain search and activate other parts of itself will allow a team member (such as an artist) to solve the problem—it's a good practice (Lehrer, 2012).

It is after the times when we have a mental block, when we let ourselves relax and indulge in distractions and stop looking, that we actually find a solution. Once we break away from being trapped by a mental block, the brain starts to consider information that was irrelevant until now, but through a series of surprising associations that information is transformed into a solution and (eureka!) the idea then becomes very obvious. That is when a creative individual realizes that the solution was always right there in front of them (Lehrer, 2012). Insight comes as a raw finding that mobilizes the process of innovation. It is the idea that sticks and needs to be shared and further validated to see if the idea can be developed.

THE LAYERS OF THE DISCOVERY CIRCLE

The main components of the discovery circle are the three layers of actions that ensure insights (see Figure 11-1). The first layer is the inner circle that has to do with the conditions that allow feelings to come out and cooperation to happen. The second layer has to do with key skills that need to be developed before looking for answers through the four specific points of view specified in the third layer. All three layers interact interchangeably. They do not happen linearly—one before another—they happen simultaneously. The layers overlap, and the constant intermittent activation of all of them generates insight.

LAYER 1: INTUITION, COLLABORATION, AND OPENNESS

Layer 1 is comprised of intuition, collaboration, and openness. This layer is the closest to insight because it combines the interaction with others and our inner thoughts. Listening to others *and* listening to gut instincts are challenging for creative individuals and professionals, but this skill must be mastered so that insights can occur. Layer 1 highlights the importance of the aspects of intuition, collaboration, and openness and having them work in balance.

Intuition

Intuition refers to the internal voice we all have that tells us if something feels right or wrong. Intuition might help open the eyes of a group to something that is not evident. Listen to your inner voice cautiously, but do not let yourself be carried away by your intuition in a biased way. Your intuition might be conditioned by past experiences or events that happened to you or in the industry in general. Sometimes we do not understand a situation correctly, so our intuition can lead us to the wrong side. That is why it is very important to always say how you feel about a particular idea and to seek clarification to avoid any confusion. When "it feels right," then we feel certain and a process flows. Feeling right is visceral. Feeling right is from our gut instincts and definitely counts.

Collaboration and Openness

The two aspects of collaboration and openness are activated by the sharing of inner feelings within a creative team. Intuitions and insights must be shared. Intuitions and insights electrify a team because the power of everyone's internal feelings generates a valid connection positively affecting the process of creation. Sharing enhances the sense of trust and belief. If someone does not believe in what is being done, then others will not either and the process will fail.

If the process fails and de-motivation takes over, innovation will not happen. Collaboration helps nurture positive thoughts and actions—it's contagious. Collaboration and openness also help maintain the flow from sources of external information. Interaction with external teams, other companies, and even with the audience is the centerpiece of collaboration and openness.

An example of collaboration is Gordon-Levitt's website HITRECORD.org (Gordon-Levitt, 2010). This website builds content through the collaboration of many artists connected online around the world. In this open website, people post ideas for stories and concepts of many kinds (music, videos, short films, animation, etc.) and other artists join in the crafting of the material until it is finished. The resulting content is showcased at the Sundance Film Festival, on its website, or at special events. This tool is a true representation of free collaboration that can be applied to the making of any kind of content.

Openness has to do with a willingness to view things differently, to receive feedback, and to listen to new ideas coming from inside and outside a team or creative circle. Openness guarantees diversity of thoughts and helps us tap into new trends and different points of view to come up with a radical solution.

Key take-away from Layer 1: Open your inner feelings to the outside and let the outside become a part of your inner circle.

LAYER 2: IMPLEMENT THE DISCOVERY SKILLS

According to Dyer, Gregersen & Christiansen (2011), the main discovery skills that teams, organizations, creative individuals, and professionals need to implement are association, questioning, observation, networking, and experimenting.

Association

Association is a very interesting exercise in which we as creators do conceptual blending (Lehrer, 2012): using the past to build a new future, combining trends to create a new solution, or applying ideas in different contexts to create breakthroughs. Association has to do with mixing up concepts or situations that no one ever thought could go together. Association is related to reordering, mixing, or shifting concepts or applying the rules from one domain to a different domain. Association occurs when we let the flow or crossing over of people with different experiences and cultural backgrounds come together to consider ideas and possibilities that do not seem worth considering (Dyer, Gregerson & Christiansen, 2011; Lehrer, 2012). Association occurs through daydreaming and during relaxation—but always maintaining a connection with the real world (Lehrer, 2012).

Association is the ability to make surprising connections across areas of knowledge, industries, and even geographies. Creativity is about connecting things. Steve Jobs once said, "Creativity is the power to connect the seemingly unconnected" (Dyer, Gregerson & Christiansen, 2011, p. 41). The result of associations is insight, eureka moments, and inventions that could become innovations.

Association also happens in a rather inductive way. The association approach to analyzing data applies to visualization and the processing of details that we collect when looking at objects in the world. An inductive approach starts with the collection of details and then looks at them from a broader perspective to obtain a result (Dyer, Gregerson & Christiansen, 2011; Zettl, 2013). This type of association approach is exactly how character-driven drama works. We first think of the specific aspects of the character and then build an entire story around this character. The story comes after a process of associating the character with other aspects of life around this character. The end result is the big picture.

According to Dyer, Gregerson & Christiansen (2011), innovators apply what is called "Lego thinking" to collect ideas, hear from diverse sources, and connect dissimilar contexts to create new ideas. They say, "If ideas come from the same source (or you only look hard in one direction) they tend to be repetitive, [and] thus don't lead to disruptive ones." (In Chapter 9, *Drivers of Content Innovation*, we explored how innovations driven by genre were the result of mixing and associating genres that did not seem to match. All subgenres in the content domain originated thanks to associations.)

Actor, director, and writer Ricky Gervais associated the single-camera comedy series genre, which has been on the air for many decades, with the docu-reality genre, which was developed in the late 1990s. Gervais associated these two dissimilar genres and created *The Office*, which became a new way to tell a fictional story thorough the aesthetics of a docu-reality show, and his association led to the creation of the mock-reality comedy series genre.

Earlier, Walt Disney mastered associational skills by joining animation with full-length films and by giving themes to amusement parks (the thematic park concept) (Dyer, Gregerson & Christiansen, 2011). Alex Kurtzman and Roberto Orci, creators and producers of the drama series *Sleepy Hollow* (Fox, 2013 –), blended the supernatural period genre with police crime investigation drama to come up with an innovative time-travel/current take on the American short story, *The Legend of Sleepy Hollow*, by Washington Irving. ABC's *Once Upon a Time* also succeeded by mixing Disney's fairy tales and characters into a current adventure drama series in which the beloved characters deal with conflict from their past in the present time.

Another example of association is when producers of game shows try to bring to the TV screen something that has worked in real life. David Hurwitz, creator/executive producer of *Killer Karaoke* (2012 –), possibly took the karaoke that we all know and associated it with elements of the reality competition show *Fear Factor* (2001 –). The result was a highly amusing show in which people tried to sing a song while facing scary, difficult challenges that distracted their attention from the song, making them lose.

Mixing the present to build the future is another type of association that leads to incremental innovations. Anything today that can be improved upon and associated with a different use can lead to a powerful innovation. For example, when a producer takes a mobile application or a video game and turns it into a TV show, the product is the result of associating two different concepts and repurposing the original digital application into a different medium, in this case TV. The *Trivia Crack* application has been turned into a game show in Argentina. The host of the show plays the popular app on live TV and incorporates people in their homes as well through a second screen complementary feature in the show. This adaptation has proved to be successful in Argentina and is spreading to other countries.

The association of new technologies with the entertainment industry is a powerful demonstration of how two originally unconnected worlds have collided to allow the proliferation of platforms of exposition that demanded the creation of content that otherwise would not have ever been made or seen (see the section *To Create New Platforms of Exposition* in Chapter 9). As an example, a creative individual realized that one way to connect the internet with TV was through prequels or complementary content to the main show seen on TV. One example of doing this is *Little Monk* (2009), a ten-part web series aired by the USA Network showcasing the life of the character Monk when he was 10 years old that was launched during the last season of the *Monk* (2002 – 2009) TV series. The creators decided to give audiences more information about their beloved character in his pre-teen days. This web series is an example of an event that complements what is seen on TV.

Note: "The more diverse knowledge the brain possesses, the more connections it can make when given fresh inputs of knowledge, and fresh inputs trigger the associations that lead to novel ideas" (Dyer, Gregerson & Christiansen, 2011, p. 49).

Questioning

To create powerful associations that lead to insights, innovators encourage creative teams by challenging the status quo through questions. To do this, Dyer, Gregerson & Christiansen (2011) recommended two types of questions:

- A set of questions that will help innovators to see a situation, problem, or what they call "the territory" and
- Another set of questions that will help creative individuals disrupt the territory.

To describe the territory, we must engage in asking "what is" questions such as: What is the problem? What is missing? What is the state of the world today? Through this initial set of questions we can define the status quo or, in other words, the world we want to change, which then becomes the problem that we want to solve. A real innovator finds problems that need solutions, not just solutions to a given problem.

A content innovator is constantly challenging the world of content "as is," asking questions that help define what is happening in the industry and specifically in the content innovator's area of emphasis. Questions such as:

- What is the most effective way to bring a story to a multiplatform world?
- What is happening in the world of awards shows that causes all award shows to look the same?
- What is a unique and differentiated reality show for TV today?
- What is a story that has not been told?
- What type of show does a weak cable channel need to propel its brand awareness?
- What is a character that people have not seen?
- What is a game show dynamic that people have not yet witnessed?
- What makes the character unique? What is her objective? How can someone win the prize? What if event X happens in the show? Why is the story different from Y? Why isn't the lead character a woman? All sorts of questions are valid.

Besides asking these direct questions, important to understand is the cause of the creation of the past innovation. We have to understand the "what was he thinking" question that triggered the idea. For example, in analyzing the state of the comedy genre on TV, we could try to define the most innovative forms of comedy on the air today. What are they? Who is doing them? How did they come about? Why were they created? What was the story behind the creation of certain new form of storytelling? These questions also apply to new ideas coming across your desk. The questioning process helps us identify reasons why an idea might be interesting to produce or worth exploration. The answer might lead to an insight that will be key during the pitch.

Questioning is about digging hard until you unravel all of the pros, cons, and possibilities. Beyond finding the situation to tap into, creators must also be aware of all of the constraints a group or company has. Creators need to ask questions. What is preventing us or anyone else from doing this? How can we develop this idea without resources? How can the task be accomplished? Why has no one done this before?

After defining the constraints and barriers that make a project impossible, we need to anticipate possible flaws through "what if" questions. Playing devil's advocate helps to understand how strong an idea might be. On occasion, producers and creators think they have found the next big thing, but at the first meeting held to pitch the idea, they face a battery of "what if" questions that could prove the concept to be weak, burying any possibility the show might have had. The sets of questions must primarily be aimed at making the concept and the idea bulletproof. Answers to a battery of questions help creators improve a creative proposal. On the other hand, questioning not only has to do with the creative aspect of the idea but also with its feasibility. How can the show be produced? For example, a producer might ask the question: "Why has a big blockbuster weekly drama series not been done in [a certain territory] by [a certain channel]? The answer might be simple: "There wasn't enough money." But then, the producer should ask: "How can we find money to do this?" Maybe the solution is to involve the audience in a kick-starter type of funding program to propel the making of certain show. The solution might be to involve two big studios in a co-production model that works. These solutions are known as business insights.

Another way to approach the questioning process is by creating many hypothetical cause-and-effect statements in the form of: *If* we do this (cause), *then* that might occur (effect). As with scientists trying to prove a formula, hypothetical thinking is also useful for creative minds trying to find what could be the next big thing in show business.

Questioning helps the creation of all of the possible scenarios. What? Who? How? What if? Why not? Why? Why? Why? These questions are just few combinations. We should try to speculate and to find the real strength in an idea, the real differentiating factor, or the real solution to the problem at hand—in other words, the insight. The questioning process has to be relentless, non-stop, and an answer might not be final—there must be something else to consider. Once an answer does appear, new questions need to challenge this finding. Questions challenge industry assumptions. If we find answers for all the questions that challenge industry assumptions, we might be witnessing the birth of a disruption.

Observation

Creators of content must keep their eyes open to get a grasp of what is going on in the world. They have to watch and listen to find out what people value. Life is composed of people, interactions, history, culture, nature, technology, hope, desires, happiness, sadness, successes, failures, processes, rules, freedom, captivity, houses, families, children, women, men, animals, and everything else. Life is all around us and we live it. Observation is oriented to detecting details or the broader aspects of life that could become sources for fantastic content. Great stories, songs, and characters and new aesthetic approaches to create content or new forms of storytelling or dynamics in a game show all come from observing people and situations in life. We try to replicate life through content and, most importantly, surprise people with it.

Observation is successful when we are surprised and something becomes suddenly interesting and fascinating. When this happens, a specific piece of information that could drive a concept that could potentially become new content might be right in front of us. The point is that as creators we need to understand how a specific fact could influence what we do and how any external fact around us could lead to something new. As an example, suppose that you spend 2 hours every day seated on a train car on your way to work or back home. While you are in that train car, you observe how almost every person in the car smiles at their phones, talks to them, or types and sends emails, messages, or pictures. At that point, you start to imagine a new way to tell a story based on these communication patterns and create a new series, without knowing the platform, in which a story is told through a series of text messages, photos, videos, and voice. But beyond that technological insight, you also come up with a powerful story and characters, maybe related to a tale you overheard from a rather peculiar person on the train. After that, you decide to develop the idea further and to work on this new concept with a team of creative individuals. You combine their observations with yours and come up with a compelling concept that could propel a new multiplatform show. Observation allows us to see limitations and to assign responsibilities. Observation helps us to identify events that seem so common and normal, events that have been happening for years, but if taken to a media outlet and adapted as an audiovisual experience, could surprise everyone. When we can make that identification, we have succeeded.

As a personal note, when I developed *All for the Crown* (*Todo por la Corona*) in 2012, a reality show to select the next Miss Venezuela, I worked with a team of experienced producers who spent 6 months observing the process of selecting and preparing potential beauty queens in Venezuela. The purpose of this observation was to adapt activities that had been happening for 50 years into a reality show. From there, we determined unique situations that would make the show entertaining and surprising because the audience had never seen where the delegates came from or how they were chosen.

Observe your viewers to see how they respond to TV, stories, and games; how they perceive content; and what "turns their interest on." How can you embrace that information to make something compelling and attractive to them? Observations do not need to happen in focus groups. Observe all the time in natural settings. Begin with your family and friends. Listen to them. Look at their behaviors. Family and friends might not be representative of the country you are targeting, but remember that you are looking for new sources of content and even the tiny universe at home or with friends might provide you with some clues. Listen to people. Pay attention to the times when they talk about or criticize what they watch on TV. They might criticize mercilessly—as if they were specialists or experts (remember the type of audience we discussed in Chapter 3, *Finding Where You Are*). Some bring radical postures and others have softer supportive critiques, but nonetheless all are meaningful. Every time I am at a party or an event and people find out that I am a TV producer, they just "go off," making suggestions, giving feedback, and talking about how much they like shows or how things could be much better. Believe me—I take those conversations seriously because these people are the audience and their validation counts.

Networking

The sources of networking are endless. Networking with people from different industries, cultures, and backgrounds is essential to the process of discovery. Everyone see things differently depending on the world they live in. Their expertise might give you an unsuspected insight into creating something new in your world. Networking has to be done with the purpose of hearing different takes on how to solve a problem. Likewise, networking has to be aimed at finding resources and possibilities for collaborating beyond your constraints.

Networking helps us to gain skills and points of view from other people and to perhaps solve a problem. For example, when a story is being set up, the story needs to be told through different characters, with different personalities and ways of thinking. To achieve that, creators need to network with individuals who can help shape up how those characters will be portrayed. The way a creator of fiction does this is through the incorporation of several writers in the writing room who besides being writers are also real people. These real people provide inspiration for the characters, based on their experiences, skills, and background. Networking can help writers reach out to other people who could inspire a situation and the traits of the fictional characters they are developing. Networking also provides validation. Positive reactions can help you assess an idea's potential.

The world is now a big social network where people participate and share ideas. Through social networks, people are closer than ever, creating communities that could be perfect ecosystems or samples of a target audience that you are pursuing and giving you the chance to get reactions and recommendations and to even solve problems together. Facebook, Twitter, Instagram, and all other social media platforms have become an easy terrain for networking with communities to get impressions, ideas, and validation.

Experimenting

The activity of experimenting provides the possibility of anticipating reactions to our creations through early prototypes or pilots. Building prototypes could require investment and usually requires the auspices of the corporations funding a project. A good pilot is costly so finding approval and financial backup might be difficult.

With the advent of the internet and social media, all has changed. Reaction by the audience is now direct, helping to identify new potential hits. The cost of an experimental production could be low. Uploading the file is free. The difficulty lies in getting a sufficient number of people to watch the production to provide validation. If you have a significant number of followers or friends, you can expose the prototype directly to them and measure their reactions through their comments or Like responses. This validation could be enough to catalyze the possibility of making a full series or a film out of the concept. The data collected through this type of direct validation adds value to a concept. If the numbers are good, they will become part of the information you give to more sophisticated windows of exposition. As an example, *The Couple* (2012), an experimental production by Numa Perrier, actress/writer/filmmaker and co-founder of the network Black&Sexy.tv, was aired online through a dedicated YouTube channel. The webisodes were very simple, were low cost, and episodes depicted particular conversations of couples. The conversations were so real that the show became an honest representation of how somewhat uneventful chats could hit a note with couples identifying with them. This type of content is raw and difficult to find anywhere on TV. Thanks to the series, the channel has developed other web series and has become an online hit, reaching more than 120,000 subscribers. HBO gave Perrier a development deal and added Spike Lee as executive producer for a version of *The Couple*.

Experiments are extraordinary ways for people to experience what you have in mind. Their reactions help to identify if what you have in your hands is a possible innovation. Another example of innovation directly validated by an online audience is the short film *Alive in Joburg* (2006). Peter Jackson (film director) noticed the South African short film and soon after turned it into a major movie event of global relevance, *District 9* (2009), which ended up garnering four Oscar nominations, including best picture, in 2010.

Another way to experiment is to take existing shows and break them down into pieces to see how they could be undone or turned into something different. For example, if we look at the talent competition genre, there are plenty of shows to choose from for experimentation by changing applications, the purpose, or the ways to go through competition. In *American Idol*, for example, contestants perform, judges criticize, and the audience votes. The *X Factor* took the same premise, but had a celebrity judge coach contestants until the end of the competition. John de Mol, creator of *The Voice*, changed the purpose of the talent competition and focused on the identification of amazing voices through a series of castings in which the judges did not see a contestant before selecting them to appear on the show. Then the judges, by turning their chairs to face the contestant, discovered the identity of the performer. de Mol mixed this casting phase with the backward-facing chairs and the full involvement of each coach to take their protégées on to win the competition. *The Voice* also gave judges the possibility of becoming the real protagonists of the show, exposing them by showing their doubts, emotions, and hesitation during the exciting chair-turning phase. *The Voice* is no longer a singing competition; it's a coaches' competition.

Experiments can include shorts, spec songs and spec scripts, and self-produced web series, etc. Important is that the experiments provide practice so we can assimilate a skill.

Practice

The more we practice a skill, the more the possibilities we have to master a formula and find a way to break it. Once we have mastered a formula, we can explore variations that might bring new insight and a different way to do something. To break a formula, we need to master it; and to master it, we need to practice. Writers, producers, and directors spend years in low-ranking jobs, writing and directing specs or shorts, until they breakthrough. Accomplished writers such as Quentin Tarantino, Charlie Kaufman, J.J. Abrams, and Christopher Nolan mastered their writing skills before deciding to experiment with different ways to tell a story.

We can experiment with characters and make them grow in surprising ways. *Orphan Black* (BBC, 2013 –) is a superb example about how a lead actress has gained the skills to play multiple characters within the same show. This drama series presents the story of a woman who suddenly sees another woman who looks exactly like her and discovers that she and the woman are part of a conspiracy that creates clones. The clones are in essence totally different women with their own experiences, skills, and traits. Through practice the lead actress Tatiana Maslany learned how to break into new characters rapidly, how to make them believable, compelling, and different, and how to collaborate in the creation of new characters. According to the creators of the series, John Fawcett and Graeme Manson, lead actress Tatiana Maslany became a source of the characters' evolution in the series because she actually participated in the creation of some of the clones. For example, Tony (also played by Maslany) is a transgender character who becomes a rather surprising clone in the established world of female clones (Thomas, 2014)

A Method for Activating Layer 2

Through imagination we can visualize what does not exist and then play with it until an idea comes up (Eberle, 2008). There is no limit to imagination and the existing diverse methods to activate it to ignite the elements of Layer 1 in the circle of discovery. The brainstorming technique, created by Alex Osborn (1953), is often the first method that comes to mind when we want to solve a problem. Brainstorming is actually the word of choice every time we want to start a creative session. This method relies on no criticizing of any idea and maintaining an open-minded spirit to hearing even the craziest thoughts until a solution is found—anything counts.

Applying the SCAMPER method, created by Eberle (2008), is also recommended by Dyer, Gregerson & Christiansen (2011). Eberle's SCAMPER method is based on Alex Osborn's checklist of activities for brainstorming and is an acronym for seven thinking techniques which together form a vehicle to challenge known notions: <u>S</u>ubstitute, <u>C</u>ombine, <u>A</u>djust, <u>M</u>odify, <u>P</u>ut to another use, <u>E</u>liminate, and <u>R</u>everse. Eberle's method (2008) works this way:

Substitute. Substitution has to do with replacing an attribute of a product that could act in the place of this attribute. In the substitution process, we must answer questions such as: what else, where else, who else, and when else could this product be or happen if something key were changed or replaced? For example, let's suppose we want to do a new studio-based trivia game show based on an existing one. We could ask:

- Who else could be a contestant besides an ordinary adult? Celebrities? Teenagers? Grandparents? Animals? Virtual contestants who only show their faces on tablets?
- Where else could the show happen besides in a studio? On a beach? In a cabin? In the middle of a baseball field?
- What else could we ask the participants to do? Could we ask trivia questions instead of having physical challenges?

The answers help merge the current situation with the substituted element and the association happens.

Combine. Combination is about bringing together or uniting two dissimilar aspects such as people, purposes, ideas, protagonists, materials, or processes.

Adjust. Adaptation or adjusting is changing the purpose of a show to suit a different condition such as a new target audience or a new time slot.

**Modify.** The modification technique deals with the alteration and change of attributes of a product arbitrarily. Modification includes changes in genre, on-camera talent, color, shape, sound, form, color palette, and size and also includes magnifying and minifying a situation. For example, an initially conceived reality show could be modified to become a fiction single-camera sitcom/mock-documentary.

**Put to another purpose.** The put-to-some-other-purpose technique challenges the original intent of a program. For example, using the same example of the show initially conceived as a reality show, its purpose will be different when the reality show becomes a fiction show. The change in purpose should be unusual, new, and unexpected.

**Eliminate.** Elimination is a technique through which we can eliminate any element of a subject and reduce it to its core or simplest form.

**Reverse.** Reverse is a technique that deals with turning around something specific about a project. Let's say an idea is very costly, but then we decide to go to the least costly possibility for that same idea. From a creative standpoint, this could imply going from comedy to drama. Reversing is about turning in the opposite direction or changing the order in which the events or the composition of the product, project, or show are rearranged. An example of this application would be _Pulp Fiction_. The story in _Pulp Fiction_ is not told in regular three-act structure, which is the usual order of arrangement of a screenplay. The story is rearranged, told in non-linear chapters, an aspect that made the storytelling absolutely unique.

**Key take-away from Layer 2:** The outside world provides the context for triggering Layer 2. Open up your senses, relate to others, and take time to experiment and practice to generate insights.

LAYER 3: LOOK FOR TRIGGERS AND SIGNS

Skarzynski & Gibson (2008) established that to unveil insights, innovative individuals need identify four elusive aspects: orthodoxy, discontinuity, competency, and unarticulated needs. The identification of these aspects also depends on incorporation of the techniques in Layer 2 of the discovery circle.

Orthodoxy

Orthodoxy is a convention that drives success in a company or an industry that is not supposed to be changed (Skarzynsky & Gibson, 2008). Unchangeable, deeply embedded traditions, paradigms, formulas, rules, and fixed practices are orthodoxies that are usually the best-known and accepted methods for doing something that prevent newcomers from doing something in a different way. Orthodoxies lead to corporate or process myopia (Johnston & Bate, 2013), which is easy way to avoid looking into the future and to prevent shakeups in the status quo to do things different and better. If it's not broken, why fix it? Examples of orthodoxies in the media industry that have been broken (and possible ways to break them) include:

- The length and act structure of a TV drama series or a sitcom: HBO challenged the act structure when HBO started producing drama series and comedy with no commercial breaks in full 60-minute and 30-minute lengths.
- Fixed programming strategies: For a weekly fiction series model, why not use a daily model? If *Scandal* works great on Thursday night, why can't we see it every night?
- Number of episodes per season: Why should a season be a maximum of 26 episodes? Why not to produce 52 episodes for an entire year?
- The windowing process: Netflix beat the orthodox vision that the home video industry was a posterior platform for showcasing content after a successful run in theaters or on TV. Netflix started producing its own content and became the first window for its own shows.
- Past successes become automatic orthodoxies: The intention to replicate current successes or victories from the past could be an orthodoxy if not handled carefully.
- Aesthetics rules: The camera cannot shake. MTV broke this orthodoxy and created a new style to visualize events through shaking cameras.

Successful innovative individuals constantly challenge the status quo. They generate surprising content that takes the industry by surprise. These innovators may act in a rather subversive way, but when finally successful, they produce the next formula to be challenged.

People with strong, biased opinions are orthodoxies on their own. These individuals are the result of years of operating with successful careers, but they get stuck by having single self-centered vision.

For innovators, orthodoxy is a gateway to breakthroughs because orthodoxies are the rules to be broken. The audience, the writers, the producers, and the programmers have a set of rules to be followed, but when these rules are broken, everyone turns their attention to see what is going on. If a new proposal is good, then an innovation occurs. Shonda Rhimes defied orthodoxies in the industry by bringing to life stories in hectic work environments that in a very organic and normal way presented relationships and people in positions of power despite their color, race, and background. In her *Grey's Anatomy* (2005 –), Latino, Asian, Black, and White characters engage in a series of stories that generate surprise and interest in a rather conservative audience. Later, in *Scandal* (2012 –), Shonda Rhimes developed a most provocative and controversial character: Olivia Pope, the most influential political fixer in Washington, DC, who has a love affair with the president of the United States. The shocking element is the interracial tacit premise of the show, making it absolutely edgy and real (as well as bringing viewers a story that had not been told with such force and lack of constraint). The relationships in her shows just happen and people "deal with it." Skarzynsky & Gibson (2008) recommended using the following to challenge orthodoxies:

- Do not follow the leader in the industry. Do just the opposite.
- Identify dogmas, rules, and conventionalisms.
- Find absurdities, the things that companies do that are absurd in the eyes of viewers.
- Go to extremes. Take a widely accepted rule and turn it upside down. (As discussed in the process of questioning, question orthodoxies to see what will happen if things are done totally differently.)
- Search for the "and." Think of content constraints and what would happen if the audience were given all that they wanted—not just one thing.

Discontinuity

Discontinuity is the convergence of different trends that could potentially create a single event that will disrupt an industry. Discontinuity is a shift in the trend line that diverts the future from its path (Johnston & Bate, 2013). Skarzynsky & Gibson (2008, p. 55) stated, "The confluence of several unrelated developments in, for example, technology, demographics, lifestyle, regulation, geopolitics and so forth together create the potential for dramatic industry change."

As an innovator you must look for patterns of trends during the processes of observation and association. For example, Netflix realized that people watched all of the episodes of a TV fiction series in a single weekend once the season was over on TV. This change in consumer behavior might have been the discontinuity that sparked the notion of Netflix to create fiction programming that people could watch and own like any other TV series, with all the episodes available at launch date. The convergence of technology and consumer trends allowed the proliferation of content in new platforms such as Netflix, Amazon, Hulu, and Crackle. The release of an entire series of episodes became the new rule.

To identify discontinuity, engage in strategic research and put into full force observation, association, and networking. You must listen to your audience and be where the competitors are not. You want to unveil the future—and the future is out there in different places; you just need to put the pieces together. Try to understand trends in their historical context and then "amplify the weak signals." For example, the second you see that men are starting to wear colorful pants, that digital devices are coming in more different colors, or that Microsoft is now more colorful than ever (ads, devices, logo, etc.), you realize that the world is going through a colorful phase that might be a hint for something new. Look for interactions between trends and see what might come up. Social trends are adopted by groups of people, and their impact might be lasting or ephemeral.

Spotting trends. According to Trias de Bes & Kotler (2011), social trends expose our behavior and, if considered in the process of creating innovations, assure acceptance and a greater chance to succeed. Depending on the length of the time frame, social trends are classified in four ways: macro-trends, trends, fashions, and fads. A macro-trend lasts between 5 and 10 years, a trend lasts between 1 to 5 years, a fashion lasts for a season, and a fad lasts for a month. A fad is usually related to short-lived events (a visit by the Pope, the Academy Awards, or the Olympic Games). If a fad turns into a fashion and if the fashion turns into a trend that lasts longer than a year or two, then the trend could become a macro-trend, which lasts between 5 to 10 years, but no longer than that given that every 7 years important changes occur in the life goals of a generation. The key is to identify trends quickly. I recommend having outside observers or engaging in social media to exchange, gather, and track emerging trends, fashions, and fads. Other valuable techniques for spotting trends are through the use of internet monitoring, ethnographic studies, and geolocation (the practice of assessing a location):

- Internet or network monitoring is an assessment of what people are reading, searching for, or talking about online. Different tools are available to monitor what is trending on the internet (such as Google Trends or Twitter Trending Topics). Automatic alerts are available on Google and Yahoo to program messages to you each time a predetermined topic is mentioned. StepRep is another tool to monitor what is said about specific individuals, companies, or brands. Scout Labs enables the monitoring of blogs, social platforms, websites, etc. and allows engagement in direct conversations with customers to listen to what they have to say. Another tool taking advantage of online information and interactions is www.wefeelfine.org, a site dedicated to registering the sentiments and feelings of people around the world. The site automatically counts and posts online anything that starts or contains "I feel" (Trias de Bes & Kotler, 2011).

- Ethnographic studies are a costly undertaking, but they allow a researcher to study individuals by using direct observation and involvement in their daily activities to get a comprehensive description of their customs, beliefs, and the main cultural premises of the individual being observed (in their natural habitat, at home, when shopping, when driving, at a party, etc.).
- Geolocation gathers information based on geographical location. Mobile social networks such as Foursquare allow users to share opinions about topics they are experiencing in their locations (Trias de Bes & Kotler, 2011).

All of these methods to gather information allows browsers and individuals engaged in the discovery process to spot trends that lead to the identification of discontinuities in people's lives, which could be the sources of an insight to build content.

Competency

Through identification of our core competences we reaffirm what our strengths are and what is it that we do not have that we need to get through having other partners, collaboration, or training. We want to create shows and we need to have the skills to do so. Be aware of your competencies and strengths. If you cannot write, then find a partner who can write. If you do not produce, then align yourself with a producer. If you need to sell your content, but do not have the contacts or the means to do so, then find a way to work with an agent. Competency has to do with skills knowledge and access to resources. Competency also has to do with assets and the possibility of realizing a positive return on them. An asset is not only a computer but also the content that you have created.

You must be aware of how unique and special your competencies are and the edge they will give you compared to the competition. If you do not have a skill, you have to learn it or find it somewhere else.

Unarticulated Needs

Identifying unarticulated needs is the most important, and the most difficult, aspect in the generation of insight. Unarticulated needs are also known as customer insight (Skarzynsky & Gibson, 2008; Johnston & Bate, 2013) or in our case audience insight—something an audience does not know it needs.

An unmet need is often a frustration that can serve as the basis for a new idea, but the problem is that a viewer does not know how to express this frustration. They do not even know that they need what you are about to create. According to Johnston & Bate (2013), people know what they value, but they do not know what they need. They are satisfied with what they are watching or experiencing in media because they do not know that there is something better. The mix of a set of aspects they value might produce an insight that leads to innovative content. For example, people did not know that they needed a show like *Gossip Girl*, but the creators of the show knew that a big group of young people valued gossip and would also value learning about the lives of the wealthy. The creators mixed these two aspects and came up with the idea for the show. This type of need is difficult to identify. Identifying it requires direct observation, customer experience mapping, and analogies from other industries. The result can be gaining understanding of customers and their unarticulated needs so that we can find solutions.

In the entertainment world, good content always meets an unarticulated need because it surprises and entertains people. Once a viewer starts searching to meet a need and then experiences a show, if they like it, they can't stop watching. The surprise comes from their response to the fulfillment of a need they did not know they had. When the story (or the show dynamics) strikes a chord with a viewer, they usually react by saying, "I can't believe no one has done that before. It's so simple, but no one has attempted that story before." People need to see stories and characters they can relate to. They need to have fun when watching a game show, they need to feel that they can play the game and "make it" and project themselves into the event, and they ultimately need to receive a positive impact and a sense of value-added to their vault of experiences. When viewers get frustrated when experiencing a content event, it is because an unarticulated need has not been fulfilled. People then do not feel the need to stick around.

To find unarticulated unmet needs, observing people and situations on the street is important. Be alert to what they say, do, and value. These insights do not happen through surveys or quantitative research but through real interactions and observations (Johnston & Bate, 2013). As an example, people using different forms of communication pave the way for a new means to tell a story. No one is actually telling you that they want to be entertained via three different social platforms all at once, but when you see how easily they engage from one platform to another, you might begin to think otherwise and find the way to entice these people to enjoy a content piece using the social platforms they value most.

Another example that I always mention in my seminars is the Facebook Timeline, which is a tremendous source of stories. People post events in their lives and soon after other people react and interact with them. That interaction is loaded with support, empathy, emotions, conflict, and resolution and thus a story. Without knowing it, a Facebook user is telling you that they enjoy the stories on

Facebook Timeline, in that fashion and in that format. This observation and realization might lead to new way to present stories on Facebook that is the result of an unarticulated need of a Facebook user.

Key take-away from Layer 3: That special need that an audience does not know it has together with strict parameters become insights on their own and the epicenter for coming up with innovations.

We have now completed our discussion of the circle of discovery in which four layers interact with each other: observation, networking, experimenting, and practice. The circle of discovery is the DNA and core of the innovation process. All four layers of the circle of discovery lead to the identification of orthodoxy, strengths, discontinuity, and unarticulated needs that ultimately derive precious insights that open the door for new content, business opportunities, and the future. The next chapter will explain how the value chain of innovation delineates a framework for achieving results.

STEP 4

IMPLEMENT THE VALUE CHAIN
OF CONTENT INNOVATION

12

THE VALUE CHAIN OF INNOVATION

Nothing is more frustrating than having ideas that don't go anywhere. Strategic creative individuals need to solve this problem and find a way to deliver a solution, otherwise innovation will not happen. An innovative idea goes nowhere unless it can be processed. I recognize the importance of providing a framework of operation—a process—to creative individuals so they can accomplish their visions. Once creative individuals get comfortable in a process, they start delivering results.

The end result of a process is what matters the most because this result represents the show, the program, the content, and if successful the innovation. As we already know, successful content is an innovation because it entertains, receives approval, and drives a business. This innovation has a utilitarian purpose and people embrace it. If that happens, the process of discovery and delivery has created magic, but if one part of the process fails, innovation will not be there.

Some innovation experts express disagreement about giving a framework of operation (or a linear process) to the generation of innovation. Nevertheless, I support the theory that there must be a reference and a number of activities that creative people must engage in to have a clear purpose in the making of specific content. If a process is not in place, then the path to follow will not be either and people will have no clear orientation about what to do, when to do it, and how to do it. As a consequence, I have put together a framework of operation that I call the value chain of content innovation (VCCI). The objective of the VCCI is to provide a working methodology not only for creative individuals but also for the executives who are managing processes of content creation. I have implemented this framework throughout my career, and it has helped me and my teams to have

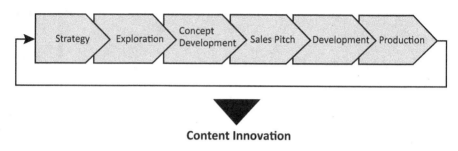

Content Innovation

Figure 12-1. The value chain of innovation.

a clear understanding of the workload, complexity of operation, goals, the accomplishments, and where we are heading.

ELEMENTS OF THE CHAIN

The VCCI is a tool for creators and organizations to deliver—to turn amazing ideas resulting from a process of discovery into meaningful, entertaining projects. The VCCI defines resources, tasks, functional activities, and the path for producing a successful, innovative show. This process of delivery is composed of several important activities and stages, each one producing an important outcome in the form of ideas, concepts, prototypes or pilots, scripts, and ultimately a show, the end result. The VCCI blends the concepts of discovery from Chapter 11 (*The Discovery Circle*) with the process that nowadays exists in the Hollywood studio system and my own approach related to content development, production, and sales activities.

Figure 12-1 illustrates the key activities in the value chain, which is a cyclical execution framework for discovering, creating, and making innovation happen. The VCCI framework is a six-part process (a methodology) that helps implement a clear vision through goal-oriented activities. VCCI is composed of these goal-oriented activities:

- Market and creative strategic research
- Exploration
- Concept development
- Sales pitch
- Development
- Production

But more than a methodology, VCCI is a philosophical framework of operation that helps creative professionals to understand what needs to be done to produce innovation. You do not need to be inside the studio system to incorporate this process. You can do it on your own.

Market and creative strategic research. Market and creative strategic research has to do with the search for information that will help creative professionals and individuals to understand their context. Strategic research provides information that helps us analyze the landscape where we are going to operate and create. The information gathered is either external to our operation or intrinsic to it. Creative strategic research goes beyond the mere concept of analytic investigation. Creative strategic research incorporates intuition and the discovery of insights, trends, unarticulated needs, and the identification of orthodoxies (discussed in Chapter 11, *The Discovery Circle*). All of the information collected needs to be analyzed and shared with all team members in the value chain. This information provides a new source of reference, trends, know-how, intelligence, and self-awareness. The outcome of the strategic research activity is a revised strategy, with solid goals, objectives, mission, and insight.

Exploration. Exploration has to do with having an open innovation architecture to search, generate, and evaluate ideas and resources. The goal of the exploration phase is to activate the funneling of ideas and the process of creative validation to receive, recognize the valuable ones, and to decide on (evaluate) the ideas to work on based on the creative strategy in place. The result of the evaluation phase defines the course of action to follow around an idea and provides a sense of the type of innovation that the idea might be, whether the idea is a breakthrough or an incremental innovation to an existing one.

Concept development. Concept development is the third activity in the value chain. Concept development is activated once an idea has been approved within the process of exploration and is the process by which meaningful ideas become valuable and tangible. Conceptualization of a show varies and depends on the platform, genre, target audience, and resources needed, aspects which define the type of operation to implement, the time frame of execution, and the resources required for the proper conversion of the concept into a valuable content. Once the concept has been fleshed out in the form of a pre-bible document containing all-important detail about the idea and its form of implementation, a feasibility analysis needs to be performed to understand the economic aspects of the concept and the best way to produce it. A feasibility analysis helps define the markets that might be suitable for the idea and the possible clients (broadcasters) to target in the next process. This process is also called "development in a vacuum" because it is not tailor-made for a client but for your catalog.

Sales pitch. The sales pitch activity represents the undertakings that activate a commissioning sales process. This activity relies on implementation of a customer relationship management (CRM) methodology to organize who, how to target them, and how to follow up with them to close deals. This sales pitch phase involves the generation of marketing elements and the preparation of a catalog to showcase what we have. Once the show has been presented and the response has been positive, a process of negotiation starts and the deal is either closed or dropped. This sales pitch phase needs the work of people who are skilled in the art of sales because during this phase we define the target platforms, which could be a channel, a digital entity, and an advertiser or could be social media if we want to launch the show directly to the public via a social media platform. Once the show has been picked and negotiation is done, then the processes of development and production are activated. For vertically integrated TV networks with the creative and production operations embedded, the sales pitch process occurs between the internal producers and the programming department. There is usually one instance that emerges within the TV channel as the client, whose role is to green-light the shows that better fit the strategy of the network.

Development. Development precedes production of the content. During the process of development the concept sold is tailored to the expectations and the characteristics of the platform that has commissioned the product—in other words, the concept is synced to be coherent with the brand. Platforms such as public TV channels, cable channels, online platforms, mobile applications, and OTT channels have specific premises that define their brands which need to be considered and understood by developers of content. For example, the premise of a TV show might be rather safe, but if the platform is edgy, then the content might need to be rewritten based on this situation so that the content better fits the identity of the platform's brand—an MTV show will be different from a CW Television Network show.

Production. Once the show has been developed and approved, the show enters the production phase. Production implies the actual crafting of the show. Production demands the coordination of different functional areas and resources both human and material. The end result will be delivered to an audience to go through the last sociocultural validation—the product faces an audience who decides its fate, with their acceptance or rejection. Whatever the outcome is, the information becomes part of the domain and the recorded data that is incorporated in the strategic research process, closing the value chain.

Stating that these activities or phases do not work in isolation is important—even though people concentrate on specific activities within the value chain, they still have to work in constant interaction and validation. In fact, people working today on concept development areas might also be a part of the sales pitch, development, and production processes as well, involvement that depends on the

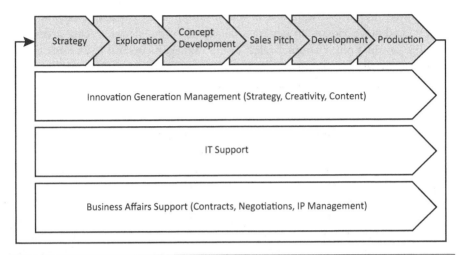

Figure 12-2. The adjusted value chain of content innovation.

degree of responsibility they have had in the project and, ultimately, their roles, skills, and interest in getting involved throughout.

ELEMENTS OF THE ADJUSTED CHAIN

The value chain of innovation also needs supporting activities such as innovation generation management, information technology (IT) support, and business affairs support to provide strategy, oversight, control, and leadership to carefully leverage processes and assets and to understand competences, weaknesses, and resources. Figure 12-2 illustrates the adjusted VCCI.

Innovation generation management. Innovation generation management goes beyond the management of idea generation, concept development, and implementation processes. The main objective of innovation generation management is to organize, in an efficient and effective way, the six main activities in the value chain of innovation (market and creative strategic research, exploration, concept development, sales pitch, development, and production) plus the supporting functional areas so that their implementation supports the strategic goals of a company.

Information technology support. IT support covers all of the activities and tools that we use to guarantee the proper storage of information, the adequate sharing of data, and the different outcomes of the VCCI activities. IT is crucial.

Nowadays different software is available to build plans, calculate budgets, write scripts, and store videos; to generate databases of people to quickly access the results of evaluations, customer relationship management, and news reports; and to ultimately to track the progress of innovations throughout. IT support helps creative individuals to keep track of everything and to access information easily and in a timely fashion.

Business affairs support. Business affairs support deals with all legal- and business-related matters—from contracts negotiation and the definition of deal terms to profitability analysis of a specific project or an entire creative operation. Business affairs professionals support the management of the entire process to validate the strategy and mission of the firm and to ensure that all content created is protected from an intellectual property standpoint. Content protection as an intellectual property is actually the most important aspect that business affairs professionals are in charge of because intellectual property rights are what ultimately determine the value of a firm. A business affairs team is in charge of establishing the premises of negotiation. The team highlights the different pros and cons a certain process or project might imply from a legal standpoint.

Implementation of VCCI requires leadership and resources. The process is not only for companies but also for creative individuals in general who can adopt it on a simpler scale. The point here is that you now know all of the functional areas that need to be activated. Each activity becomes a potential reason for collaborators to come into place until the show is done. VCCI is ultimately a chain of collaboration and execution. Throughout the value chain, different types of professionals are activated. Based on their roles (to be discussed in Chapters 13 through 19) activators and facilitators manage the entire process:

- Browsers are in charge of strategic research and exploration activities, whereas creators conceptualize the projects.
- Content developers produce ideas, ideate concepts, find new solutions, and locate possibilities throughout the process.
- Facilitators contribute in the sales pitch and sales process.
- Developers and executors are the writers and producers who actually deliver the final product.

This chapter has been an overview of what the value chain of content innovation implies. Upcoming chapters in Step IV will present in depth how to implement each activity and the expected outcomes and processes they entail. The next chapter discusses the market and strategic research activity.

13

MARKET AND STRATEGIC RESEARCH

As explained in Chapter 1 (*The Importance of Being Strategic in the Process of Innovation*), to have a solid identity and a differentiated path for embarking on the creation of content, a creative individual needs to define a personal strategy. Not only is defining *who* you are and *what* you have important, but also important is defining *where* you are. Market and creative strategic research helps with keeping up with the always-evolving industry by reshaping and redefining your objectives and strategy.

Strategic research helps you look for discontinuities and discrepancies between the past and existing conditions; to observe internal and external business environments; and to discern unexpected events, deviations from planned procedures, shifts in social or technical processes, and shifts in economic- or market-related mutations, alterations, and demographic changes. This creative strategic research process entails internal and external scanning for threats and opportunities for change and can be sustained by a forward process of creative development and production (dal Zotto & Kranenburg, 2008). For example, the results of market research could lead to an insight that helps you see the type of content you need to develop and the most suitable target market to pitch this content to—possibly a "blue ocean market" (a market with uncontested space)—which will make you a leader in a certain genre.

To define a strategy, for example, before embarking on a think tank operation, implement a system for gathering and generate three clusters of information:

- Cluster 1: Context assessment
- Cluster 2: Target audience identification

- Cluster 3: Competitive advantages identification

Let's now review each cluster of information in detail and then discuss the reports that could be generated as a result—reports that will help you define your strategic identity and goals.

CLUSTER 1: CONTEXT ASSESSMENT

Context assessment is achieved by gathering information from news reports, the competition, client performance indicators (broadcasters), and programming and industry practices.

News and Information Updates

The entertainment world produces massive quantities of information related to creative, market, business, and technology matters. These four aspects are covered at conferences and in books and publications that range from sophisticated journals, industry trades, and online newsletters to gossip magazines and simple conversations with an expert in the field. All sources count, but first let's concentrate on print and online publications:

- Entertainment business publications for industry professionals
- General business publications for the general market
- Entertainment publications for the general market

Entertainment business publications for industry professionals. Business publications for industry professionals encompass important trade information sources, such as *Hollywood Reporter* (http://www.hollywoodreporter.com), *Variety Magazine* (http://variety.com), *TBI Vision* (http://tbivision.com), *C21* (http://www.c21media.net), *WorldScreen* (http://www.worldscreen.com), *Cynopsis* (http://www.cynopsis.com), *TheWrap* (http://www.thewrap.com), and *The Wit* (http://www.thewit.com). These sources provide a business-driven overview of what entertainment companies and producers are doing around the world. Information ranges from business models, executives taking about leading positions, new production companies being launched, creative trends in the world, and new technology applications. Other multiplatform specialized publications include *Script Magazine* (http://www.scriptmag.com), the *American Cinematographer* (http://www.theasc.com/ac_magazine/), and the *Creative Planet Network* (http://www.creativeplanetnetwork.com), comprised of publications such as *Video Edge Magazine* and *Video Edge Newsletter* (http://www.videoedge.net), *TV Technology* (http://www.tvtechnology.com/index), and *Connect2Media* (http://www.c2meworld.com), that cover best practices in the creation and delivery of video content. Other specialized research firms build periodic reports about the entertainment and media industry and make them available for a fee or in the form of a subscribed service. Examples include The Wit, Informa, Price WaterhouseCoopers, and FRAPA (the Format Recognition and Protection Association). *The Wit*, for example, is one of the most sophisticated tools out there. *The Wit* is dedicated to collect, in one single platform, all information about TV shows and digital multiplatform initiatives produced and aired across the world. The amount of information *The Wit* manages is just stunning. *The Wit* offers reports that summarize what is hot and fresh in the world or in specific territories, analyzes trends, and makes available programming grids and show performances. *The Wit* has become one of the most important references in the world for finding out about anything related to content. Other companies such as PricewaterhouseCoopers provide periodic research reports and reviews of the TV and digital industry around the world, contributing tremendously to the generation of creative strategies.

General business publications for the general market. Publications for the general market include journals such as the *Harvard Business Review*, the *Financial Times*, and *The Wall Street Journal*. These sources provide information on best practices, business models, and macroeconomic news about the state of the economy worldwide and highlight what is new in terms of technological implementations across industries.

Entertainment publications for the general market. These publications include magazines (now multiplatforms), such as *Entertainment Weekly* (http://www.ew.com/ew/) and *TV Guide* (http://www.tvguide.com) in the United States, that provide valuable information in terms of what to watch and what is popular and relevant in the market. These entertainment publications are a bridge between the industry and viewers. *Entertainment Weekly* has a great sense of assessing what, who, and where content is airing and the faces (on-camera talent) that audiences are embracing or the critics adore. *Entertainment Weekly* is an outspoken source of validation about what is coming out of the pipeline across the different U.S. platforms of entertainment (film, TV, books, theater, music, digital, etc). *Entertainment Weekly* is another great multiplatform for learning not only what actors, producers, and entertainers think in general and where they came from, but to also foresee and spot trends coming from Hollywood. *TV Guide* is a multiplatform guide for "saiing through" the landscape of content available on linear TV (regular programming) in the United States. *TV Guide* gives a visual, informative overview of what each channel offers and is a source for identifying the nature of competition in the populated TV and cable spectrum.

Gossip magazines. On the other end of the spectrum, gossip magazines are valuable sources of celebrity information because they let us see who is out there getting the attention of the public in a positive or negative way. Gossip magazines are funny, dramatic, and outrageous. They are a type of pop culture thermometer at any given point in time. A former boss once told me about the importance of gossip magazines when I noticed that he had an immense pile of all sorts of magazines that I would not even buy at the time. He told me that the best way to stay current in the important matter of pop culture was by reading gossip magazines. When we were discussing the potential cast for a series we had in development, I realized his deep knowledge about actresses and actors who were relevant for a particular market. These magazines not only give us information for casting purposes, but they also provide ideas for stories and potential triggers for different types of content insight. Now I look at these magazines as sources for casting. By just looking through them, I can identify faces, talent, and people who, depending on the type of content I am making, might become the next star of a show. Some people don't want to be seen buying that type of magazine or don't even consider them to be important publications, but as a creative professionals, we need to be aware of the pop context and the universe of talent out there. So in strategic research for content creation in media, it's OK to gossip.

Networking. In regard to conversations with peers at conferences, seminars, and professional presentations and simple conversations with experts, these always give fresh insight about what other people in the industry think. Absolutely key is to interact and network to get information because not everything is published.

Social media. Today, social media also plays a crucial role in spreading thoughts and articles, filtering information, and building communities of people sharing our same professional or personal interests. The proliferation of free or low-cost webinars on all sorts of topics; remote access to conferences or presentations, such as *TED: Ideas worth spreading* (a site offering programs and initiatives on technology, entertainment, and design) and others of the same type; and the opportunities that schools provide to the general public to gain knowledge by enrolling in college courses remotely at no cost also open a new realm of possibilities to gain knowledge and intelligence and learn what others are thinking and doing.

We have to have a sense of creative strategic research activated all the time. Read, watch, listen, take walks, watch people talking and see how they interact and engage in fun activities, and go to a bookstore to see what is on the shelves. Items in bookstores that people are reading are *what* is being published. Take a look at your Facebook Timeline and see how people open up their lives to others. Be aware of new ways of communication. Step out of your own context and see it from the outside. Exploring beyond your comfort zone is vital. Check out what other industries are doing. Ask, interact with people who have nothing to do with entertainment, and join online communities of people who are exploring different aspects of life to gain real world insights as well. This type of overview will provide you with a different perspective, which is ultimately going to help you understand where you are.

How do we access all the information? We can purchase publications online or in stores. In the case of journals, we can subscribe to weekly, daily, or monthly newsletters, printouts, and downloadable assets. Some of these publications are costly so getting access might be an important consideration unless you are in a corporation or possess the means to purchase them. Nevertheless, there are always ways to get around the cost. I recommend to at least go to the websites of key publications such as the entertainment business publications mentioned at the beginning of this section (*Variety, Hollywood Reporter, TBI Vision* (world), *TheWrap, Cynopsis,* and *The Wit*) and subscribe to free newsletters that you will receive on a daily basis with highlights (one liners) of the state of the industry. You might not get access to an entire article (unless you pay a fee), but at least you will be able to get a grasp of what is happening in the entertainment industry. Another way to get information is by following these publications as well as influential thinkers via Twitter, LinkedIn, and other social media sources that provide daily reports in the form of tweets or other kinds of social media posts. People share the information they get from their sources, thus facilitating knowledge and intelligence gathering. From these sources you will be able to get information about the competition, who is who and who is working with whom, talent, successful practices, failure, and the economic landscape. Remember: Everything is a source, the sources are out there, and there is no excuse for not using them.

Competitive Analysis

The information collected from news and information updates also serves as a basis for preparing reports on what competitors are doing and how you stand when compared to them. Competitive analysis helps you answer questions such as:

- Are you doing exactly the same type of content that others are doing?
- Are you on the right path of differentiation and innovation?
- Are you teaming up with the right people?
- Are you costly?
- Do you offer the right quality?
- Are you ahead of the curve in specific ways to pitch content?

Features	Competitor 1	Competitor 2	Competitor 3	Competitor 4
Genre of Expertise				
Successful Story				
Main Clients				
Main Territories				
Key ATL				
Production Capabilities				
Development Slate				
Pilots				
Platforms of Exposition				

Figure 13-1. Competitive analysis matrix.

From a competitive standpoint you must be aware of where you stand in reference to the competition—to see what is it that you do not have and others do, and vice versa, and to identify the precise competence that you can develop ahead of everyone else.

Competitive analysis can be done by preparing a simple matrix showing your key important features versus the features of competitors. The features in Figure 13-1 are a sample of a few you could use. The more differentiated the features are, the better the panorama you get will be.

Content creation analysis helps identify companies or people doing similar content and how successful, or not, they are. Competitive analysis helps to identify who is the best in the field and who is selling what and to spot trends in terms of content and business among other aspects. Knowing your competition is a must.

Programming Grid Analysis and TV Guide Features

Programming grids are visual representations of all programming that a TV channel or a content viewing outlet has scheduled for a period of time, usually for a week from Monday to Sunday from 6 a.m. to midnight. Figure 13-2 presents an excerpt of a hypothetical programming grid.

The programming grid tool is highly useful for allowing creative individuals to understand the flow of content throughout the day and to also understand the platform's brand. The type of programming and the order in which the programming appears on the schedule also serve to identify the flow of the audience in terms of demographics. Programming grids may present all-day programming or be broken down into day-time and prime-time programming. Depending on the type of programming you want to concentrate on, the evaluation should focus on

TIME	Monday	Tuesday	Wednesday	Thursday	Friday	Saturday	Sunday
18:00	Newscast	Newscast	Newscast	Newscast	Newscast	Newscast	Sports Update
19:00	Sitcom	Sitcom	Sitcom	Sitcom	Sitcom	Entertainment News	Movie 1
20:00	Reality Show	Talent Show	Drama Series	Drama Series	Drama Series	Game Show	Movie 1
21:00	Drama Series	Talent Show	Comedy Series	Comedy Series	News Special	Variety Special	Movie 2
22:00	Drama Series	Drama Series	Comedy	Comedy Series	Hidden Camera Show	Variety Special	Movie 2
23:00	Newscast	Newscast	Newscast	Newscast	Newscast	Newscast	Newscast

Figure 13-2. Hypothetical programming grid.

a specific part of the day and the shows that comprise that specific programming block.

Programming grids are available on a channel's website, in mobile apps containing information about a specific channel, or via programming guides with information for multiple channels featured by cable and digital satellite services. A programming grid is the offerings a channel makes to its audience—the product "wrapped and ready" to be consumed.

With the proliferation of different content platforms and the changes in viewing habits thanks to DVRs, video-on-demand, and rental digital platforms, programming grids are no longer the only way to locate content in a given platform. Instead, we need to know about the lists of programs, or categories of programs, within the platforms. People can scan within a category, select a TV show or a film, and watch it right away, using dedicated sites for video rental or sell-through outlets such as Amazon and Netflix that feature list of categories with content to choose from. The same as a programming grid, the list of programs a digital platform contains helps to define the nature and identity of the platform, which is exactly what the creators of content need to understand to direct their creative efforts more effectively.

Programming grids showcased by cable services (Figure 13-3) enable us to compare what competitors are offering at the same time and to see how TV channels can use programming to challenge each other (*TV Guide*, 2014). A programming grid also allows visualization of opportunities that could bring new content to a competitor at a disadvantage, which could also lead to locating an underserved market or an unmet need, thus becoming a content insight. The TV Guide feature shown in Figure 13-3 also lets us see the competitive landscape of

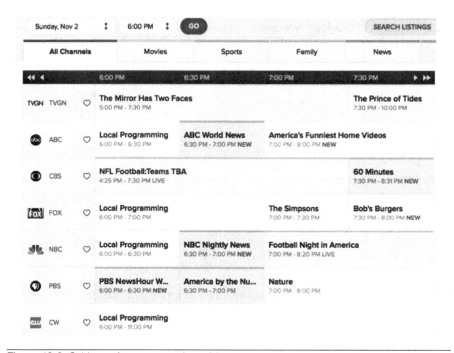

Figure 13-3. Cable service programming grid.

broadcasters and the different types of channels that exist and proliferate. The full list of the channels that a cable provider offers is an immediate tool for picturing the diversity of outlets that exist on traditional media.

Not only standalone digital platforms offer an opportunity to watch content in this fashion. Cable operators are also integrating their programming into all platforms (tablets, TV, cell phones) to offer viewers an opportunity to catch up with their favorite shows after the shows have aired. We can watch live TV wherever we are just by clicking on a cable service's app icon on a tablet or a smartphone. The way TV programming is presented today complies with nonlinear on-demand consumer viewing habits. From the different ways to access and use guides, we can get a sense of what each platform offers and how people access these platforms, either live or streamed.

A new list of platforms has emerged with the advent of smart devices. OTT channels, apps, and dedicated websites with video capabilities are new competitors for traditional broadcasters. When we look at all of the options in the set-up box (e.g., a game console) or a smart TV, we realize how the offerings of OTT channels have grown dramatically, widening the opportunities and possibilities to showcase innovative content. All connected devices (smart TVs, cell phones, tablets) allow the possibility to scan, select, and watch programming of different durations and origin. YouTube, for example, offers the possibility of watching user-generated content and high-profile TV series or films according to your profile and online behavior. YouTube's OTT channel on smart TV devices features the most popular videos and also offers them in categories for users to choose.

By looking at programming grids, we can determine:

- Channel landscapes and profiles
- Programming per time slot
- Competing channels and channels programming against each other
- Holes in the competition (who's losing, who's winning)
- Brand identities
- Viewer profiles per time slot and for an entire channel

The information collected in a programming grid lets us see what is already out there that could be similar to something we have or what is a hole in the marketplace. Maybe you have the perfect missing piece for a particular programming grid.

TV Show Analysis

TV show analysis helps us to identify the life cycle of a given show and to explore its strengths and weaknesses. The combination of these aspects leads to a conclusion as to whether the show is a strong performer with a long run ahead of it or whether the show is an ailing program that soon will be cancelled. If the show is a poor performer, then an opportunity in the time slot will be open for content generators to either improve the show or replace it. Figure 13-4 presents a graph with the four stages of the life cycle of a TV show.

A TV show goes through a phase of introduction and grows until it achieves maturity to then enter a final stage of decline. As shown in Figure 13-4, the introduction of a show occurs during the pilot season, a period in which no ratings are registered, but when the reactions of executives in the network (or channel) green-light production and airing of the show. The growth period occurs during the first two seasons of the show. The growth period is determined by increases in the number of viewers until there is a crossing of the threshold of audience acceptance—a time for the channel to decide if the show continues on the air or not. Once the show's fate is decided, if it is picked for a new season, maturity starts (usually during Season III) and could last for several seasons until the show starts to fade. This fading stage is known as the decline phase. Depending on how steep the decline slope is and how soon it crosses the threshold of audience acceptance, the show will be cancelled quickly or given a couple more seasons.

The life cycle of a given show varies because not all shows achieve maturity. Some shows start with a declining performance, pushing their cancellation in

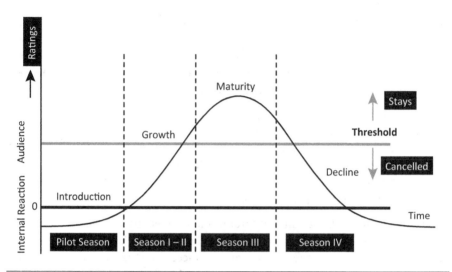

Figure 13-4. Four stages of the life cycle of a TV show on any platform.

the first season. A show also has a threshold of acceptance when it launches. According to the audience's reaction, a show will have a full life cycle or it will be over in the initial stages.

Audience Measurement

Audience measurement is the quantifiable result of audience validation for a specific show. On TV, audience is measured by ratings, which express the actual count of people who watched a show. Ratings are an overnight measurement of success. The audience, however, is not necessarily in front of a TV but instead may be online or engaged with other devices and interacting with the show's platform or other people while the show is actually on the air. The audience therefore has to be measured on TV, online, and on mobile devices and through the impact on social media (social TV measurement) (Nielsen, 2014).

Social TV measurement indicates how many relevant interactions or reactions the show is causing via Twitter, Facebook, and any relevant social media platform or through a dedicated online platform created for the show. For example, Twitter offers a great tool for measuring the relevance of a given topic. So if a show becomes a trending topic in a territory and the comments are mostly positive, the show might be a hit. Twitter is certainly reenergizing TV and becoming a powerful audience driver and tune-in propeller. All of these metrics are indicators of social cultural validation. They are a direct indication of people's responses. Likes, downloads, sales, views, followers, number of friends, retweets, etc. all serve as metrics to understand how people react to an entertainment experience and how all of these platforms are activated simultaneously.

Free newsletters from publications such as *Variety* provide overnight ratings for the United States. The *Variety* newsletter, for example, states the top ten prime-time shows in the United States. The data collected by *Variety* becomes part of the domain and the background information that experts in the field use to make decisions based on what worked in the past. Nielsen ratings in the United States also provide reports on multiplatform viewing habits, social TV, and other indicators to give you a sense of how an audience enjoys content. Ratings and overall audience measurement are part of analytics, but always necessary is balancing out ratings and audience measurements with your intuition. Use the information you find to build context and always look for ways to change it. This is the purpose of strategic research.

In recent years, U.S. ratings system did not include U.S. Hispanic networks. Hispanic networks are now included. Interesting to see is how prime-time telenovelas featured on Hispanic networks in the United States such as Univision have outperformed some general market programs. Telenovelas air in a stripped-down fashion and have an average of 3 to 4 million viewers every night. As a result, telenovelas appear frequently on the top-ten list of shows in the 18- to 49-year-old target group. Looking at this fact from an out-of-the-box perspective, we might infer different things. For example, if daily emissions for series with continued storylines work in prime-time in U.S. Hispanic markets, could they work in the general market as well? Using *Scandal*, a continued soap-style drama series that has an average of approximately 10 million viewers every week (Nielsen, 2014), as an example, what if the series were aired daily? Would that mean that potentially 10 million viewers would watch every day? This line of thought is an out-of-the-box application of what is happening in the context of U.S. TV, a context in which two different audience groups watch TV differently, but if we were to cross their viewing habits and TV forms of emission, together with multiplatform patterns, then something interesting might happen. When we discussed unmet needs in Chapter 11 (*The Discovery Circle*), we mentioned that we have to pay attention to what people value. *Scandal* fans obviously value the story, and they might even value having the ability to watch the show every day, as if they were binge watching it from Netflix or Amazon once a season is over. But who is willing to break through the orthodoxy imposed in prime-time television in the United States, where all series are aired weekly and presented in seasons?

Nickelodeon in the United States realized the power of daily continued series when the network decided to adapt *Grachi* (2011 –), a telenovela that ran for more than three seasons with more than 200 episodes in Latin America with outstanding success, as a daily series called *Every Witch Way* (2014 –). Nickelodeon took a chance and their "daily exercise" paid off, so the network has activated a second season for the show.

Audience assessment analysis provides an idea about how we can use ratings, viewer habits, and reaction information to come up with concepts and ideas that might sound a bit crazy but that could surprise viewers in a positive way if the content were given a chance. Audience assessment is also how we measure risk and realize that we have something new in front of us.

Understand Development Cycles

Every territory in the world has what is called a development cycle, primarily defined by upfront presentations, which is the time when channels pitch to advertising clients the new content being prepared for a new season. Upfront presentations have a main purpose of allowing advertising clients to buy TV airtime "up front" or several months before the next TV season begins. If advertisers like the new content, they pour money into the bucket and the process of production gets assured funds and continuity. This revenue also guarantees activation of a new development cycle.

No matter where we live, we need to find out when an upfront is happening and start counting backward. The United States is very organized in that sense. Every August, a new process of development is activated. Ideas and scripts are evaluated and developed between August and December, and the best ones are turned into pilots between February and March. In April a final selection is made, and the best finally make it to the upfront in May, to be ultimately launched in the next prime-time fall season. Each country has a similar process.

Be aware of emission patterns. It's important. Network TV, cable, and digital platforms have different strategies when launching shows. Network TV is more traditional, with big releases in the fall, mid-season premieres in January or February, and summer releases in June. Digital platforms follow other viewing patterns and release new shows in February (winter), June (summer), and in the fall. Digital platforms either release content all at once or week after week. Amazon is even giving an opportunity to its Amazon Prime viewers to vote for the best pilots so that Amazon can develop content that people really want to see. What is important about being aware of emission patterns is to recognize the platforms and know when the platforms present their new products in the market. Once you figure that out, count backward and identify the right moment to pitch the next big hit.

CLUSTER 2: TARGET MARKET IDENTIFICATION

Once you know *who* you are, *what* you have, and *where* you are, you need to know what market you are going after. You need to collect information about different markets and how they are being served and by whom. Content creation has two markets: the clients and the audience.

The Clients

A client is a platform of exposition, an advertiser, or an entity supporting and providing the resources to do a show. Target definition helps us understand the characteristics of clients: traditional media (TV outlets), digital media platforms (online, IPTV, OTT, mobile TV, PPV, video rentals), and non-traditional media (newspapers, magazines, celebrities, corporations, brands that produce content directly). Once a client has been identified and signs on to a show's economics, resources are then secured and work can focus on making a good impact on the client's audience.

The Audience

Find out what different types of people are watching what and figure out intuitively or analytically what might be an underserved audience. A market is defined by communities of followers who are channeled through a funnel of interest-based social media platforms such as YouTube, Twitter, Facebook, and Instagram and also by demographic and psychographic information.

If you are generating content by yourself that is to be exposed on online platforms, then your target audience will be the online public. How are you going to get the attention of communities of potential followers for your content? What is going to drive their interest? How are you going to use social media power to drive their attention? You have to understand "how" they are and "what" is going to drive their attention to your content. Your target market is the most important element in social validation, precisely because the reaction from this market will seal the future of your content.

Audiences present a mix of habits for the consumption of content. There is no single criterion but instead a combination of aspects that the five different generations (Baby Boomers, Gen X, Gen Y/Millennials, and Gen Z/Next), all connected at various degrees, engage to enjoy content in a traditional and multiplatform fashion. Overall, the "connected generation" viewers (Gen Y/Millennials) are always in search of original content. Their behavior is determining the future and evolution of television. According to a study conducted by the German consulting firm Booz & Company, the TV genre has to make a special effort to gain relevancy by growing its offerings tied to second and third screens that better reflect the nonlinear communication and entertainment lifestyle of today's consumers (Friedrich, Peterson, Koster & Blum, 2012). This investigation points out that more than a lifestyle the "always-on generation" (Gen C) has a short cycle of attention given that for each hour of free time, a digital person changes platforms up to 27 times. As a result, TV stories and shows that allow multiplatform engagement and simultaneous storytelling will rule and help redefine the industry and process of revenue generation (Todotvnews, 2012).

Remember that valuable tools to gather information about your target market also comprise internet monitoring, ethnographics, geolocation, and social trend spotting (see the *Discontinuities* section in Chapter 11).

CLUSTER 3: COMPETITIVE ADVANTAGES

To define your strategy, you need to understand clearly what you have and what you do not have. This analysis will result in a list of competitive advantages that define your strengths—what you have and know to be your key assets. Your weaknesses are the aspects you do not have that make you vulnerable versus the competition. For example, if you are a skillful independent fiction writer, you have a competence that is very important for creative companies that are developing fiction content Despite having this strength, your knowledge and writing skills, however, you might not have the ability to sell your content because you just don't know how to sell or you don't have connections in the market. In that case, lack of marketing ability or no connections in the market are your weaknesses, so you have to team up with individuals who have access to clients. As you can see, the creative process leads you to work with complements to fill the gaps that your weaknesses have in the procurement of content. An honest self-evaluation of your strengths and weaknesses helps you to identify areas with room for improvement.

Keep a personal human resources databases. When reading news sources, the names of professionals pop up all the time. Executives, writers, producers, agents, advertising agencies, directors of photography, story consultants, story gurus, actors, production companies, investors, etc. Those are the names of people you might need at some point in your career to propel a project. As we have already discussed, collaboration and cooperation are two essential aspects that you must incorporate in the process of innovation to find solutions through others. I recommend that you build a list of people. In this list, write a note next to each name in the list stating the key strength of that person. Your personal human resources database could even be organized using Google+ or LinkedIn groups that share the same interests. Professional networks also help locate people who might be interesting and interested in working with you on a certain project. The purpose of having these lists of people is to improve your capacity to react and the possibility to deliver.

THE INFORMATION

What do you do with all of the information you find? Processing a large amount of information when there is almost no time, either because you are too busy or just too focused on getting the best out of your free time, is difficult. Processing information all depends on who you are. Remember that question about defining your macro-strategy? Your macro-strategy will help you orient the research process and the type of information that matters for you. The important issue here is not to be too focused on one single type of information but to be open to the many sources and different types.

My first advice is to not let information "eat you up." Embrace it. Do not try to learn or read everything all at once. Learning takes time. So start with few sources at a time. Read what you can. Anything helps and provides context.

If you are on a creative team, ideal is that you will have a group of analysts who are dedicated to processing all of the information. Their function is to collect data from publications and gather information that the other team members bring to the table and to turn it into a report that everyone can relate to and read. Processing all of the information could be lengthy, but it is doable. I recommend structuring information in the form of SWOT reports. A SWOT report classifies all information into four quadrants: strengths, weaknesses, opportunities, and threats (Figure 13-5).

SWOT news reports. If a SWOT news report is completed on a monthly basis, you will have a solid monthly report that will give you an overview of the world of entertainment news and how all of the events happening in it affect or ignite the generation of your content. The analyst assigned to a SWOT news report could be an intern from a business school or someone with a marketing background who has knowledge about this framework of analysis.

SWOT information reports. For a SWOT information report, the analyst assigned to preparing this report reads a publication and immediately fits the information into a quadrant of the report. For example, an online newsletter usually presents short sentences in headline reports. Each headline provides sufficient information to understand in which quadrant the information goes, however, by clicking on one of these headlines, the entire report can be accessed. The same needs to be done with all other information collected. The analyst has to read and process this information as well. Create abstracts and be able to

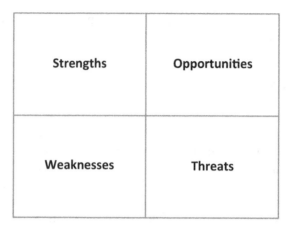

Strengths	Opportunities
Weaknesses	Threats

Figure 13-5. SWOT framework for classifying information.

summarize, every month, all quadrants for easy consumption. If you get information via an oral communication, then it has to be written down. Sketch it or save it in your mobile device so that you can then merge it with the rest of the information. Brainstorming sessions are also necessary for team members to share what they have heard from other individuals within or outside the industry with other team members.

Who should be hired to work on the data information and information classification process? These individuals should be browsers. When looking for these professionals, find people who are passionate about the collection of data and information and who are skillful in the art of classifying information within the quadrants of a SWOT report. I usually prefer to incorporate people with professional marketing and business backgrounds (business development in the entertainment industry) who are keen to do strategic research. These individuals know how to gather information. They have been trained to make sense out of it, using not only the SWOT framework but also other frameworks that are taught in business and marketing schools. If an individual also has experience in the entertainment industry, the process will be faster and the results will be presented to the team more promptly. Also incorporate people with an open sense of collaboration who are capable of listening and sharing. Although the area of data collected and analyzed could be set in a very refined fashion, with professionals who are highly trained in the subject matter, interns, junior analysts, and senior analysts could also work together to identify opportunities.

If you are on a creative team, the final report could be a sophisticated document, but it could also be a large whiteboard with information that combines the state of the industry and your position within it. You do not always need to come up with complex reports. What is important is to look at the information and always classify it in your head as a strength, opportunity, weakness, or threat. Every piece has a fit. Try it and you will see—your strategic thought process will be sharper.

THE OUTCOME OF THE MARKET AND STRATEGIC RESEARCH PROCESS

If you are in an organization, based on the market information collected, a creative group or the company will identify where to concentrate development efforts. The nature of the markets to target and the portfolio of innovations to be pursued must therefore be defined. To be innovative, creative individuals in the group or company must aim for content that could potentially be a game changer. They must try to find the next radical innovation that will turn the world around. The process of discovery and the subsequent value chain of innovation must have that objective active and nurtured, along with the resources and time to develop and find the next big thing.

With the information collected, form a clear strategy that will let all of the individuals involved in the process know *what* kind of ideas, in what areas and for what purpose, are to be generated and *how*, with what resources and in what time frame, *what* type of innovation, with what effect, are to be developed. The resulting strategy is a written statement of who you are, what you have, where you are, and what type of content you are going to do, why, and for whom. This strategy when communicated provides employees with a clear direction and enhances and sets the dynamics for a goal-oriented frame of creative operation (dal Zotto & Kranenburg, 2008).

14

EXPLORATION

The main objective of the exploration activity is to find the best possible ideas and trends, to manage references, and to ultimately filter and evaluate them in an efficient and methodical way to create an excellent pool of ideas that might eventually enter the concept development stage. As explained in Chapter 13 (*Market and Strategic Research*), a clear definition of the type of pipeline that we want to have is needed. Is it a pipeline of original breakthroughs or do we want to incorporate incremental innovations as well? A company's portfolio of innovations should include incremental and radical innovations. It is at this point that you need to find the content that best fits the strategic criteria. Depending on the strategy, select the type of source and ideas that are most convenient for the company's or your portfolio.

The exploration process is led by browsers and covers the following aspects:

- Identification of sources for creative ideas
- Implementation of a process of submission
- Evaluation
- Selection
- Rights negotiation
- Generation of a database for ideas considered

An exploration team has to tap into as many sources as possible to select a wide variety of ideas before making decisions about what should be developed. Sources have to be diverse and numerous to ensure that the ideas selected have strong differentiating factors and the potential to become an innovation. The material collected during this process could come from anywhere in the world. Ideas are everywhere; they could work in your territory if adapted. The process is then a funnel-like process through which all of the ideas transit (Figure 14-1).

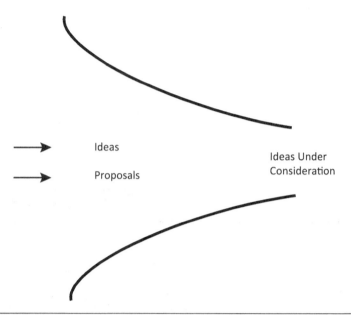

Figure 14-1. Funnel of creative exploration.

Once ideas enter the funnel for creative exploration they go through an evaluation process, which is none other than implementation of a system of creative validation. The best ideas survive and enter the concept development stage.

The process of exploration is a stage-gate system used to sort good ideas from bad ones. This sorting method was developed by Robert Cooper in the late 1980s and consists of a series of assessment gates that aims to eliminate weak ideas and concentrate on speeding up the potential "winners." Each gate is a point of validation within a group or a company that determines if a project should be killed, sent back for more development, or advanced to the next development stage (Harvard Business Essentials, 2003, p. 65).

TYPES OF CREATIVE IDEAS

Based on the strategy in place, the browsers look for ideas that fit the portfolio criteria, which must also entail both radical and incremental innovations, and are classified as:

- Blockbusters
- Bread and butter
- Niche

Blockbusters. Radical innovations, the main purpose of the innovation process, can receive the name "blockbusters." Blockbusters have content with global and lasting impact. Examples are *Big Brother*, *Pop Idol*, the *CSI* franchise, which became some of the most-watched TV shows around the world, and *Sex and the City*, the TV series that also became a major film event. The media industry depends strongly on blockbusters. To create tomorrow's blockbusters, the focus is on innovation rather than imitation (Aris & Bughi, 2005). Even so, blockbusters rely heavily on talent, development can be costly, and not all ideas have blockbuster potential. Incremental innovations also need to have market possibilities to drive and generate revenue for the company.

Bread and butter. Other ideas to look for are those with "bread and butter" potential. Bread and butter ideas have a lower profile, become steady performers, are commissioned in high volumes, and represent an important revenue-generation machine. They could be prime-time shows in some territories or fillers in other daytime programming slots. Examples of these shows include *Wheel of Fortune* and *Family Feud*, shows that programming executives recall as ones that never fail. If you can spot an idea with that kind of potential, you might have a winner.

Niche. Other types of ideas to look for are those that target more niche-like markets. This type of content has grown with the proliferation of multiple platforms of expositions. For example, some cable or OTT channels are dedicated to car collectors or dogs flying or other very specific interests. The truth of the matter is that these new platforms have opened opportunities to tie content directly with brands aiming at a very specific market and with content that would not ever have been made in the general market (Aris & Bughin, 2005). Among these programs are docu-soaps, lifestyle programming, factual programming, and live music performances such as *MTV Unplugged*, etc.

SOURCES OF CREATIVE IDEAS

Browsers for ideas might find ideas in a variety of resources such as those shown in Figure 14-2: in-house, print, digital, creative communities, non-entertainment related, previously produced, formats, databases of formats and references, international content trends/trades, urban areas/countrysides, on-camera talent, and an idea on a napkin.

In-house. In-house ideas are prepared within a group or a creative company. These ideas can come from anyone in a corporation, not just from an elite group

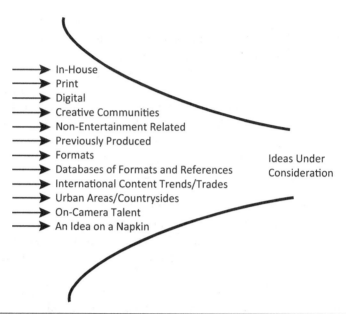

In-House
Print
Digital
Creative Communities
Non-Entertainment Related
Previously Produced
Formats
Databases of Formats and References
International Content Trends/Trades
Urban Areas/Countrysides
On-Camera Talent
An Idea on a Napkin

Ideas Under
Consideration

Figure 14-2. Sources of ideas going through the funnel of exploration.

of individuals. Anyone could be a source for an innovation. First find ideas "inside the house." (Browsers need to look in-house first and then open up to the outside world.) This activity motivates people and enhances collaboration within a group. People feel that they can share their ideas without hesitation; otherwise, they might shut down and take their ideas somewhere else. Internal ideas could come in the form of full fleshed-out proposals on paper or they could come from successes or failures from the past that could be readapted and revamped for today's audiences. Internal ideas can also come from writers, producers, directors, creative people in the marketing department, creative executives, CEOs, production assistants, coordinators, and interns, anyone. Other functional areas within a corporation might also have people with ideas for TV shows. Open the doors for them to pitch their concepts. Let them feel there is opportunity to present what could possibly be a successful endeavor. (This type of idea exploration is also based on the process of discovery explained in Chapter 11, *The Discovery Circle*, which produces insights and ideas that could be turned into TV shows.)

Print. Print resources can be novels, magazines, and newspapers—sources that are fictional or non-fictional in nature. Fictional sources such as novels are usually turned into films or TV series. Non-fiction books and articles in newspaper and magazines can also be the genesis of fictional content. Biopics, or films based on current or historical events, are made from the information found in books, manuscripts, articles, and other printed material. Another example is

Hola TV, the adaption of *Hello Magazine* into a TV channel in Latin America, which uses sections of the magazine as inspiration for original programming. Non-fictional sources can also lead to the generation of documentaries, special news reports, educational training videos, and even game shows. All publications are sources of information to help figure out new content. Non-fictional types of magazines covering different interests such as fitness, mechanics, travel, business, baby care, and lifestyle have been translated into content for a variety of platforms and channels. If you feel that ideas are not flowing, that you do not know what is happening in the world, or that you are disconnected from reality, then stop by the nearest news kiosk, or any place where you can still find print information, to open your realm of possibilities.

Digital. Apps, websites, Twitter accounts, Facebook pages, and blogs can also lead to the creation of content. A game show could derive from a mobile application (e.g., *The Trivia Track* app has been turned into a game show in Argentina by Televisa International). Match-making websites can be the genesis for a reality show. A Twitter account from a funny but previously unknown person with a strong follower base could lead to an online or TV talk show featuring the owner of the account. Facebook pages are filled with stories of real people and could be the source of fiction or non-fiction shows. These digital sources also have implicit new ways to communicate. User-generated content on YouTube or independent shorts released online could become major film or TV events with global impact. The same notion applies for actors, singers, and songwriters who upload their content online. People validate these performers and this initial acceptance might be the indicator of success that you need to move an idea forward.

Creative communities. Creative communities are also called third parties because they are not part of your company or group of creative individuals. A third party can be a person, a group, or a company doing the same as you—generating ideas. Teaming up with third parties helps extend your realm of possibilities for finding new ideas without necessarily investing more money on infrastructure. Working with third parties is a fundamental mandate in the process of open innovation. Apple would not have developed the iPod if it were not for Apple's open exploration process. Pitch sessions and creative rallies also encourage the creative community to present their ideas and concepts. Periodically organize pitch sessions and creative rallies and let people in creative communities know that you are searching for new ideas.

Non-entertainment related. Non-entertainment-related sources are individuals from other industries who have great knowledge on a specific topic that could be valuable for building a TV show. For example, a doctor could be the source of the next hospital drama; a golfer could become the next anchor for a specialized TV show about golf; a scientist could use a very unorthodox method to unveil a truth behind certain aspect of life and then become the source for a documentary series; a psychologist might be the inspiration for a new type of reality show; a sports event could be the source for another reality show. Look for sources everywhere. Anyone around you could have a compelling story to tell that you could turn into an audiovisual event.

Previously produced. Previously produced content, such as movies, old series, current series, and theater plays could lead to the creation of new content. Films have always been a source for TV content. Many movies have made a successful transition into the TV medium (Perebinossoff, Gross & Lynne, 2005). For the creation of new content, the process is a matter of assessing the franchise potential of the title and seeing if the story could be told in more than 88 episodes (the magic number for syndication) or in the lapse of four seasons. Examples of movies that became the source of TV content include *Moonrunners* (1975), which led to the successful TV series *The Dukes of Hazard*, *M*A*S*H** (1970), *9 to 5* (1980), and *Buffy the Vampire Slayer* (1992)—all became TV events. Old series or series currently on the air could be remade and adapted to current times. A spin-off of a series based on a character could trigger a new series. Examples of spin-offs include *Laverne and Shirley* and *Mork and Mindy* which were spun-off from *Happy Days*. Another high-profile example is *Frasier* which was spun-off from *Cheers* (Perebinossoff, Gross & Lynne, 2005).

Formats. Shows that have been produced successfully in other territories leave a recipe behind that could be replicated elsewhere and become an innovation in a new place. A format opportunity could be described as the "selling of remake rights which enables buyers to produce a local remake tailored to suit their domestic television market" (Fey, 2012). Game shows, reality shows, TV series, etc. could be replicated with success in other territories or adapted to match the cultural idiosyncrasy of a market. Key aspects to take into consideration when evaluating a format are the success track and adaptation feasibility. For those reasons, important is gathering information on the performance the show in its original territory of emission and assessing the number of countries the show has aired in, how many episodes were produced, and if new seasons are in the making. After gathering information on the success track of the format, evaluate how a show can be produced in your territory. What resources are required to make it happen and what type of adaptation does the show need to fit the cultural premises in your territory? Companies selling formats should provide all success track information and a bible with all of the creative specifics and resources that you need to have in place for a proper implementation. If the show is suitable for your market, then you move to the concept development stage to work on the version for your territory. Today, producers are using formats from fiction and non-fiction shows to create successful shows in their territories. Examples of remade formats in the United States include *Shameless* (from *Shameless*, United Kingdom), *Elementary* (from *Sherlock*, United Kingdom), *Ugly Betty* (from *Yo soy Betty, la fea*, Colombia), *Devious Maids* (from *Ellas son ... la alegría del hogar*, Mexico), and *The Mysteries of Laura* (from *Los misterios de Laura*, Spain). Among the non-fictional formats are *Survivor* (from *Survivor*, Sweden), *American Idol* (from *Pop Idol*, United Kingdom), and *Rising Star* (from Israel).

Databases of formats and references. Research firms such as The WIT compile information about content produced and aired worldwide. The WIT, one of the most complete sources in the industry, compiles information about TV programming and new digital endeavors. The information is reliable and up to date. Access to The WIT database is by subscription. Other publications such as *TBI* and *C21* also provide extended reports about content from around the world. All shows stored in databases of formats become references in the market that could be useful for a creative team during the concept development process, not only to become inspired but to also create awareness of what is out there in the market.

International content trends/trades. These sources include festivals, fairs, conventions, and international or local events where content providers such as distributors, producers, and writers present their ideas and formats. These events are also called markets. Notable gatherings are MIPCOM, NATPE, MIPTV, NATPE Europe, and the Asia Pacific Media Forum.

Urban areas/countrysides. Every place represents a source of content. The streets offer all sorts of hints and signs of things that could translate into new content initiatives. A taxi cab, a store, street performers, traffic surveillance cameras, a park, a nightclub, people interacting with their mobile devices in the subway, a bus, people running in a park or walking their pets, a poster, a billboard, a karaoke bar, a concert, a conversation between teenagers, a skateboarder, and an idea on a napkin—everything has the possibility of producing an insight that might become an innovation.

On-camera talent. Big or small celebrities might come up with an outstanding idea. Just the fact of having a major talent behind a concept could be a big selling proposition. Tom Hanks, Steven Spielberg, and Jerry Bruckheimer are some of the most successful godfathers of content in the last century. Artists in general are crossing over their comfort zones as performers and are becoming more active in terms of content generation. They use their star power to gain access to networks and channels and even use their personal monetary resources to build platforms of exposition. On-camera talent can range from singers to actors to presenters or from sportscasters, newscasters, and sports players to reality stars. Examples of stars making content include Eva Longoria, Justin Timberlake, Madonna, Angelina Jolie, Brad Pitt, Ben Affleck, and Wilmer Valderrama.

An idea on a napkin. I always say that ideas can come from anywhere. They could come up in a formal creative meeting or could happen while on vacation with your kids. An idea could be sketched on a napkin and a great concept might materialize afterward. Do not let any idea slip through your fingers or get lost on your desk. Embrace them all. Do not expect all ideas to be fine tuned and ready to air. Look beyond that and make sure that your evaluators of concept can see beyond the initial pitch.

THE SUBMISSION PROCESS

Submissions can come in several forms. Submissions can be in the form of a script, a paper treatment, a short demo or trailer, a pilot, a graphic representation of a series (storyboards), a bible, episodes produced in another territory, and previously produced material for any platform (print, TV, online, etc.).

The process of submission needs to be rigorous. Companies and individuals need to protect themselves from copyright infringement situations, which might come as a result of receiving an unsolicited idea. Some producers just refuse to review unsolicited material, whereas others will agree to review unsolicited material if the person submitting the material signs what is known as a submission release (Blumenthal & Goodenough, 2006). As a creator of ideas who receives many ideas from various sources, you must protect yourself by telling a writer submitting material that there might be something similar in the making already within your creative division. Better is not to receive an idea if you think you have something similar. Conversely a writer needs to copyright their material and ensure that they can claim ownership before sending a pitch to anyone. Ownership of the material entitles the writer to be compensated for the utilization of that material by a receiving party.

The way the process usually works is that after a submission release has been signed, the producer or an executive negotiates the rights for the show material that has been selected. If, however, the show material is rejected, the writer will have no claims to make if something similar is eventually produced. A submissions release is a waiver of *all* claims.

Figure 14-3 presents a sample submission release letter. In this document the writer acknowledges that the producer might be working on or might come up with similar ideas and that the producer or the writer will not take legal action if

[Producer's Letterhead]

[Date]
[Name and Address]

Dear _____

As you know,_____ ("Producer") is engaged in the production of television programs for exploitation in any and all entertainment media. In this context, Producer reviews various sources of ideas, stories, and suggestions. Such material may relate to format, theme, characters, treatments, and/or means of exploiting a production once completed. In order to avoid misunderstandings, Producer will not review or discuss ideas, scripts, treatments, formats, or the like submitted to it on an unsolicited basis by persons not in its employ without first obtaining the agreement of the person submitting the material to the provisions of this letter.

By signing the enclosed copy of this letter and returning it to us, you hereby acknowledge and agree as follows:

1. You are submitting to Producer the following material for its review:

   _____

   _____

2. You warrant that you are the sole owner and author of the above described material and that you have the full right and authorization to submit it to Producer, free of any obligation to any third party.

3. You agree that any part of the submitted material which is not novel or original and not legally protected may be used by Producer without any liability on its part to you and that nothing herein shall place Producer in any different position with respect to such non-novel or original material by reason hereof.

4. Producer shall not be under any obligation to you with respect to the submitted material except as may later be set forth in a fully executed written agreement between you and Producer.

5. You realize that Producer has had and will have access to and/or may independently create or have created ideas identical to the theme, plot, idea, format or other element of material now being submitted by you and you agree that you will not be entitled to any compensation by reason of the use by Producer of such similar or identical material.

Very truly yours,
[Producer]

By:
AGREED TO AND ACCEPTED
By:
Date:

Figure 14-3. Sample submission release letter.

so. Of course, the entire document is based on trust so many lawyers recommend that writers never sign these documents to maintain the protection of their ideas from any type of copyright infringement. The best advice for a writer is to seek legal representation or representation by an agent who has established relations with studios and producers and who has an understanding of how to protect the work they pitch on behalf of a represented artist. A submission release letter (or form) usually contemplates several aspects:

- Specifies the name of the person submitting the material and information about the author
- Specifies the title of the project and the type of material being submitted (e.g., a script, a demo, a pilot)
- Provides a warranty of sole ownership by the author
- Notice by the producer receiving the unsolicited material making clear to the other party that the producer, the company, or the group the producer represents constantly reviews and receives unsolicited submissions of ideas, which might be similar to or identical to those ideas developed or owned by the producer, in which case the person submitting the material will not be entitled to any compensation because of the use of such similar or identical material (Litwak, 2002; Blumenthal & Goodenough, 2006).
- Acknowledgement that the producer will not review the unsolicited material if the release is not signed
- Notice that the producer will evaluate the material to decide whether to acquire the rights
- Notice that the author will not receive any compensation if the producer uses any material that is not protectable and contained in the submitted material
- Notice that the author will receive compensation if the producer decides to use the submitted material created by the author

Another document used is a Non-Disclosure Agreement (NDA). An NDA allows the parties involved to exchange creative confidential work with the understanding that each party will respect the work of the other from a legal standpoint. In this case, the parties promise to one another not to share the information disclosed with a third party, also respecting the rights the other individual has over their own material. Once the releases or the agreement to exchange documents have been signed, the ideas enter a process of evaluation and market verification, through which not only you evaluate the potential the idea has to succeed in the market, but also you check with the research team if there is something similar out there.

THE EVALUATION PROCESS

The purpose of the evaluation process is to assess the innovative potential of an idea and to determine the possible effect it will have in the market should the idea be produced. The evaluation process should answer whether the idea is a possible game changer, a radical innovation, or an incremental innovation.

Coverage Evaluation

A coverage evaluation form is used by evaluators or readers of content as a place to record comments, conclusions, and recommendations after reviewing an idea. Evaluators spot strengths and weaknesses in a proposal and make a final recommendation which might be: *recommend*, if the concept has clear innovative potential and is almost ready to move into the sales stage with little conceptual development; *consider*, if the idea has potential but needs to be reworked; or *pass*, if the idea is not suitable. An evaluator could definitely pass on a submission but could also recommend that the writer, producer, or another artist involved in the project under evaluation be considered for another project. Evaluators of content are experts in the field and possess objective criteria to assess the weaknesses and strengths of a proposal. An evaluator has to be fully trained in the concept of innovation, in innovation classification according to the degree of novelty, and in the key drivers required for content innovation to occur (see Chapter 8, *Classification of Media Content Innovation According to Degree of Novelty*, and Chapter 9, *Drivers of Content Innovation*).

A coverage form is a powerful tool for executives or people who have almost no time to read a content submission to get a sense of what a show is about and what its potential could be. For that reason short and concise evaluations are preferable, and welcomed, by creative executives. A coverage form differs per genre. A fiction evaluator (or reader) concentrates on different aspects than a non-fiction evaluator. I have designed evaluation forms for each genre. Figure 14-4 represents a coverage form with four elements for a fiction proposal:

- Header: The header section of the form contains the name of the author, the entity representing the project, the type of materials submitted, and person who received the submission. The header also has a space for the name of the evaluator (the analyst) for future reference.
- Brief Summary of Show: The summary section has two parts:
  - Logline: Describes in two sentences what the show is about
  - Synopsis: Describes the story in one paragraph (maximum)

- Analysis: The comments summary area usually contains one paragraph that assesses the innovation potential of each aspect and highlights weaknesses and strengths of the concept. Gauging the following aspects within a story is recommended:
  - Plot and structure: The plot and structure area has to do with originality and the way the story flows and progresses. How is the story structured? Are the turning points clear? Is the story sustainable? How innovative is the story? Is this innovation unique? Is this innovation a potential breakthrough? Has the story ever been seen?
  - Characters: The characters area has to do with characterization and the character arc.
  - Momentum: Momentum refers to the possibility the story has to create anticipation and the audience's desire for more. How innovative is the story? Is this innovation a breakthrough or incremental?
  - Style: Style has to do with dialogue and the description of actions and the characters.
  - Genre elements: The genre elements area is for describing how the distinctive elements of genre are depicted in the proposal. If the project is an action-driven concept, a horror story, or a romantic comedy, an evaluator expects to find the elements of the respective formula.
  - Type of innovation and key drivers: The type of innovation and key drivers area identifies if the innovation is incremental or radical and what the key drivers of this particular innovation are.
  - Conclusion: The conclusion area is for a very short statement about whether the show is worth consideration (or not) and why.
- Evaluation: The evaluation section has a survey to be filled by the evaluator, which helps an executive reading the coverage form to see a matrix summarizing the degree of innovation and the key strengths of the project. The aspects considered are the same as in the comments summary and consider some specific qualities:
  - Innovation potential: Depending on the type of innovation specified in comments summary area, the innovation potential area is to assess how innovative an evaluator thinks the proposal will actually be.
  - Franchise potential: Franchise potential has to do with longevity and the possibility that the concept could have to be extended for

several seasons or be reproduced without cannibalization (e.g., as the CSI and NCIS franchises have).

- Cinematic/production values: Is the show set to breakthrough in terms of production design and visual imagery? (This aspect helps anticipate the budget range.)
  - Audience potential: Would this concept be well received by a specific audience? Is this concept serving a new niche or does it have general market potential?
- Results: The evaluator not only evaluates the project but also the writer/producer involved in the submission, with one of three possible outcomes—*recommend, consider,* or *pass.*

An evaluation form for a non-fiction project is presented in Figure 14-5.

Intellectual Property Rights Evaluation

The value chain of content creation is based on the production and distribution of intellectual properties created by artists with the expectation to profit from them. The key element that artists sell when offering an intellectual property is the rights to own the property. The problem with media content is that " … copying them is usually easy and cheap, so multiple forms of unauthorized usage can occur generating copyright infringement and piracy of media contents or the parasitical imitation of media formats as, for example, TV formats" (dal Zotto & Kranenburg, 2008, p. 37).

An evaluation team has to obtain all relevant information about property rights, including:

- Who owns the property rights?
- Who bears interest in the intellectual property?
- Has the content been produced somewhere else?
- Is the content an imitation of something made in another country?
- Are several individuals or companies involved or just one individual?

You must ensure that you get the rights needed for all territories and platforms you intend to target. Major studios usually negotiate worldwide rights and perpetuity to secure that the property becomes an asset they own. A major studio might request such a level of ownership and, depending on the leverage the rights holder has, the rights holder might get some revenue participation resulting from the rights exploitation of the content. Important to understand is how much of the project you can actually own and then request the proper certification of ownership just to ensure all information provided by the rights holder is backed up by documentation.

Title:		Form (treatment, eps, etc.):	
Author(s):		Length/Pages:	
Submitted to:		Date:	**HEADER**
Submitted by:		Analyst:	
Company/Agency:		Genre:	
Elements Submitted:		Locale:	

Logline:

BRIEF SUMMARY OF SHOW

Synopsis:

Comments Summary:
a. Plot and structure:
b. Characters (characterization and character arc):
c. Momentum:
d. Style: **ANALYSIS**
e. Genre elements:
f. Type of innovation and key drivers:
g. Conclusion:

Evaluation:

	Excellent	Good	Fair	Poor
Innovation Potential				
Premise/Concept				
Franchise Potential				
Plot/Structure			**EVALUATION**	
Characterization				
Dialogue				
Cinematic/Production Values				
Audience Potential				

Budget: Low: _____   Medium: _____   High: _____

Writer/Producer Evaluation: Recommend: ____   Consider: _____   Pass: _____

Project Evaluation: Recommend: ____   Consider: _____   Pass: _____

Suitable for: _____   **RESULTS**

Figure 14-4. Coverage evaluation form for fiction/drama programming. eps, episodes.

Entertainment/Reality/Variety

Title:		Form (treatment, eps, etc.)	
Author(s):		Length/Pages (#):	
Submitted to:		Date:	
Submitted by:		Analyst:	
Company/Agency:		Genre:	
Elements Submitted:		Locale:	

Logline:

Description/Show Dynamics:

Genre Elements:

Type of Innovation and Key Drivers:

Comments Summary:

Evaluation:

Criterion	Excellent	Good	Fair	Poor
Innovation Potential				
Premise/Concept/Originality				
Structure				
Cinematic/Production Values				
Franchise Potential				
Audience Potential				
Overall Writing-Dynamic of Show				

Blockbuster _____   **Bread and Butter** _____   **Niche** _____

Budget: Low: _____   Medium: _____   High: _____

Project Evaluation: Recommend: _____   Consider: _____   Pass: _____

Conclusion: _____

Figure 14-5. Coverage evaluation form for a non-fiction project (entertainment, reality, and variety). eps, episodes.

Evaluation Team Members

Field experts comprise the group of people who validate and evaluate the ideas while the ideas advance through the funnel of selection (see Figure 14-1). To guarantee an objective, balanced, and unbiased process, recommended is to assemble a team with a team of browsers who are members of the field and who have various backgrounds and levels of expertise. The opinion of these browsers will seal the fate of a show. I propose a team formed by:

- On-air/online-promotion creative copy producers: Creative copy-producing professionals have powerful skills in identifying the strengths a given show has because they are used to identifying the key selling proposition that makes a show worth watching and that will become the centerpiece of promotional campaigns to invite audiences to tune in. These individuals can spot weaknesses and bring up interesting intelligence regarding shows that have worked in the past. Because they have processed so many types of projects before, these individuals have developed an objective sense for recommending what is good or bad. Copy producers could become part of the evaluation team or only be invited to assess projects outside of their regular hours as copy producers. (This arrangement could be a great opportunity to apply the 80/20 rule, involving 20% of a copy producer's work time in evaluation.)

- Critics, journalists, and analysts of content in publications: Critics, journalists, and analysts are accustomed to watching, reading, and listening to anything being released (or to be released) in the market to provide advice about whether to watch or not. Some critics have developed an excellent connection with audiences. They know the market and can therefore be used to provide objective comments. Other critics, however, are biased and have become pseudo-celebrities with strong points of view that might contaminate the process—avoid them.

- Marketing and sales individuals: Marketing and sales professionals develop a strong sense of what audiences do and want. They possess information and data from the past that allow them to anticipate what will sell well in a market. Marketing and sales professionals are good allies to have and even more so when you incorporate them into the process first as viewers and then as marketers. Marketing professionals also like being creative and expressing their points of view even though their world is sometimes so analytical that they can lose perspective and disconnect from reality, becoming pessimists. By combining both their analytic and creativity abilities, the recommendations of marketing professionals might be more honest and worth consideration.

- Creative professionals with production backgrounds: Individuals with creative and production backgrounds provide insights on the potential a project has from a creative and a production standpoint. They can identify the complexity of a show on paper or by watching demos or pilots and can predict how difficult (or feasible) making the show might be under any given set of conditions related to resources, budget, efficiency, etc.

- Top and creative executives with business strategic vision: Even though the strategy has to be clear throughout, executives can help filter out ideas they consider to not be a fit in the strategy of the company. They explain why, and the information becomes a premise to be considered in future evaluations. Important, however, is that their vision or strategy does not become orthodoxy within the process. If so, many innovations might just be passing by—and the company will be doomed.
- Writers/developers with no hidden agendas: Writers are the ultimate members of any evaluation team. Writers tend to be precise in terms of story, characterization, genre, and show dynamics (non-fiction) evaluation. They can spot the quality of a writer and make recommendations. Be careful when selecting writers to evaluate ideas. Ensure they can remain objective when evaluating ideas from fellow writers or creative individuals. Ensure that they do not carry the frustration of a project that failed for lack of opportunities to a new idea. If so, this frustration creates vengeful lines of thoughts that may bias the process of evaluation.
- Entertainment lawyers and business affairs experts: Entertainment lawyers and business affairs experts can help to assess and analyze intellectual property rights.

THE SELECTION PROCESS FOR NEW IDEAS

The selection of new ideas is a result of a process of creative validation that started with the evaluation of each submission by members of the evaluation team. The recommendations made needed to be validated among the team members through implementation of the circle of validation initiative, which consists of holding periodic round tables for selection of the ideas that will enter the concept development stage.

Bogart (1995) and Gans (2003) indicated that decisions in media firms depended on a combination of factors such as public service and cultural factors, established relationships, and intuition (dal Zotto & Kranenburg, 2008, p. xvi). For public service organizations, we can understand that people are willing to create content for free and how established relationships could overshadow or favor the content evaluation process. We can also understand how fights or clashes between intuitions and the economic rationality behind a decision make the evaluation process difficult. Risk-taking firms will bet on real breakthroughs and take more chances, relying on intuition, when selecting from their pipeline of ideas, sometimes defying economic criteria. For other companies, however, if a show is too far out-of-the-box, the time frame for deciding whether the show is suitable (or not) might be very long because the decision makers do not want to take on the extra risk, the unpredictability of success, and the difficulty of determining reliable tests for everything that might influence the decision. The more therefore that decision makers can "see," the better the chances are for them to anticipate what an innovative idea might be.

Another aspect influencing the decision can be the commercial viability of a product. A channel considering the product might have an actual need to decide whether to replace inexpensive re-runs with original programming that even if not costly would create a distortion in the channel's budget and bottom line.

Decisions in the media industry are not easy. That is why understanding your market, the players that are actually investing in programming, and the monetary dynamics in the market will help you to move an innovative idea forward are so important. Remember: The more innovative an idea is, the higher the risk and the more difficult it is to accomplish moving the idea forward. Decision makers have the ultimate word—their support helps propel the making of new shows.

Use a Circle of Validation for Selection

To ensure an unbiased selection process, you need to have a circle of validation in place formed by a mix of evaluators with various backgrounds. Recommended is to have at least three rounds of evaluation per project, meaning that you let three evaluators review the same project. Projects that receive two evaluations as "pass" are out of consideration, whereas projects with two or three "considers" might move on to the next stage, which is a roundtable for selection that involves several individuals who may or may not have been involved in the process of evaluation.

The circle of validation starts with an initial reader or evaluator. Once the initial evaluator submits a coverage evaluation form, a second evaluator reviews the show and adds comments to the coverage form. A third evaluation is then performed and the final coverage evaluation form includes the consensus of at least three evaluators. The final coverage form will then be used during roundtables for selection.

The circle of validation needs to develop a series of key questions about the project. The answers to these questions must be positive before the project can be selected for concept development (Trias de Bes & Kotler, 2011). Trias de Bes & Kotler (2011) and Skarzynsky & Gibson (2008) proposed a list of questions that has been adapted for the purposes of this book and can be used as a validation checklist:

- Is this project necessary?
- Is this project truly innovative? Is it a before and after? Is it a radical or an incremental innovation?
- What benefits will this project, when complete, bring to the company and the clients?
- Is this project going to place the company in a better position?
- Is undertaking this project now suitable and appropriate? Will there be any adverse repercussions if we postpone undertaking this project?
- What are the end objectives of this project and how practical are they?
- What is the overall time frame? What resources are necessary? Do we have these resources? Do we have the competences to develop the project or do we need to hire people or team up with another company?
- Is this project cost-effective? What are the projected benefits and advantages?
- Do we have the means to or the possibility to negotiate the intellectual property rights for the concept under evaluation?
- Do we have the means, distribution channels, and the right people to sell the product/property?
- Do we have access to clients or do we need to develop a new task force or expertise to bring this project to the market?

The answers to these questions complement the creative aspects contained in the coverage of the show. This ultimate evaluation needs to be recorded and archived together with the coverage forms to maintain a record of why the project was one to pursue or why it was not.

Schedule Periodic Roundtables for Selection

Roundtables are quarterly or bi-monthly meetings that have the purpose of selecting the projects that will enter the conceptualization stage. Roundtables provide an opportunity for attendees to discuss content-based strategies and to choose the projects that match the criteria of selection. Changes in strategic direction could derive from these meetings after identification of a breakthrough idea. That is why roundtables are so important and crucial. Attendees of these meetings should be an extension of the evaluation team together with the incorporation of executives and individuals from other functional divisions who did not participate in the evaluation process. Having fresh eyes and ears to sense reactions and potential is vital. The leader of the roundtable process has to make a final recommendation to move the project to the next stage.

SECURE THE RIGHTS TO DEVELOP THE CONCEPT: THE OPTIONING OR PURCHASING PROCESS

When a project or show has been selected from among the ideas that entered the funnel for creative exploration, you must ensure that you have the rights to further develop the concept. Depending on the source of the material in question, you will have to negotiate the rights that will allow you to work and exploit the concept. Important: Before pitching the project to anyone in the industry, or posting your concept on the web directly for an audience, ensure that you have the intellectual property rights to do so.

Optioning. Rights optioning means "obtaining exclusive ownership and/or rights to a script, book, or story for a period of time long enough to develop and hopefully sell as a project" Kellison (2009, p. 289). A rights option agreement usually includes the names of the parties involved and the nature and duration of the option; compensation and payment terms; verification of ownership; specification about on-screen credits; if the purchaser can assign the rights to another party; and if the writer or producer is attached should the show get green-lit (Perebinossoff, Gross & Gross, 2005). Option duration agreements vary from periods of 3 months to periods of 18 to 24 months.

Purchasing. The purchase price depends on the negotiation and the type of material being negotiated, including but not limited to formats, third-party originals, and other previously published material.

Ideas from in house. In the case of original ideas generated inside a group or company, have a standard procedure in place to ensure that you have ownership over what is/has been done within the group or company. Different strategies to ensure ownership include:

- Register your material in a writer's guild, the copyright office in your country, or any other institution that will ensure that your material is secure in an intellectual property archive.
- If you are developing only original material and are hiring writers and creative individuals to develop the show, ensure that all of these individuals sign a work-for-hire agreement so that you keep the intellectual property rights. The writers will receive credits and compensation, but you will keep ownership of the intellectual property rights.

Name	Skill	Speciality	Relevant Work	Reference	Suitable For
AAAAA	Writer	Sicoms	*Frasier*	Worked with XXXX	Any Sitcom
BBBBB	Producer	Entertainment (Variety)		Newcomer	Project X
CCCCC	Production Coordinator	Variety			Project A
DDDDD	Writer	Game shows	*Wheel of Fortune*		Project Y

Figure 14-6. Sample production resources database.

- If you cannot pay for the work of the writers you need to engage to develop a show, the writers could be made partners in exchange for a posterior payment and a revenue share, but with you keeping the intellectual property rights.

INFORMATION MANAGEMENT WITH DATABASES

An important database to maitain is a creative and production resources database that compiles in one document all information about the writers, producers, and other important key individuals or companies that might be suitable for the content you are producing. In this database, highlight the previous work that these individuals have done and if possible include links to samples or demo reels for future reference. Specify the strengths the individuals being evaluated possess related to genre, skill, and quality of execution so that you can identify each individual later if they are a great fit for another project. To assess the other human resources you need, collect résumés, credits, personal contact data, demo reels, excerpts of previous work, and references from other individuals. An example of a creative and production resources database is shown in Figure 14-6.

All ideas submitted, releases signed, and evaluations made must also be kept in a database of documents. The database could be called an evaluations database. This database has to be accessible and clearly show information sorted by different criteria. Recommended is preparation of a workbook using spreadsheet software or, if you have the means, hiring an expert who can prepare a tailor-made solution that could be implemented and shared with other team members. Figure 14-7 is a simple representation of this database.

Project	Date Evaluation	Company	Location	Writer(s)	Evaluator	Genre	Sub-Genre	Material	Result
Project 1	8/1/14	AAA Productions	Mexico	FFF, GGG	GB	Variety	Late Night	Episodes 1, 2, 3	Recommend
Project 2	7/1/14	BBB Writers	Spain/UK	GGGG, HHH	GB	Sitcom	Mock Reality	Demo	Consider
Project 3	10/17/14	Writer AAA	Spain/UK	AAAA, GGG	AI	Sitcom	Traditional	Demo	Consider
Project 4		BBB Prod	UK	BBBB, PPPP	AI	Drama	Anthology	Demo	Consider
Project 5		CCC Prod	UK	JJJJ, IIII	AI	Drama	Telenovela	Scripts 1, 2, 3	Consider
Project 6		DODD Prod	Ireland	FFFF, RRR	AI	Drama	Teleseries		Pass
Project 7	10/30/14	EEEE, FFFF	USA	EEEE, CHHHH	GB	Reality	Franchise	Paper Format: 2 pp	Pass
Project 8	10/21/14	GGGG, HHHH	USA	NNNNN, OOOO	MR	Reality	Docu-Soap	Demo	Pass
Project 9	10/22/14	Writer AAA	USA		MR	Reality	Competition	Paper Format: 1 to 4 pp	Consider
Project 10	10/21/14	KKKKK, HHHH	USA	KKKK, UUUU	MR	Reality	Competition	Demo	Consider
Project 11	10/21/14	NNNN Media	USA	DODD, YYYY	MR	Reality	Competition	Paper Format: 1 to 4 pp	Consider
Project 12	10/22/14	TTTT Media	Netherlands	ZZZZZ, VVVV	MR	Game Show	Studio	Paper Format: 1 to 4 pp	Pass

Figure 14-7. Sample evaluations database.

15

CONCEPT DEVELOPMENT

Once an idea has been selected during the exploration process, the idea then enters a process of refinement and conversion. The process of refinement and conversion is also called "development in a vacuum" because development is done within the constraints of your creative bubble, without a definite client or a platform in mind. During this process, creative professionals put into practice the circle of discovery to procure differentiation and a unique value proposition (Figure 15-1). The end result is the project that will be pitched. In the pitch, the project is presented through key materials in print or in an aural/visual form.

Conceptualization entails three stages: think, write, and develop (Kellison, 2009). *Think*, the first stage, contemplates a definition of the nature of content, key target market selection, and anticipation of the resources that will be needed. *Write*, the second stage, involves preparation of a pre-bible. *Develop*, the third stage, includes feasibility analysis, creative validation, the preparation of specific sales materials, and updating of the catalog. Figure 15-2 presents all of the activities that the concept development process involves. All of these activities need to be taken into consideration to ensure conceptualization of a fiction or non-fiction project for any platform. These activities will now be discussed in detail.

CONCEPTUALIZATION STAGE 1: THINK

Define the Nature of the Content

The first step in the conceptualization process is determining a definition of the type of innovation the creative team will be working on. To do that, several actions are recommended:

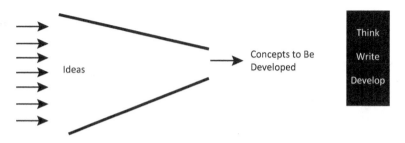

Figure 15-1. Funnel of exploitation and concept development stages.

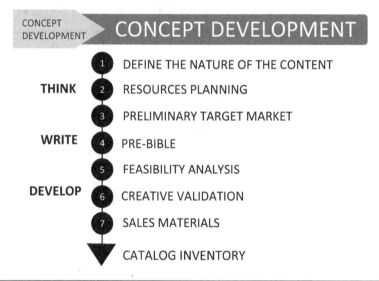

Figure 15-2. The concept development process.

- Assess the status of the idea selected and the recommendation made at the conclusion of the roundtable for this idea during the process of evaluation in an activity that entails these actions:
  - Assess the stage of development of the concept, either acquired from a third party or created internally, and determine the work needed to be done.
  - Assess the creative needs required to pursue the concept (writers, experts, and producers).
  - Ensure that you understand the nature of the rights. Indicate if the concept is 100% original. Has the concept been copyrighted? Does the concept come from a source or is it a format remake? Do the rights need to be negotiated? How long do you have the rights to work on the idea?

- Define what material stays and what goes. Make a complete analysis of the strengths and weaknesses the concept currently has in terms of story, characters, writers, and production house.
- Define the type of innovation: radical or incremental:
  - Is the concept a radical innovation, meaning an original or a potential breakthrough, or is it an incremental innovation to an existing genre, content, or program? Is the content a format that will be remade in the market?
  - Define the "it" factor of the concept. What makes it special?
- Identify the main drivers of the innovation: product (genre, characters, aesthetics, concept), technology, or business (see Chapter 9, *Drivers of Content Innovation*).
- Decide on the type of show this concept will be within your portfolio:
  - A "blockbuster" with global relevance, format potential, and the opportunity to establish a new business practice
  - A "bread and butter" that could be produced in a large volume of episodes with long run potential
  - A "niche" for specific audiences, thematic channels, or platforms
- Define the genre and the format of emission for the show. Is the genre clear or is it a hybrid? Experiment with variations of genre and decide about the best fit for the concept. For example, you might have a concept that seems to be a good fit for a reality show, but when you start thinking about it you realize that the concept is a better fit as a fiction show. Most concepts have a clear genre from the beginning, but some are susceptible to "what if" questions that can lead to creation of new interesting possibilities for exploration. During this phase of defining the genre and the emission format, a creative team looks at references (but not to copy them) and evaluates established genres and successful shows (or failures) from the past. Some of the most popular fiction genres include family drama, medical drama, romance dramedy, soap-style drama, teen drama, cop/investigative drama/action, and procedural or courtroom drama; teen sitcom, children's sitcom, prime-time sitcom, and mock-reality sitcom; single-camera comedy; telenovelas, teleseries, and soap operas; and mystery, science fiction, period, war, horror, and fantasy (Webber, 2005). Popular non-fiction genres are game shows, variety shows, talk shows, reality shows, talent competition shows, lifestyle shows, home improvement shows, educational shows, and award shows; documentaries and docu-soaps; newscasts, news specials, interviews, and sportscasts; musicals and special musical events.

FORMAT	DRAMA	COMEDY	DRAMEDY	REALITY
30 Minutes		X		
1 Hour				X
Weekly × 13				
Weekly × 24				
Daily × 60 (Teleseries)			X	
Daily × 120 (Telenovela)				
Webisode			X	
Movie		X		
Anthology				
Theater				
Music				

Figure 15-3. Matrix of genre and format of transmission.

A tool to evaluate genre and format of emission is the matrix for genre association shown in Figure 15-3. The columns correspond to genre. You determine them (drama, comedy, etc.). In the rows, mark the cells in which the show might be a good fit. The matrix in Figure 15-3 represents a show concept that could be developed as a half-hour sitcom or as a 60-episode teleseries, a webseries, a movie, or a reality show. This combination of possibilities defines the different paths available to you. Each of the different ways to exploit the show represents a business opportunity.

Once the genre is defined, you will be able to write a logline with a summary of the concept, including the key selling proposition of the show and the basic information of genre and alternative formats of emission. This information is for you only and is not to be given to clients.

Once you decide who you will pitch the show to, highlight one platform that is relevant for the client/channel. Highlight other platforms if appropriate. As an example, a drama series concept could be produced as a weekly soap drama series for the general market in the United States or as a three-part miniseries in the United Kingdom or as a 120-episode telenovela in Latin America with daily emissions. The concept of the show is the same, but from the beginning the different ways the show could be produced are defined. Another example would be a film that could be turned into a reality competition. Recent movies such as *The Hunger Games* and *The Maze* are examples. Of course, in a TV show version, the contestants will not suffer as in the movies, but the basics of competition and elimination could be pretty much the same.

Concept Variation	Platform							
	TV	Cable	Online	Mobile App	OTT	Print	Theater	Film
Children	X-						X	
Teen								
Teen adults		X	X	X				
Family								
M/F 18–49	X+		X	X	X	X	X	X
M 18–49		X						
F 18–49		X						

Figure 15-4. Matrix of broadcasters and audiences for a single concept.

Review the Market Potential

Once the show has been selected, review the role of the target market and define an objective, both in terms of potential buyers of the show and the audience. The target market helps define the edge and the tone of the proposal and becomes the basis of defining the on- and off-camera resources that could be employed. Market potential can also be defined using a matrix in which the creators can experiment with the different options at hand. Once again, some concepts have a clear target market embedded in the idea, but others can be adapted for various audiences to create more possibilities in terms of broadcasters and clients.

After defining the target market, define the target audience. For example, is the content for adult audiences in the open market or is it for a niche audience? Likewise, define the platform and potential clients who would be able to finance the show. Is the show for a cable channel, an on-line platform, or a mobile application? Figure 15-4 presents a matrix for assessing how a specific content could be exposed on different platforms and audiences. Each cell marked in the matrix as a possibility creates a business opportunity. Even if the show is launched for a specific audience, by using this matrix, variations of the show that could be rolled out afterward can be anticipated. Figure 15-4 shows that the concept is perfectly suitable for males and females ranging from 18 to 49 years old and could be exposed on traditional free TV (network), online platforms, mobile, and OTT and in variations that could be created for print, theater, and film. The matrix provides a full spectrum of what could be done with an innovative concept. Other cells with an X indicate that a version for children or another one for teen adults might be possible, of course with the necessary adjustments demanded by the target markets.

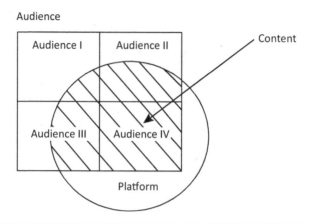

Figure 15-5. Intersection of markets (audiences and platforms).

The audience breakdown comes from analyzing the type of audience the content appeals to. Look into the demographic aspects and lifestyle information related to the habits, routines, and activities of your audience. Breakdown of the audience is of course made using the sense of discovery analyzed in Chapter 11 (*The Discovery Circle*) and has to do with identifying the values and interests you might be able to match in the show.

In regard to channels, the breakdown in Figure 15-4 contemplates the linear and non-linear platforms of exposition now available. Linear platforms include traditional free TV (network) and cable channels, whereas non-linear platforms include VOD, video rental and purchase services, dedicated websites, OTT channels, mobile applications, social media platforms, etc. This mix of channels allows you to evaluate the multiplatform aspects of the show and to also define at inception the need for different types of content to meet the needs of one or many platforms.

As with content assessment in Figure 15-3, each platform will intersect with various target audiences, so you can also experiment with the visual representation in Figure 15-5. As shown, content can span several audiences or be for a specific audience. In this example, the content serves four different audiences in different degrees, with Audience IV being the key audience for the show. Audience composition can have more than four quadrants, so use as many audiences as you need to explore the possibilities.

Let's suppose you are designing a TV game show, which producers envision as being a big family show for many audiences in prime time and in syndication time slots in the United States (Figure 15-6). So as a producer you could define family as being the primary audience, but also visualize the show as being done for other audiences. You could create a version for children or a purely teenage-

Concept Variation	Platform							
	TV	Cable	Online	Mobile App	OTT	Print	Theater	Film
Children	X		X	X (APP)			X	
Teen	X		X	X				
Teen adults	X		X	X				
Family	X+	X	X	X (APP)	X			
M/F 18–49								
M 18–49								
F 18–49								
MF > 50	X	X						

Figure 15-6. Examples of the different variations and platforms for a TV show that could be exploited throughout the life of the product.

driven show. You might even decide to come up with a version targeting older generations (50+) that could air on nostalgia-type channels or through Facebook communities of that generation. *The $10,000 Pyramid* is an example of a U.S. TV game show that began in 1973 as a single show and subsequently went on to air in seven versions. As shown in Figure 15-6, different versions could be exploited throughout the life of the product. By anticipating these possibilities, you can build a more solid business model around them.

Each possibility becomes a creative opportunity and becomes part of an umbrella title that could give birth to different versions of the same show. If we look at a second visual representation of the audience possibilities for a pyramid-type game show for TV (Figure 15-7), we find that family can still be defined as the primary audience but that older and teen audiences have almost as much potential opportunity. The children's market is also promising, so four different content and business opportunities could be pursued.

Plan the Resources

Based on the type of innovation conceptualized, you will need to engage creative professionals with different backgrounds and capabilities to work on the idea. Your team should be composed of:

- Content developers/writers
- Researchers
- Producers
- Production designers

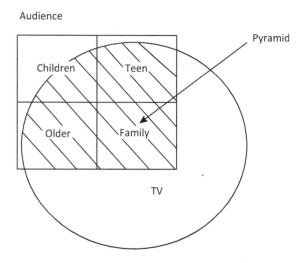

Audience

Pyramid

Children Teen

Older Family

TV

Figure 15-7. Audience possibilities for TV.

Content developers. Content developers write a description of the show without going into the details of the story, whereas scriptwriters engage in the writing of the scripts of the story that will be produced. In the case of a fiction program, a content developer works on the story first (the premise of the show), collects information, and prepares the characters and then engages in writing the episodes. A content developer is not necessarily the person who writes the show. Sometimes a writer does not have the patience to engage in the initial process if the idea is not their original idea. Therefore, a content developer might write the initial premise of the show and then have specialized writers to join the team to give the premise proper form in terms of genre and screenwriting; or a writer might have crafted the initial premise, but then a content developer(s) joins the team to prepare the pre-bible of the show before engaging in the actual writing. In the case of non-fiction content, fully writing the dynamics of the show is important. Game shows, for example, require significant scenario planning to contemplate all of the possible outcomes. This type of writing is done by specialized content developers.

Researchers. Researchers collect all necessary information for writers to consider. Researchers basically accumulate facts and keep diaries of brainstorming sessions and the information provided by writers (and content developers), such as life experiences that are connected to the concept to be developed.

Producers. Producers usually anticipate the nature of the production and work together with content developers to anticipate the strategy needed to produce the show, the complexity of the operation, and how to bring the concept to life.

Production designers. Production designers work on the visual concept of the show. They create sketches and collect references for set designs, locations, graphics, visualization aspects, photography, characters, etc. Production designers include directors, directors of photography, and set designers as well as other professionals.

CONCEPTUALIZATION STAGE 2: WRITE

Put the Pieces Together

The most important aspect of creating TV or multiplatform content is putting together all of the different elements that comprise an idea and what you have at hand to give it purpose. Before engaging in any script or synopsis writing, or anything else, collect and organize all elements of the idea. They allow you to spot insights that will help you to make a unique show (as discussed in Chapter 11, *The Discovery Process*).

During Conceptualization Stage 2, conducting research is of utmost importance. According to McKee (1997), research must be conducted at three levels: from memory, imagination, and facts. Research provides the knowledge that will lead you to creation of a show. To master the research concept, you have to fully examine your background.

Memory. First, put into perspective what you know from personal experiences that is related to the material you are preparing. What do you know? Where does it come from? This type of research has to do with memory. As McKee (1997) assured, this type of research is not about daydreaming but about writing down information that you remember from pertinent experiences and turning it into working knowledge.

Imagination. Second, activate your imagination. Put on paper details about what you would like the characters or participants to experience in the show. Imagination brings into context dreams, unrelated events, and hidden connections that you can only visualize, but when translated into scenes and events connected to the concept, they become the mass of your registered working imagination.

Facts. The third aspect of research is composed of facts, the information available all around you. Think about the sources of ideas we reviewed in Chapter

14 (*Exploration*). They all apply here as well. Look at sources that could provide references or information. Seek out studies and documents prepared in the field that will provide important tools and findings that could help to build the characters, the story, the setting, and the overall context of an entertaining experience.

Once you have completed your research and collected knowledge from personal experiences, your imagination, and the facts, the creative and writing process can be activated. This moment of activation propels the writing and design of the show. Remember that research does not replace creativity but instead fuels it. What is important during the writing and design process is that application is made of all of the methods related to the discovery process. The resulting elements need to be written down and organized in the form of a pre-bible.

Prepare the Pre-Bible

Pre-bible preparation is the actual process of creating a show, which occurs in a vacuum because only the nature of the content, the target market, and the resources at hand are considered. No definite client or platform is in mind. A pre-bible is generated *before* the show is commissioned and produced. A pre-bible contains a combination of creative information, specific production methodology, and budget and resources information. This document states the characteristics of the show and how to produce it and contains all of the information you need to give to clients during the sales process. Once the show is produced, the pre-bible is revised and becomes the bible.

Brainstorming and discovery sessions help to define the elements comprising the pre-bible. During Conceptualization Stage 2, addressing the importance of originality and avoiding the utilization of any references for the copying of sections, characters, or dynamics are important. The reason for using references is to know what is in the market and then to intentionally stay completely away from it. Pre-bible preparation must occur based on a plan and have specific deadlines. The content of a pre-bible depends on the genre of the series.

Fiction pre-bible. A fiction pre-bible contains:

- Concept/series description: The content description is a brief statement about the story and the quest the main characters will follow until the end of the series. Depending on the type of series (continued, episodic, self-contained, anthological, etc.), the concept must reflect the nature of the sub-genre and be clear to an individual reading the description.

Genre:	Specific genre and sub-genre
Format:	Number of episodes x duration of episodes
Target:	Key demographic to target
Frequency:	Emission strategy
Status:	Make reference to the stage of the process and the elements you have ready to share such as treatment, scripts, character description, etc.
Created by:	Author
Written by:	Writer

Figure 15-8. Summary of concept information.

- Summary of the show: The summary of the show contains the genre, format, target, frequency, and status and the creator and writer (Figure 15-8).
- Full synopsis: The full synopsis must state the entire story arc. In an episodic self-contained series such as *CSI* or *NCIS*, the synopsis is replaced by a description of the series and how the status quo of the main characters becomes the framework for showcasing an array of cases. If a show is both episodic and soap-style, such as *Scandal* or *Grey's Anatomy*, the synopsis revolves around the evolution of the characters. In an auto-conclusive drama series, the synopsis presents an opening statement of what the characters will go through but does not necessarily lead to revealing the ending. A teleseries or telenovela has a finite structure, so the story synopsis reveals the ending.
- Character description: The character description contains a full description of the character mix of the show. Likewise, depending on the nature of the show, the characters described here are usually main and regularly recurring characters in the series. In a soap-style continued series, the character list will be longer. For example, the list of characters for a telenovela ranges from 20 to 30 actors.
- Franchise potential: The term *franchise potential* has to do with the possibility the show has to be on the air for a long period of time. To analyze franchise potential, engage in making a projection of at least three seasons. This projection lets the creator know if the show being developed is for a long run or if it is more suitable for shorter installments such as miniseries, movies, and anthology series. A three-season projection is a good exercise for identifying how strong the premise is for the show to stay on the air for more than three seasons. If the premise of the show revolves around a gimmick, then its longevity will be in question.

- Sustainability: "Mapa de Ruta" (or story route) is a term used in Latin America to analyze the sustainability of teleseries and telenovelas. A creator needs to anticipate how the story will flow throughout (the story route) by producing a three-act breakdown and providing episodic loglines within each act. An individual reading the pre-bible should be able to see the episodic progression and evolution of the story. A story route is a great instrument for projecting how long the run of the show could be in terms of episodes (40, 60, or 120).

- Treatments and beat sheets for 101–105: Once the story route and the three-season projection have been completed, writers need to generate treatments and beat sheets for the first five episodes (101–105) of the season. This will allow visualization of the narrative formula of the show, the main events, the turning points, and the cliffhangers characterizing the narrative. Likewise, creators can experiment with new narrative structures that could lead to narrative breakthroughs in storytelling.

- First scripts: Just one great script could sell a show, but a group of three scripts can provide an even better understanding of the series and the story route ahead.

- Production design: Once the scripts are in place and the story is clear, producers might engage art directors and designers to work on the visual aspects of the show. Visual references are always welcome by clients.

Other elements in the pre-bible are the product integration capability analysis, budget template, production resources plan, tentative production plan, and the multiplatform design.

Non-fiction pre-bible. A non-fiction pre-bible contains:
- Content description: The content description is an explanation of the program and its objective. For a game show, you must specify the challenge and the prize that contestants will pursue.

- Summary of the show: The same as with fiction, the summary of the show clarifies the sub-genre, number of episodes, frequency of airing, locale of production, and the names of the creators and producers. If the show comes from a known successful source, ensure that this information is pointed out in the concept description.

- Rules of the game: If the content is a game show, prepare a complete scenario analysis of the dynamics of the show, exploring the possibilities of every single outcome, to come up with the rules, the do(s) and the don't(s), of the game. Remember: Cover every weak spot in the game so that the host always has the answers.

- Act structure: The show could be a continued elimination-type process week after week or a self-contained event that resolves in every broadcast. In either case, you need to define the act structure or phases of the show. The audience needs to enter a journey. Changes and phases will open the possibilities for surprises or more challenging situations for the audience while the show progresses. Reality competitions, for example, are usually set in a three-act structure in which the first phase concentrates on casting, the second phase focuses on the competition, and the final phase of the show selects the winner in a series of semi-finals and finals. The structure of a game show such as *Wheel of Fortune* is different. The structure is self-contained because all phases of the show occur in a single episode and each episode has a winner. For docu-soaps such as *The Kardashians* or *Jersey Shore*, a season might be based either on a three-act structure, so that events have the characters evolve as they do in a fiction show, or the characters could stay in status quo situation and face a series of circumstances that resolve within the same episode. The structure of non-fiction content varies, but the basis is conventions that are already established in the industry. Remember: If you master a formula, you can also "break it" to have a new way of structuring this type of content.

- Role of contestants: The same as when writing character descriptions in a fiction program, the characteristics and the role each contestant or participant plays in the show must be specified. Making recommendations about the type of individuals needed on the set and the mix of participants that will ensure conflict, drama, and entertainment is important.

- Role of the presenters: The host is key for a non-fiction show. The host is the master of ceremonies. The host is the "conductor" and also the person who causes the characters to showcase their true colors and perform according to their traits and roles within the show. The host leads and controls situations. The host knows the rules.

- Visual references in terms of look and sound: In non-fiction, art design is very important. Art design allows you to predefine the magnitude of the event you have envisioned. Is the program going to be a big visual undertaking such as *American Gladiators* or *Dancing with the Stars*? Will the program have something unique that deserves an engineering design such as the turning chairs on *The Voice* or the lifting curved screen in *Rising Star*? Is consideration being given to shooting the show at a remote location such as in *Machu Picchu* or *Patagonia*? Visual references let a reader and a client project what the show will look like on the air.

- Commercial appeal for product integration: Specify the potential the program has to integrate brands and sponsors.
- Resources: The same as with a fiction pre-bible, work on preparing a budget template, a production resources plan, and a tentative production plan with the length of the production.
- Multiplatform design: Ensure that you conceptualize the multiplatform nature of the show and present how second-screen integration comes into play, how online and mobile platforms complement the main platform, etc. Conceptualizing the multiplatform design also contemplates music, theater, radio, and other platforms of exposition (even traditional) that the show might be suitable for as well.
- Franchise potential: The franchise potential of a show is related to its global impact, longevity, international rollout potential, and adaptability as a format. The pre-bible is also called a "paper format" because it pre-establishes the recipe for making the show elsewhere. Once a show is produced for the first time, the recipe is proven and the paper format then turns into a format ready to be rolled out. As a result, the franchise potential is demonstrated.

Conceptualizing a format. If you are not conceptualizing an original TV show but instead are working on a format to be used in a new territory, a *new bible* adapted to conditions in the new territory will need to be created. The writers first assess the original bible and come to fully understand all of the creative and production aspects of the original TV show, do a market match, and identify possible weak spots that might need to be changed. The original bible contains a series of premises, procedures, and rules that guarantee that the show is done properly. The original bible contains the "recipe for success," which if changed might be a deviation from the original idea that made the show a success in the first place. The original bible also contains the formula for making the show, specifies the methodology, and provides rundowns, a database of activities, challenges, games, engineering specifics, software, security aspects, and copies of all of the original episodes. For fiction content, you might not receive an original bible but only the original scripts and screeners. In that case, you will have to plan for creating a bible that has character descriptions and a rewritten synopsis following the original aspects of the series but suiting the cultural expectations of the territory. Requesting deliverables from the original version, such as video episodes, pictures, scripts, ratings, press coverage, promotional strategies, and ancillary exploitation records, is recommended. With creation of a new bible for the format, the writers then become the specialists for the product in the new territory. The new bible must contain:

- Adaptation and a localization strategy: For fiction shows, assess and localize the elements of the story, the characters, and the episodic structure and nature of emission and establish if the new show will be a mirror adaptation or a work based on a format. In other words, will you use and replicate the scripts, stories, and dialogue from the original series? Will you make the same number of episodes? Will you air the show with the same frequency as the original? Will the show air daily or weekly? If the show is to have fewer episodes and air with a different frequency than the original, then you need to strategize and put in place a process of conversion to translate the original series into the new form. To illustrate, let's take the case of a conversion from a daily series such as a telenovela to a drama weekly series. In this case, you will need to simplify the world of the characters and rebuild the story progression to fit the number of weekly episodes per season. Usually, writers take the original premise and rewrite the episodes based on the original story, but they add new events or situations to make the premise culturally relevant. If this is the case, the show can end up growing on its own and finding a different path. An example of this type of adaptation is *Ugly Betty*, which was adapted from one of the most successful telenovelas of all time, *Yo soy Betty, la fea*. If a weekly series is being adapted into a daily soap, then you need to add additional layers of characters to the story to fit a 60- to 120-episode run. Other examples of this type of adaptation include *Nip/Tuck* in Colombia and *Grey's Anatomy* in Colombia and Mexico. Examples of mirror adaptations include *The Nanny* and *Married with Children* in several territories. Producers of non-fiction formats need to analyze the original set design, the visual infrastructure required, and the dynamics of the format to determine if the adaptation will mimic the original work in all regards (creative and production) or if it will have variations that better suit the market. These changes are usually approved by the rights holder. Changes might include adjustments to the set or if flexibility is in place, a total new set design may be required to fit the market constraints or capabilities.
- Production strategy for a new market: Production strategy for a new market has to do with production methodology. In the United States shooting is usually one episode at a time in a film style, while in other countries, producers might use a more efficient process by shooting several episodes at the same time, using a cross-boarding model

based on location. Producers also come up with innovative formulas to produce a show by combining the methodologies of the country of origin with their personal custom methodologies. These new processes bring innovative production approaches, called hybrid formulas of production, which incorporate the best practices from different countries.

CONCEPTUALIZATION STAGE 3: DEVELOP

Obtain Validation

The scripts and creative materials being prepared as part of the pre-bible need to be validated. Find internal sources of validation to help anticipate client reactions that might lead to improvements to the proposal before it even reaches a client. Review scripts, the synopsis, and the show dynamics to bring the material to a client as strong as it possibly can be. Do the same type of internal review for the validation of a program being conceptualized. You can use the same circle of validation that was discussed in Chapter 14 (*Exploration*). The process is iterative until the final material is agreed upon.

Part of the validation process requires information beyond scripts and paper. The more visual the validation process is the better the understanding will be of how the show flows. Depending on the resources you have, consider generating full pilots or tests. Each of these elements then needs to be run through a circle of validation to anticipate opportunities for improvement. Once validated, the material might need to be tweaked to make it better for a client. Self-produced pilots and tests should represent a full episode of the show. These elements are costly and risky. With the understanding that innovations are usually risky pilot endeavors, a pilot production still might be the most important element you could produce that would cause decision makers to take the concept straight to a series. So, if you have the means, and you believe the show is a breakthrough that people need to see, then make a pilot.

Feasibility analysis. A feasibility analysis entails analyzing all information gathered and developed and contained in the pre-bible to verify that the show is feasible to produce. The feasibility analysis process requires preparation of a budget, a production plan, and scenarios for making the show. The producers need to select a single location where all production could take place because the geographic location of the show will define part of the cost structure and the methodology of production—different location scenarios generate different budgets. Each budget represents a scenario. Buyers of content usually prefer to review different setups for producing the show. At this point, the budget does not need to be precise but instead an educated approximation using a ball-park figure that can be used when pitching the program or the content to a target platform.

Sales materials. Presentation of a project is one of the most important defining moments in the entire process. The materials you bring to a client are a summary of all of the creative efforts that support the project in a convincing and appealing way:

- Sales pitch: A sales pitch is a short version of the pre-bible. The sales pitch basically focuses on key creative elements, such as the concept, the synopsis, and the characters. For non-fiction programs, the pitch should briefly describe the dynamics of the show, specifying what happens in each episode or what the elimination or winning strategy is for a game show or a reality competition. For a character-driven reality, the pitch is all about the cast members and how unique they are. The sales pitch serves as a tool to open interaction with a client until the show is commissioned. The pitch must contain a summary of why the show is innovative and why it could be the next big thing. If you can say this in few words, then you have a winner. Always highlight the insight behind the idea and the origin of the idea because this is important background information that connects you with a client at a more honest and even an emotional level.
- Demo production: A demo (also known as a promotional trailer) must be a selling tool. Nothing is more convincing than an audiovisual representation of a project. An approximation of what the show is going to look like and be could explain in only few minutes what many pages might require. Having a great demo as a key selling tool could save time and get you a deal right away. A demo can be put together from original footage or from existing footage from other references.
- Pre-bible: If the pitch is successful, you could decide to deliver a full fleshed-out pre-bible for a client to further evaluate the show. Because the pre-bible contains detailed creative and conceptual information and also an approximation of the production design of the show, it gives the client a better sense of the show.
- Pilot (if self-produced): A pilot is a full-length representation of episode 101. The pilot will let the client see the concept in its full extension. Shooting a self-financed pilot is risky, however, because the feedback of a validating entity such as a client is always helpful in the process of refining the concept and mitigates one-sided influences. A good idea is to find partners or even engage the client in the making

of the pilot. If you are absolutely certain about the concept and idea, then go for it. Others involved could cause the concept to deviate from its innovative path. It's your call.

Update the Catalog

The end result of Conceptualization Stage 3 is updating your catalog of content with the new show. The concept joins all of the shows that you have developed and produced in the "pay," in other words, in your pipeline of content. The catalog needs to be organized and succinct. The information must be brief and presented in an orderly fashion, usually organized by genre or sub-genre. Each page in the catalog should state in a visually rich form, the title, logo, a brief description of the show, the production auspices, and a summary of the show properties (number of episodes, genre, author, locale, production house, etc.). (*Note*: The catalog also keeps track of different materials you have developed and serves as inventory of the scripts, pre-bibles, demos, and pilots. If a show has already been produced, the catalog has information about the trailers and promos and the best episodes to show clients.) When updating the catalog is complete and materials are ready to be presented to clients, the sales process will begin.

This chapter has presented in detail the activities that need to be taken into consideration to ensure the conceptualization of a fiction or non-fiction program for any platform. The next chapter will discuss the sales pitch and marketing considerations needed to move the concept through the value chain of innovation.

16

SELLING THE CONCEPT

When the entire catalog (the shows you have developed) is set and the materials are ready to be presented to clients, the sales process begins. The value chain of innovation now enters a fourth stage that entails pitching and closing deals. During this stage, a process of direct validation begins with the clients or platforms, brands, and any entity that may be able to contribute the resources needed to produce the content. This process of validation leads to responses that could lead to four possible outcomes:

- Commissioning of the show (i.e., straight to production of a series)
- Further development of the product
- Revision of the concept
- Total rejection of the product

Commissioning of the show. The first outcome, or commissioning of the show, is related to closing a deal with a platform, which activates subsequent development and production of the series.

Further development of the product. The second outcome of the validation process derives from a client who likes the product but considers the idea to need further development before the client is willing to agree to enter the production stage. During this process, the idea is adapted according to the client's needs, but production is not guaranteed. This outcome might be accompanied by a pilot deal.

Revision. The third outcome, revision of the concept, occurs if the idea is received in the market with mixed responses. In this case, you take constructive feedback and redevelop the concept if you consider that the revised premise has potential and you sense that the client might welcome the revised idea at a later time. Revision of the concept also opens up an opportunity for you to present the project to a different group of platforms. For example, a show might have been pitched as a reality, but soon after starting the selling process, you receive feedback from various platforms or a key client suggesting that the show might work best as a comedy. By paying attention to what a key client says, you might secure a second chance to present the revised concept to that specific client or to a different pool of platforms that were not included in the initial identification of possible commissioning entities.

Total rejection. The fourth possible outcome of the validation process is total rejection, obviously indicating that the project will not be commissioned within the array of possible clients you have selected. At this point, you could proceed in one of two ways: not pursue the project or redevelop it.

Now that we have a clear understanding of the four-outcome validation process, we are ready to activate the activities that define the sales endeavor.

THE SALES ENDEAVOR

Three different activities define the sales endeavor: preparation, customer relationship management (commissioning), and closing the deal:

- Preparation
  - Identify the right people to sell the content.
  - Know your inventory (the catalog).
  - Set objectives and goals regarding the client's landscape.
- Customer relationship management
  - Client validation
  - The pitch (bringing what is relevant to a client)
  - Building and managing relationships
  - Follow up
- Closing the deal

Preparation

If you are the creator of the content, you are the main sales person responsible for moving the show forward. Because you are responsible for the selling efforts, you must have a database containing the rights' availabilities, restrictions, summaries of concepts, and potential clients. As the main seller of the show, you must also have ready a 5-minute "elevator" pitch with reasons why the show is "worth it" and unique. If, however, you have the means to activate a sales force, then you must ensure that you have the right people to lead and handle the selling process.

Identify the right people. The right people should mainly be facilitators who specialize in the task of selling content. They also need to be trained. The sales team needs to know what it is selling. They need to understand the number of elements you have available and what is it that these elements offer.

Know your inventory. Know your inventory refers to catalog control. As part of the sales strategy, be aware of the life cycles of all of your products in the catalog. How long can you keep these products relevant? If you are pitching to all networks, titles could be "alive" until the pitch season is over, so the life cycles could be rather short. If the territory is vast and includes many countries, depending on the territory where you are pitching the show, consider using an average life cycle in the catalog that could go range from 2 to 3 years. Within the catalog you will have to put whatever is fresh upfront. (Note that the life cycle of the shows in a catalog is different from the life cycle of a show in production and a show on the air. The life cycle in a catalog is tied to the number of options you can devise for the concept in the market. For example, if a new outlet appears, then the life cycle of the product might be extended. You can keep shows in the catalog for as long as you wish—the life of a show all depends on relevancy, reactions, and ultimately the number of people who see the show. The catalog is your list of assets, so do not discard anything because you never know when a concept you thought was dead might be the right fit for another window of exposition.

Set objectives and goals. Setting the right objectives and sales goals is important. How many shows do you intend to pitch, sell, and eventually have on the air at a given time based on the bandwidth you have to process it? You might already have a clear view of your potential market, but ensure that you estimate properly and set objectives that are achievable. Do not build plans around excessive speculation. Start slowly, grow, and then speculate based on your personal resources and the tangible reactions. You must select the shows you think have the greatest chance to make a strong impact. Make selection your special emphasis and dedicate the necessary time and resources.

Once the catalog is ready and the objectives are clear, the sales operation is activated. At this point customer relationship management (CRM) strategies need to be implemented to guarantee efficient and successful sales efforts.

Customer Relationship Management

Customer relationship management (CRM) is a concept that ranges from the emotional aspects of customer relations to automated marketing tools with profit projection capabilities. From a quantitative and marketing standpoint, CRM has to do with follow up, quantification, and realization of opportunities and leads. CRM also urges you to conduct research and market matching.

Client validation. Nothing is worse than bringing the wrong concept to a client, something they do not need, or bringing a project to a client who has no financial resources. For that reason, market matching is crucial. Market matching consists of matching content with the profile and identity of the brands that distinguish your clients from one another. Understand who a target client is. Gaining understanding of a target client is when strategic research comes into place. At this point, you already know the channels that might be suitable for your concept. Convey that during your meeting. Be knowledgeable and prepared. Otherwise, a commissioning client will not see the value in your proposal and your product will be rejected at an extremely important validation point.

The pitch: bring what is relevant. Understanding your clients will allow you to define what you need to bring to a certain client. Depending on the nature of a meeting, you could come prepared with anything ranging from a verbal pitch to a very sophisticated presentation of a fully produced pilot for a series. You must come ready to impress. My recommendation is to always bet on visual materials, either in the form of a demo or a well-designed slide presentation. Short demos of projects are the best way to convey a message quickly. Short demos provide a sense that the show is actually happening. Clients become more enthusiastic. Strongly suggested is having the following materials as part of your sales kit:

- A sales pitch that is a short version of the pre-bible, including a basic description of the show and the main elements that make the show a potential innovation
- A demo that includes an aural/visual short video about the content
- The pre-bible with a folder anticipating the look and feel of the series
- Script 1 for fiction
- An estimated budget

For the first meeting, just bring whatever you have that is the most visual. A sales pitch and a demo will be perfect. The sales pitch could also be prepared using presentation software such as PowerPoint or Keynote. Make the presentation memorable, visually relevant. If the client is interested, bring other appropriate material. For example, does the client want to read more? Does the client want to know the cost of producing the show? Does the client have a specific place where production of the show is preferred? Does the client need to have various cost scenarios? You must be ready to provide the answers so that you do not lose momentum.

Build and manage relationships. Building and managing relationships entails dealing with customers. Customers think they are always right even if they are totally wrong. They know best. Their approach, feedback, and willingness to share who they are and what they want, however, will lead you to knowing them well. So at this stage, you also need to be willing to "let them manage you" if they love your idea. The instant customers become involved, they think they own you, so you must be ready for that—in other words, teamwork expands with customer involvement. Encourage a client to tell you what they need so that you can incorporate their expectations and deliver in a very effective way. If you are targeting a commissioning entity, for example, you have to come up with ideas that are relevant to their core values, brand, and target audience. Building and managing relationships with your clients is not just key but also the ultimate strategy to improve your possibility of succeeding and being funded. The process defines what you will be producing, exposing to an audience, and maybe turning into an innovation. A client has the keys to the kingdom, so you need to understand the client in such way that the client feels that you are part of their team and not just a vendor. When a client says "yes" to your pitch, the client *wants* to do the project with you, triggering a process of collaboration with the client. This obviously triggers the question: how far can you let a client manage the relationship if their feedback is turning the concept into something else? This is a very difficult question to answer. Sometimes the best approach is to keep moving forward, putting the original project aside for a better occasion, embracing the new, and hoping for the best. Nevertheless, you must also raise your concerns with the client and seek a solution that works to the advantage of the project. The idea is to work in collaboration as one big team. The client is buying your show because the client believes in it. You must maintain an open mind that things can change—flexibility is key. Pay attention to the signs when a show is taking a sudden U-turn. Internalize and analyze the implications. At that point it is up to you. If what is coming out as a result of their feedback is great as well, then embrace it, but if not and you anticipate trouble, share your concerns. Always try to find a solution before leaving a deal on the table. As you can see, it is all about managing the relationship. If there is no agreement, then it is your call about continuing or not. I always say that there are projects for clients and clients for projects. There needs to be a match. Usually a show does not move forward if the match is not there—which in the end is the healthiest solution to the situation. Everyone moves on, and you continue looking for that perfect match.

Clients are not only TV channels but also brands or a person or an entity with financial resources. You will be working with their money, so they have to be, and feel, in control. If a relationship is already in place from CRM, a client could end up handing you full creative control.

For TV channels with production and programming vertically integrated processes, the client is an internal department or division. In-house producers pitch projects to their programming counterparts and the process of validation and sales are pretty much the same as explained earlier. The same CRM principle applies.

If you are making your own content that you intend to post directly to viewers on Facebook, then you are in control and can do what you consider is best. In this case, the audience has a rare direct first opportunity to tell you whether they like your content or not. Amazon has taken this type of audience validation very seriously and is launching a slate of original programs in the form of pilots that target their Amazon Prime clients, giving them the chance to provide direct feedback on what they like. Based on the responses, Amazon selects the shows that will be produced. Amazon is bypassing rounds of internal validation and betting on increasing its chances to succeed by creating engagement that involves customers in the decision-making process at the pilot stage. In this scenario, Amazon is the client for submitted content but is making the decision of creative control and acceptance in association with the audience.

Clients know very well what they want, and even if they cannot say so upfront in a conversation or a survey, they know that if you pitch something that does not fill a need they have with an audience, they can reject the pitch and the show will not happen. The audience therefore becomes your main client when you have the means to produce content and showcase it directly to them. The client in this case might be a user-generated platform such as YouTube or Vimeo.

Different terminology exists to describe customer relations. Some call it customer relationship management (CRM). Others such as Newell (2003) call it customer management of relationships (CMR). I am adding *customers in charge of the relationship* (CCR) to the terminology. The interesting concept that Newell (2003) brought to the table, which I fully support, was that clients want to be in control and you have to be willing let them be in control. When you have established a name in the industry for yourself and people have come to expect a certain highly creative product from you, then you have grasped the validation of your audience and the client and the process will balance out. You might say that you are now in control. Nevertheless, the audience and the customers constantly change and evolve, so their needs change. You must ensure that you evolve with them and anticipate what they might need soon.

The CRM process is not just about validating, pitching, and selling. It is about building relationships and understanding the nature of these relationships to make them sustainable, robust, and profitable.

Follow up. CRM helps you to compile information on your clients, track your conversations, and make plans for what to pitch and when. Follow up is absolutely crucial. If you cannot undertake the follow-up function, find time to do so or delegate this important task to a qualified individual. Sometimes you even get so embedded in your own creative processes that you forget to follow up. When that happens, you start "fading out" from a project. People forget and then the project is off.

Another important aspect of CRM is that it helps you concentrate on the most important projects, those that will ultimately represent 80% of your business. You can keep track of the most important projects by quantifying the revenue that each prospective business opportunity might generate. Anticipating potential revenue allows you to give extra care to the projects that might be a turning point for your economic bottom line. CRM is a tool that can be implemented both as a philosophy and as a software application. Inexpensive mobile applications that help you keep track with your follow up are available for downloading.

Closing the Deal

The closing the deal activity comprises the iterative process of negotiation between the rights holder and the entity wanting to produce the show. Contracts are prepared. In these contracts, all key aspects of utilization, exploitation, and revenue sharing tied to the property are laid out.

Other Key Personnel in the Selling Process

Another key activity within production is the assurance of funding and the partners necessary to make the show. During the negotiation stage, commissioning entities or financiers of the show provide the economic resources to turn an idea into a tangible asset. Once these resources are locked in, the development and production processes are activated. The resources are secured by the individual in charge of the sales team, an individual who must have the profile of a facilitator.

RECOMMENDED READING

The Result Driven Manager Series (2006). *Connecting with Your Customers.* Boston: Harvard Business School Press.

Dyche, J. (2002). *The CRM Handbook: A Business Guide to Customer Relationship Management.* Upper Saddle River, NJ: Addison-Wesley.

17

DEVELOPMENT

When a show has been selected and commissioned by a client, the development process starts. To make a show fully relevant for a client, the development process entails working very closely with the commissioning partner. The development process is all about creativity, innovation, and meeting expectations at the client level. The process demands the application of the discovery circle throughout to come up with insights that will surprise the client and make the show stronger. You have to make the client part of your innovation circle and explain how you operate. At this point, you have already enticed the client thanks to an innovative concept with innovative features. Now is the time to make these innovative features even better from the client's point of view. If the client buys into the collaborating style of your operation, then the probability of making a successful show will be higher. Remember: According to the discussion in Chapter 16 (in the section about customer management), the client must be part of your process and you must be part of theirs.

Not all clients of course open up in the best possible way or understand that they need to collaborate with your work so that you can do it "right"—to their satisfaction. Some clients just assume that you will solve every matter with no major feedback or details provided by them about what they consider to be wrong. These clients might not approve of a certain aspect of the show, but they do not tell you clearly what is not working for them. These clients are difficult because they do not want to compromise their position—they would rather play it safe than to express an opinion. Maybe they don't think they are responsible for telling you what to do. Most of the time, believe me, these clients *do* know what's wrong—what's not working for them. You just have to encourage them to voice their feedback and concerns so that you can deliver what *is* right.

Clients such as studios and networks like to be in control and for that reason they involve creative executives in the development process. These executives are knowledgeable in both the creation and the production processes and will provide specific feedback throughout the making of the content. They actually want to produce the show—and that actually is great. When you get that level of commitment from a client, the show is going to happen. Clients "gone wrong," however, are those who think they are so savvy. These clients are controlling and bring so many no-no's and rules to the process that they end up killing the creative empowerment of the team. The writers no longer feel good about the quality of their work. The development process suffers and stalls. Ideal is finding balance. Balance is what you need to attain. By establishing good relationships with challenging clients, you get to know them and they get to know you—and magic happens.

Development is about structuring and giving depth to what has been created in the concept development stages (discussed in Chapter 15, *Concept Development*). Depth is accomplished by working with a client to find out what needs to be addressed in terms of brand values and audience expectations. Usually what happens in this process is that you find some orthodoxies or rigid rules that could affect the edge and differentiating factor that the show had when conceived and pitched to the client. Working with a development process based on orthodoxy is a recipe for failure because orthodoxies prevent creative producers and writers from taking real chances. The more open and willing a client is to break the mold, the more innovative the content will be. When orthodoxy is identified, you have to talk to the client about it. Let the client know that you are all about taking advantage of any possibility to innovate. You and the client might have an opportunity right in front of your eyes.

Sometimes brand values that are auto-imposed by the heads of a channel become orthodoxies that do not allow the channel to succeed. When you identify orthodoxy of this type, use the strength of your content to help the client understand the opportunity that is right front of them.

An innovation can get stalled in what is called "development hell" as a consequence of some mismatched criteria between the creators of a show and a commissioning entity (for example, how decisions are made, the measurements of success, etc.). Many concepts do not pass this impasse. Precious ideas are then shut out and never make it to the production stage. On occasion the rights revert to the creators of the developed content who may take it to another production house that will green-light the content.

DEVELOPMENT TYPES

Show development is of two types: a show picked up for a series and a show under consideration by a commissioning entity.

A show picked up for a series. For a show that has been picked up for series, either by a commissioning entity or by the owner of the rights who has the capital means, development entails the design of a full series or a show. This process might take 2 to 12 months, depending on the complexity of the show and the affinity and interaction between the creators of the show and the commissioning entity. During the development process, depending on the genre, the elements to generate are:

- Fiction: The synopsis, treatment, character descriptions, season projection, and beat sheet for all episodes (The writing process then goes on until completion of the last episode of the series.)
- Non-fiction: The treatment for the show, season projection, dynamics or mechanics, breakdown of content per episode, and casting (if a character-driven reality) (The writing process then goes on until completion of the last episode of the series, a process tied into preproduction of the show.)

A show under consideration by a commissioning entity. For a show still under consideration because the commissioning entity wants to first see the show developed and piloted to decide if it is a clear fit for the brand, development entails the designing of the core elements of the show. For a fiction show, development entails writing at least three scripts, a projection of the full series, and production of a full pilot tailored to the needs of the brand. This process might be shorter, but it usually takes between 3 and 4 months. In the United States, shows are developed first and a first script is written. If approved, the show enters the pilot stage. If the show succeeds, it then enters the production stage.

THE DEVELOPMENT PROCESS

The development process applies to both fiction and non-fiction programming and entails several steps:

- Prepare a development plan. All processes need a timeline—deadlines and activities that are mapped out in the order in which they need to occur—prior to activation of the production process.
- Assemble the writing and creative teams by genre and functionality.
- Implement the creative process.
- Revise the pre-bible and adapt it to the brand.
- Define the type of innovation (genre, character, story, narrative, aesthetics, production process, technology, or business, etc.). What is needed to turn the show into something unique? At this point, explore

different ways to enrich the story. Remember: What is in the pre-bible was done *before* any feedback from the client. Now, things could have changed, so be ready for that possibility. Without giving up what you think to be unique in your show, make the show relevant for the brand that will ultimately accommodate your idea. Use an iterative process of feedback to make the show stronger. This is the time to explore. Create an atmosphere of fun with the client when analyzing different ways to make the show not only relevant for the brand but also unique.

- Start writing:
  - Work with drafts of scripts, run downs, and the dynamics of the show that need to be validated first by the internal group and then by the client. This process of validation generates revisions and notes that will enrich the show. When individuals with fresh eyes read or review creative material, they might see what you did not.
  - Review production constraints. When the script, rundown, and structure of the show have been approved, they need to be normalized based on production constraints such as the size of the set, number of locations allowed per episode, number of characters that can be incorporated for budget reasons, etc. The best-case scenario is when the constraints are minimal. Unfortunately, there will always be at least one.
  - Conduct table reads. Table reads are of two variations, one for fiction and another for non-fiction content. After the table reads are finished, the writers will deliver a shooting script:
    - Fiction: Table reads for fiction are done with the writers and the creative producers who are involved in development of the story and the actors who will be in the show. These table reads occur throughout the writing process because the writers need to discuss and exchange ideas, collaborate, and detect possible weaknesses. Table reads with the creative producers target soft spots in the story and give the writers an opportunity to collect ideas so they can make the situations depicted in the story more surprising and believable. Table reads with actors involve reading the scripts with the actors. During these table reads, the actors finally give a voice to the characters in the scripts. The actors can provide ideas regarding how a character might speak, think, and behave. This validation with the actors helps to redefine the characters and improve the nature of the script.

- Non-fiction: Table reads for non-fiction do occur, but they are dependent on the sub-genre: news, game shows, documentary, reality, reality competition, sports, etc. For game shows and reality competitions, beyond reading the script, you must do field or studio testing to evaluate the concept for flaws. Studio testing can be done in an open space with props that emulate the different elements you are planning to have in place for the show. Members of your production team and people who do not know anything about the concept can be used to run through the dynamics of the show and validate what was written.

- Write, plan, and produce a pilot. A pilot is usually the first episode of a series or what is known as episode zero. Producing an episode zero allows decision makers to assess the power of the show's concept. This pilot needs to be as close as possible in quality to what the show will be if accepted. Do not go for the safe choices. A pilot should have the elements that will make the series stand out.

- Evaluate production design. If applicable, explore new aesthetic formulas: a new set design, revolutionary wardrobe design based on recently spotted trends, a different take on photography or camera framing, etc.

- Assess and finalize the budget and production resources plan for the series based on a new development.

- Deliver a new creative bible of the original show tailored for a specific customer and audience and get ready for production, the next step.

At this point, you are one step away from producing the magic and getting close to an audience that might ultimately give you the thumbs up. The production process starts when the development process has been completed and the team has been hired and is ready to implement the execution plan. Production, the sixth activity in the value chain of content innovation, will be addressed in the next chapter. Production is the final execution—the realization of the strategy, the idea, and the months of effort spent developing the show that will be packaged and presented to the audience.

18

PRODUCTION

After completing the development process for a show, the concept enters the production stage, which is composed of three phases:

- Preproduction
- Production or principal photography
- Postproduction

WHO IS IN CHARGE OF THE PRODUCTION PROCESS?

Individuals who deliver—executors—should be in charge of the production process. Executors include the show runner, the production team, writers, engineers, operations and logistics specialists, the cast, musicians, editors, and special effects artists. In other words, the entire team should be comprised of people who deliver. During the making of the show, additional functional areas, each with the specialized capacities that are needed to realize the original dream of the creator of the show, include administration, engineering, business affairs, information technology, etc.

PREPRODUCTION

The preproduction plan kicks in when the development process is over. Purchasing, hiring, and writing are essential activities at this time. Preproduction phase duration varies according to the type of show. A good producer anticipates and negotiates the best possible time frame needed to be able to prepare all of the necessary details to make the production process a smooth one.

During the preproduction phase, the producer secures all of the resources needed to make and deliver the show. A production resources plan was prepared during the development process, but with the activation of preproduction, the producer needs to start looking at what is feasible under the economic conditions that received final approval from the commissioning entity.

The preproduction phase serves as a backdrop for discovery and embraces the generation of insights. People are inspired, motivated, communicating, and connected thanks to having the opportunity to make a show. When people share the same goals, an overall positive atmosphere opens the path for finding, developing, and designing creative solutions. Not all of these solutions will work, but they represent attempts to make something better even before the cameras roll.

Progression of the entire preproduction phase is based on creative validation, administrative control, and logistics. In terms of creative considerations during the preproduction phase, assimilation of the discovery circle throughout is a must. During this phase, all creative personnel will be participating in a process of internal and external validation. Internal validation occurs within the team. Writers, producers, directors, etc. intervene and make decisions about the story, the dynamics, and the overall aesthetics of the show. Once these elements have been validated internally, they will be presented to the client for external validation.

Internal validation. The process of internal validation ensures that whatever is going to be placed in front of the camera is in near-perfect shape. On occasion, however, excessive preparation and revisions change the essence of what the concept was intended to be and derails production.

External validation. The process of external validation helps production get "in sync" with the commissioning entity. From the beginning, if both groups are not clear in terms of expectations, the show could end up in an endless process of revisions that will cause the show to take a nonorganic direction. For that reason, understanding when revisions have achieved their goals and ensuring that the process does not take the initially validated concept down an unexpected nonorganic path is important.

In the case of fiction programming, writing that started in the development process continues. Design of the series is in full force, the cast is contracted, and table reads start. Actors read the scripts. In the case of non-fiction shows, the dynamics are tested. This is when the director and the director of photography establish the visual strategy for the show. Set and production design artists anticipate the look and feel and the aesthetics approach for the show. Editors and audio designers anticipate the rhythm and type of sound design that will be featured in the show.

Administrative control. In the preproduction phase, administrative control has to do with the producer ensuring that the proper production resources plan is in place and being executed. It is during this phase that the cash flow is activated in full force. Close attention to cost control is essential. The state of mind during this phase is anticipation of deviations and cost control.

Logistics. During the preproduction phase, logistics entails coordination of the entire team and finding new ways to be efficient throughout to make production progress smoothly. Logistics in this sense helps anticipate the best ways to produce the show. This anticipation produces insights for finding revolutionary ways to do things that either usually take too long or traditionally have been difficult or impossible to produce. Logistics in this context involves transportation, operations, utilization of resources, use of calendars, etc. Once the preproduction phase is fully executed, principal photography starts.

PRODUCTION/PRINCIPAL PHOTOGRAPHY

The production phase is also known as principal photography. Once principal photography starts and a show is on the air, the producers must ensure sustainability through the constant injection of high-energy and high-impact events. Constant revitalization of the show occurs through use of the discovery circle process, which helps to revamp the show and make it sustainable over time. This revitalization process ensures that surprises and new insights keep the show alive through the generation of twists and turns in the story. Figure 18-1 is a graphic representation of how creative sustainability is maintained through constant reinvention and revamping of a show. After the show has aired, you can start the rollout of the final product as a finished product to be distributed internationally as a "can" (finished and ready for viewing by audiences) or as a format.

Anticipate plateaus in the show and boredom in the audience. You must provide a worth-waiting-for viewing surprise every time the show airs if you want the audience to engage and stay connected with the show. Revitalizing or reinventing a show that has reached a plateau, however, does not mean changing the show completely. Remember: The show already has an essence that must be honored throughout, so proposed changes have to be related to assuring the longevity of the show. Reinvention is to extend the show's life cycle.

As a creator, you must also be able to anticipate when a show can no longer continue. Better is ending the show's life cycle on a high note than to be almost forgotten or worse to be cancelled.

When a show is on the air, the process of validation occurs every time an audience in any platform watches an episode. The viewers react and decide

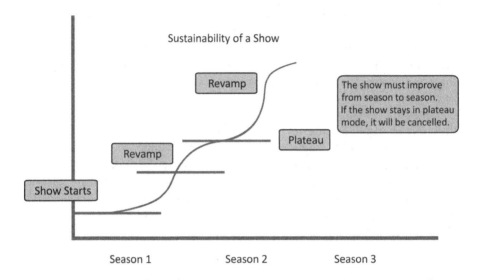

Figure 18-1. Creative sustainability maintained through constant reinventing and revamping of a show.

whether what they watched was good or not. If they liked it, then the "ratings are in" and the show stays on the air.

POSTPRODUCTION

When a show has been recorded in the field, in a studio, or as a combination of both, the video collected is processed in what is known as the postproduction phase. The postproduction phase entails visualization of the material recorded, organization and selection of material, video editing, addition of video special effects, colorization, and overall sound and video post (synchronization). This process serves as a validation platform of the material that has been shot. It is in the postproduction phase that we realize if a show has been perfectly shot or if mistakes have been made. During this validation process, the producers in charge of the process might decide to reshoot something they consider to have not come out right. In this situation, the editor and associate producer in charge of the process make recommendations if they notice inconsistencies or the need to add material that could help clarify and identify the intended message.

Although going back to the field is often not an option, doing so is possible if visualization of an inconsistency(s) occurs when a show is still in production. If the principal photography phase for the show has been completed, however, the possibility of fixing or reshooting the material could be much more difficult or represent extra costs. Video editing is, of course, the best way to optimize material that has already been shot, but if the shooting was inconsistent or poorly done, then there is nothing the video editor can do but accept the results.

The postproduction phase is the last process before a show is presented to the audience. This is the time to "make sense" out of the entire process of development and production. This is the moment of truth. If the moving images do not depict what looked like a great idea on paper, then the content will not succeed—it might even be stored or cancelled. This is why all of the processes of strategy, creativity, discovery, preparation, and execution must be so well connected. If any process is poorly implemented, it will certainly show in the end. Video editors are not magicians. One person and one computer cannot salvage the work of an entire team. All processes must be done right so the video editor's work can also shine.

Once postproduction is completed on a show, the final product is presented to the client, ultimately loaded onto the platform (broadcast, cable, digital, etc.), and exposed for the final validation test—the audience. This is when an invention hits the market and becomes an innovation if the market embraces it. If embraced, the process implemented to produce the show becomes a process validated by the industry and diffusion starts.

Once the show has been completed and the innovation has been certified, the whole process starts all over again. Further exploitation also starts and diversification of the concept through different platforms is achieved.

This chapter will now explore securing innovation, incremental innovations, reinventing and reengineering a show, franchise potential, and extending the life cycle of a show.

SUSTAINING INNOVATION

How do we create innovation and sustain it? The work of sustaining a show is definitely a task of creating incremental innovation all the time. Taking from what we learned in Chapter 9 (*Drivers of Content Innovation*), content innovation has several drivers:

- Story-driven: New seasons always demand new stories and new character revelations by the introduction of new plots that surprise audiences and extend the life cycle of the show:
  - Be aware of the effect of "story killers." Story killers eliminate the signature tension of a show. For example, when Mr. Sheffield and Fran Fine got married in the sitcom *The Nanny*, the tension was gone, the surprise was gone, and the mission had been accomplished by the characters.

- Reinvent during an emission period. Telenovelas always have a beginning and an end but on occasion go beyond the final episode of the first season for a second season. For example, a telenovela can start with an 80- to 120-episode run and if successful could be extended within the same run and stay on the air for up to 3 years. Reinvention of the story occurs within the same period of emission—the first and only run—but once the characters accomplish what they have been fighting for the entire time, the show is over. We do not need to see the characters have a happy ending.

- Understand the life cycle of the show you are producing. As the creator of the show you need to project for at least three seasons what will happen in the course of the story. In the case of game shows, however, the situation is different. For example, if a game show starts as a prime-time sensation, then you must find ways for the show to survive in the programming grid by anticipating repurposing, other windows of exposition, and different time schedules.

- Know where to introduce surprises. One way to analyze where to introduce a surprise is by looking at the show's structure in a three-act way. In the case of a fiction series with a 24-episode run per season, for example, every 8 episodes you could do a special episode in which something unexpected happens that apparently changes the course of the story. In that episode, a beloved character could die or a new status quo could be set up without changing the essence of the story. But be careful with these special episodes because if you change the status quo too much you might be changing the premise of the show and the audience could reject it. Ensure that you introduce characters and stories that enhance the status quo but do not change it.

- Character-driven: Introduce a new set of characters to generate a new plot and to extend the life cycle of a show. In the case of a game show, changing the host triggers a new era for the show.

- Aesthetic-driven: Introduce a new technological and visually surprising element that makes the show modern and more appealing, bigger, and better. The show might become so successful that you celebrate by scaling up aesthetics.

- Technology-driven: Add elements that reflect current technological advances to make the contestants interact within the game or make the audience at home participate and interact with the show. Technology could also be incorporated in fiction programs through second-screen initiatives, multiplatform narratives, and the showcasing of new ways of communication within the show.

- Game dynamics-driven: Introduce new surprises, improve the prize, or add a new twist in the path to winning the prize.
- Programming strategy-driven: Maintain a show on the air is by moving it to a more suitable time slot. For example, beloved shows such as *Wheel of Fortune* and *Jeopardy* started as prime-time successes. These game shows had very successful runs in prime-time schedules, but erosion of their audiences put them at the edge of cancellation. These shows were reinvigorated when they became daytime must-see daily shows. Likewise, the syndication model of television allows shows to survive. In syndication, a show goes from being a weekly special to becoming a daily viewing habit throughout the year (a bread and butter show). The *Wheel of Fortune* and *Jeopardy* game shows have been on for generations. They became proven concepts with a formula that did not necessarily die. If you get to create and produce a show like one of these, believe me, you have made it.

Even though many valid strategies can extend a show, the most important aspect of these improvements is that they must feel organic, not forced. People realize when you are forcing the extension of a show.

Examples of incremental innovations season after season that sustained shows include:

- *American Horror Story:* Ryan Murphy created a new formula to sustain a franchise through an anthological strategy, showing totally different horror stories season after season but using the same cast and new guest stars. The formula has proven successful. This formula generates anticipation for the audience that they will see something totally new every season.
- The *CSI* franchise: *CSI* shows stay afloat season after season because of the infinite bank of cases to be solved. Audiences know they will not be disappointed. The sustainability of the *CSI* shows relies purely on the quality of the cases.
- *Survivor:* In The United States, the *Survivor* has had more seasons than years on the air. This wonderful franchise has traveled the world with contestants facing different and surprising tasks every time. Likewise, the right mix of participants and the generations of real people who are turned into celebrities on the show and are invited back again to participate in all-star match-up seasons make the show a constant source of surprise for fans. The shows do not disappoint. Even though *Survivor* no longer reaches the audience levels of the initial seasons,

the show has reached a point at which a legion of followers still want to see what producers have in store for them in the next season. The show has maintained an average audience level, managing to survive for a long time in prime time.

- *Real World* from MTV: New participants, new locations, and new generations of participants ensure freshness every time a new installment hits the air.
- *Scandal*: The twist and turns that Shonda Rhimes knows how to create provide impactful surprises on the air. She knows how to move the pieces of the story in such way that momentum and longevity are secured.
- *Doctor Who*: The *Doctor Who* show is definitely one of the most innovative approaches to revamping a franchise over and over again. Over the show's several seasons, and written into the plot, the Doctor goes through a process of transformation and comes back as a different person (transitioning to another actor). The extraterrestrial being that travels through time and from body to body has become the signature way for the creators to maintain the show for more than 40 years.
- *Wheel of Fortune*: New hosts, new sets, and new technologies applied to the traditional dynamic of the program have secured novelty.
- *Everybody Loves Raymond*, *Married with Children*, and *The Big Bang Theory*: The quality of the stories and events make these shows appealing week after week. Jerry Seinfeld, however, realized that the *Seinfeld* concept was running out of innovative events and decided to end the show on a high note.

Ensure innovation all the time. To secure constant innovation, you must ensure that the environment where operations take place is always evolving in the procurement of improvements for the show. The leader of the show (the show runner) must always be on the lookout for fresh minds that will infuse freshness into the creative team. Not unusual is for the same team working on a show year after year to run out of ideas or get stuck creatively. The audience notices and switches to another more entertaining and surprising proposition. Audiences want to be surprised to justify that they are still vested in a show night after night. If you fail to infuse freshness and creative surprises, the audience will just not watch your show any longer. Infusing freshness into a creative and production team is essential. The weakest link has to go voluntarily or be replaced. For that reason, from day one, you must always have team member options in mind. You need people who know the show and who will complement the work being done and take the show to the next level. Back up team members are not necessarily individuals who you have under contract. These are individuals who you, as show runner, must start to locate before it is too late. You need to know who is out there who could infuse originality and trigger new positive directions in the show that the internal team can no longer generate. All shows bring in new writers through-out their run—it's how you stay ahead of the curve and make sure you don't get stuck in an orthodoxy that audiences don't want to see anymore.

The ultimate validation test. After the show has been produced, you face the ultimate validation test—validation by an audience. If the audience has provided positive feedback, then validation turns to a field composed of critics who may back up validation of the show and even provide the show with nominations and awards. If you succeed with validation from the audience and the field, your show will become an innovation. If not, you will become "domain history" and a refer-ence of something that either did not work or was ahead of its time. Examples of shows that were successfully validated by the audience and the field and became innovations of our time include (Cagle, 2013):

- *I Love Lucy* (1951 – 1957)
- *The Twilight Zone* (1959 – 1964)
- *The Jeffersons* (1975 – 1985)
- *Saturday Night Live* (1975 –)
- *Cheers* (1982 – 1993)
- *The Cosby Show* (1984 – 1992)
- *Roseanne* (1988 – 1997)
- *The Simpsons* (1989 –)
- *Law and Order* (1990 – 2010)
- *Seinfeld* (1990 – 1998)
- *The Real World* (1992 –)
- *The X Files* (1993 – 2002)
- *Friends* (1994 – 2004)
- *Sex and the City* (1998 – 2004)
- *Big Brother* (1999 –)
- *Yo soy Betty, la fea* (1999 – 2001, Colombia)
- *The Sopranos* (1999 – 2007)
- *Survivor* (2000 –)
- *The Office* (2001 – 2003, United Kingdom)
- *Arrested Development* (2003 – 2006; 2013 – on Netflix)
- *Mad Men* (2007 – 2015)
- *Breaking Bad* (2008 – 2013)
- *Veep* (2012 –)

Once a show is produced you have created the formula for a TV show. The ups and downs, the successes and failures, all become part of the memory of the show that will be in the bible for a new format.

EXTENDING THE LIFE CYCLE

When a show is over, you might consider exploring different ways to continue milking the success of the original show.

Spin-offs. One proven formula is doing a spin-off that creates a derivative work based on a previous innovation. The series *Frasier* is an example of a spin-off from the series *Cheers*. *Frasier* went to become one of the most successful sitcoms of all time, after deriving from a character in the original cast of *Cheers*, a series that was on the air for 11 years. The character Frasier Crane appeared in season 3 and became a regular on *Cheers* for 9 years. Adding these years to the 11 seasons of the series *Frasier*, Frasier Crane (the character portrayed by actor Kelsey Grammer) became the longest running character in TV history with a staggering run of 20 years on the air (Angell, Casey & Lee, 1993).

Format distribution. Format distribution is a way to extend the life cycle of a show beyond the original series produced (particularly from an economic standpoint). *Married with Children* had a successful run in the United States but has continued generating business for Sony thanks to remakes of the format worldwide. Fiction formats are a very innovative way to replicate a scripted show that was successful following a model that initially existed for new game shows to reproduce a success, but instead using scripts as the formula. Sony was a pioneer in this approach. Soon after the world embraced the Sony model, fiction formats now come from Asia, Latin America, Europe, and the United States and travel from one country to another. If a show is successful in one territory and suitable for being remade in other countries, then you have a format in your hands. The format is the recipe for other producers in other countries to replicate the show. They then add their own cultural values and make the show unique and relevant for their countries. The flow of formats around the world is very dynamic. Once production is wrapped up, the company that distributes the show will be able to generate additional revenue and business opportunities by diffusing the original franchise around the globe.

The final bible. For format distribution, a bible for the show is required to summarize all production, creative, and business aspects that made the show a hit in the original country. The final bible must contain:

- A synopsis or description of the show
- All scripts from the original version of the show
- A database of games, pranks, etc. that define the show
- A detailed dynamic of the show (if the show is a game show or a competition)
- The "rules of the road" (for reality shows) stating established practices to minimize misunderstandings and conflict
- A specific description of the types of characters needed
- Recommendations for all processes: casting, preproduction, production
- Templates for production plans
- A production resources plan
- Set floor plans
- Technical recommendations
- A security assessment for locations or the building of sets and scenery
- Track records of ratings and success
- What works and what does not

The next chapter will discuss the support needed by the creative process from functional areas.

19

SUPPORTING ACTIVITIES

The creative process cannot sustain itself without the support of certain functional areas. The creative team needs experts in different areas to achieve the creative vision of the writers and creators. The value chain of innovation has three functional areas:

- Innovation management
- Information technology support
- Business affairs

INNOVATION MANAGEMENT

Innovation management concerns the management of strategy, creativity, and innovation within the entire value chain of innovation. The innovation management task is led by a top executive in a creative organization who is able to set the goals, objectives, and mission. This individual leads the strategy as both an activator and a facilitator. The individual also manages all the tasks of the innovation value chain, sets the proper environment, and advocates for collaboration and openness throughout. In essence, the innovation management leader is a creative individual that has the managerial skills required to plan, control, create, discover, and deliver. This person might have been a writer or a producer who understands all of the processes. Shonda Rhimes, J.J. Abrams, and Steven Spielberg are examples of leaders in charge of value chains of innovation. They lead by example, articulate their creative visions, and set up groups of people to accomplish goals. Although not all innovation managers have such profiles as these well-know individuals, within many corporations, executives leading creative operations can be found with titles such as (but not limited to) Chief Creative Officer, Chief Content

Officer, Creative Director, Head of Development and Production, Head of Drama, or Head of Alternative Programming.

If you are an independent creative individual, you are the head of your innovation management process. You have to implement the process in such way that you collaborate with individuals throughout all of the different activities of the value chain so that they help you to accomplish your goals. You have to be the driver who finds people who are willing to accompany you in your quest for success.

Innovation management encompasses the implementation of strategy, creativity, innovation, and discovery in the value chain, all concepts and processes that have been reviewing in this book. Management entails creative aspects and resources planning. With the right team and resources, everything can be accomplished. Otherwise, promises will be made, but the desired outcome will not happen. Innovation management is about envisioning the impossible but doing so through possible, creative solutions.

INFORMATION TECHNOLOGY SUPPORT

Information technology (IT) entails the tools needed to store, administer, and communicate via software results and information needed by groups operating with common objectives such as creative teams and corporations. Tools that define this IT support are databases, social media platforms, intranet sites, spreadsheets, tablets, personal computers, telephones, etc.

Having a visual system for communication helps an innovation process leader to convey information and to provide a clear snapshot of what is happening at any moment in the tasks and inventory of titles and projects that are moving through the production value chain. A representation of the value chain of content innovation using IT support can provide this overview of the production process. The value chain in Figure 19-1 shows all of the activities that need to be undertaken and also provides a repository for recording all of the information that flows through the value chain.

IT departments can design software applications for you that will help store information. You can also build basic databases yourself using spreadsheet applications and word-processing software. If you are not a techie, an alternative is to use a database file to create a visual representation of the value chain that will help everyone in the company understand how titles are progressing. For example, a large whiteboard can be used to record the progression of a creative operation. Sticky notes in different colors and sizes can be placed on the whiteboard to show the elements of the value chain and their relationships with various tasks.

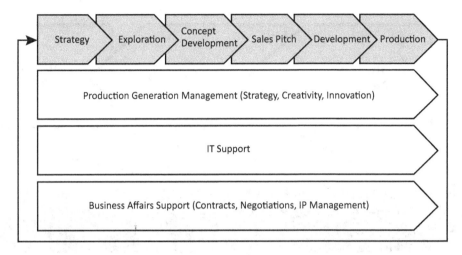

Figure 19-1. The value chain of content innovation.

Value chain databases. Value chain databases contain files with information that has been generated throughout the innovation process. These files are indexed and categorized in such a way as to allow easy access and information sharing with other team members. Databases that need to be set up are files for an overall value chain snapshot report and other specific report files for the various functional areas.

Value chain snapshots. Snapshot files provide at a glance what is happening in each process of the value chain of innovation. These snapshots also let us see what each team is working on and how a title is progressing overall. Figure 19-2 represents a snapshot of a sample value chain. The file is structured in six different sections, each one representing one of the activities featured in the value chain of innovation. The snapshot in Figure 19-2 starts with columns for strategic research and exploration and ends with a column for wrapped projects with the status of bible preparation. (*Note*: I do not always include a strategic research column because the strategic research process generates specific reports, not specific shows.)

- The first column in Figure 19-2 (Strategic Research) simply states the reports being prepared with hyperlinks to the most recent document with information. In this column, point out important strategic information such as key clients, audience demos, important dates related to development cycle, key competitors, etc. Figure 19-3 is a closer look the Strategic Research column.

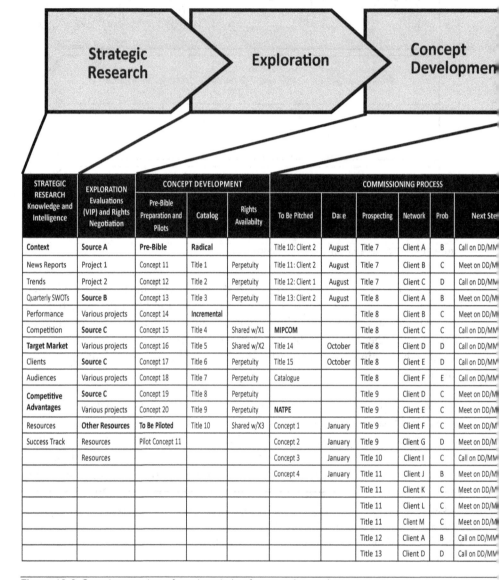

STRATEGIC RESEARCH Knowledge and Intelligence	EXPLORATION Evaluations (VIP) and Rights Negotiation	CONCEPT DEVELOPMENT				COMMISSIONING PROCESS					
		Pre-Bible Preparation and Pilots	Catalog	Rights Availabilty	To Be Pitched	Date	Prospecting	Network	Prob	Next Ste
Context	Source A	Pre-Bible	Radical		Title 10: Client 2	August	Title 7	Client A	B	Call on DD/MM
News Reports	Project 1	Concept 11	Title 1	Perpetuity	Title 11: Client 2	August	Title 7	Client B	C	Meet on DD/M
Trends	Project 2	Concept 12	Title 2	Perpetuity	Title 12: Client 1	August	Title 7	Client C	D	Call on DD/MM
Quarterly SWOTs	Source B	Concept 13	Title 3	Perpetuity	Title 13: Client 2	August	Title 8	Client A	B	Meet on DD/M
Performance	Various projects	Concept 14	Incremental				Title 8	Client B	C	Meet on DD/M
Competition	Source C	Concept 15	Title 4	Shared w/X1	MIPCOM		Title 8	Client C	C	Call on DD/MM
Target Market	Various projects	Concept 16	Title 5	Shared w/X2	Title 14	October	Title 8	Client D	D	Call on DD/MM
Clients	Source C	Concept 17	Title 6	Perpetuity	Title 15	October	Title 8	Client E	D	Call on DD/MM
Audiences	Various projects	Concept 18	Title 7	Perpetuity	Catalogue		Title 8	Client F	E	Call on DD/MM
Competitive Advantages	Source C	Concept 19	Title 8	Perpetuity			Title 9	Client D	C	Meet on DD/M
	Various projects	Concept 20	Title 9	Perpetuity	NATPE		Title 9	Client E	C	Meet on DD/M
Resources	Other Resources	To Be Piloted	Title 10	Shared w/X3	Concept 1	January	Title 9	Client F	C	Meet on DD/M
Success Track	Resources	Pilot Concept 11			Concept 2	January	Title 9	Client G	D	Meet on DD/M
	Resources				Concept 3	January	Title 10	Client I	C	Call on DD/MM
					Concept 4	January	Title 11	Client J	B	Meet on DD/M
							Title 11	Client K	C	Meet on DD/M
							Title 11	Client L	C	Meet on DD/M
							Title 11	Client M	C	Meet on DD/M
							Title 12	Client A	B	Call on DD/MM
							Title 13	Client D	D	Call on DD/MM

Figure 19-2. Sample snapshot of a value chain of content innovation.

Sales Pitch > **Development** > **Production**

COMMISSIONING PROCESS

In ...tiation	Client	Episodes	Notes
...le 4	Client X	6	Closing co-development
...le 5	Client Y	TBD	Pending pilot approval
...le 6	Client D	13	Full commission

DEVELOPMENT/PRODUCTION

Commissioned	Client	Episodes	Producer/ Supervisor
In Development			
Title 2	Client W	3	Scripts commissioned (3)
Title 3	Client D	8	February start
First Production			
Title 1	Client A	13	Current

WRAPPED

Project	Episodes	Network	Year	Bible Status
Project A	6	Network X	2014	MM/YY
Project B	6	Network X	2014	MM/YY

EXPLORATION Evaluations (VIP) and Rights Negotiation
Source A
Project 1
Project 2
Source B
Various projects
Source C
Various projects
Source C
Various projects
Source C
Various projects
Other Resources
Resources
Resources

STRATEGIC RESEARCH Knowledge and Intelligence
Context
News Reports
Trends
Quarterly SWOTs
Performance
Competition
Target Market
Clients
Audiences
Competitive Advantages
Resources
Success Track

Figure 19-3. Strategic Research snapshot.   **Figure 19-4.** Exploration snapshot.

- The second column, Exploration, is for titles under evaluation and in rights negotiations (Figure 19-4). Key projects/titles or companies under consideration are in this column.
- The third section, Concept Development, concerns projects in the concept development stage (Figure 19-5). The Concept Development section is divided into three columns. The first is for titles being conceptualized, the second is for titles in the catalog, and the third specifies the inventory of sales materials and the types of rights owned. (*Note:* If a title is yours alone, then the rights are yours in perpetuity.)
- The fourth section, Commissioning Process, is related to customer relationship management (CRM). This section includes the shows that will be pitched and to whom, the shows that are in the prospecting stage (business), and the projects that have entered the negotiation stage (Figure 19-6). The probability of being commissioned, in the Prob column, is just a guess about what could happen. An exploded view of the Prob column shows a scale used by the author (Figure 19-7).
- The fifth section, Development/Production, shows the development and production status once a show has been commissioned (Figure

CONCEPT DEVELOPMENT		
Pre-Bible Preparation and Pilots	**Catalog**	**Rights Availability**
Pre-Bible	**Radical**	
Concept 11	Title 1	Perpetuity
Concept 12	Title 2	Perpetuity
Concept 13	Title 3	Perpetuity
Concept 14	**Incremental**	
Concept 15	Title 4	Shared w/X1
Concept 16	Title 5	Shared w/X2
Concept 17	Title 6	Perpetuity
Concept 18	Title 7	Perpetuity
Concept 19	Title 8	Perpetuity
Concept 20	Title 9	Perpetuity
To Be Piloted	Title 10	Shared w/X3
Pilot Concept 11		
Pilot Concept 12		
Pilot Concept 13		

Figure 19-5. Concept Development snapshot.

19-8). Financial information can also be added to this section to provide a clearer sense of the size of the business related to a title (Figure 19-9).

- The sixth section, Wrapped, is a list of the wrapped shows with status dates for the bible for each show (Figure 19-10).

Specific reports for functional areas. For tracking purposes, each process requires a set of reports and databases:

- Strategic research:
  - Monthly news reports
  - Quarterly SWOT reports
- Trend reports:
  - A database of international content references (formats, TV shows, digital success stories)
  - A casting database
  - A database of the competitive landscape with clients
  - Ratings and programming grid databases with hyperlinks to different shows

				COMMISSIONING PROCESS					
To Be Pitched	Date	Prospecting	Network	Prob	Next Step	In Negotiation	Client	Episodes	Notes
Title 10: Client 2	August	Title 7	Client A	B	Call on DD/MM/YY	Title 4	Client X	6	Closing co-development
Title 11: Client 2	August	Title 7	Client B	C	Meet on DD/MM/YY	Title 5	Client Y	TBD	Pending pilot approval
Title 12: Client 1	August	Title 7	Client C	D	Call on DD/MM/YY	Title 6	Client D	13	Full commission
Title 13: Client 2	August	Title 8	Client A	B	Meet on DD/MM/YY				
			Client B	C	Meet on DD/MM/YY				
MIPCOM		Title 8	Client C	C	Call on DD/MM/YY				
Title 14	October	Title 8	Client D	D	Call on DD/MM/YY				
Title 15	October	Title 8	Client E	D	Call on DD/MM/YY				
Catalog		Title 8	Client F	E	Call on DD/MM/YY				
		Title 9	Client D	C	Meet on DD/MM/YY				
NATPE		Title 9	Client E	C	Meet on DD/MM/YY				
Concept 1	January	Title 9	Client F	C	Meet on DD/MM/YY				
Concept 2	January	Title 9	Client G	D	Meet on DD/MM/YY				
Concept 3	January	Title 10	Client I	C	Call on DD/MM/YY				
Concept 4	January	Title 11	Client J	B	Meet on DD/MM/YY				
		Title 11	Client K	C	Meet on DD/MM/YY				
		Title 11	Client L	C	Meet on DD/MM/YY				
		Title 11	Client M	C	Meet on DD/MM/YY				
		Title 12	Client A	B	Call on DD/MM/YY				
		Title 13	Client D	D	Call on DD/MM/YY				

Figure 19-6. Commissioning Process snapshot.

Project	Prob
A (Signed)	100%
B (Agreed)	85%
C (High)	65%
D (50%)	50%
E (25%)	25%
F (Early)	10%
G (No discussion)	–
P (To be pitched)	–

Figure 19-7. Exploded Prob column with probability scale.

DEVELOPMENT/PRODUCTION			
Commissioned	**Client**	**Episodes**	**Producer/Supervisor**
In Development			
Title 2	Client W	3	Scripts commissioned (3)
Title 3	Client D	8	February start
First Production			
Title 1	Client A	13	Current

Figure 19-8. Development/Production snapshot.

DEVELOPMENT/PRODUCTION						
Commissioned	**Client**	**Episodes**	**Total Revenue**	**Margin (%)**	**Net**	**Notes**
In Development						
Title 2	Client W	3	$$$	15	$$$	Scripts commissioned (3) + pilot
Title 3	Client D	8	$$$	10	$$$	Production, February; air, April
First Production						
Title 1	Client A	13	$$$	10	$$$	On stand by

Figure 19-9. Development/Production snapshot with financials.

WRAPPED				
Project	Episodes	Network	Year	Bible Status
Project A	6	Network X	2014	MM/YY
Project B	6	Network X	2014	MM/YY

Figure 19-10. Wrapped snapshot.

- Exploration:
  - An evaluation database containing the results of each evaluation and links to results of the actual coverage or evaluation given to a title or idea (Figure 19-11)
  - A creative and production resources database showing names of individuals and production companies that could be allies on a future project (Figure 19-12) (Important: In the report, highlight why a person or a company is of interest or under consideration.)
- Concept Development (an extended database of information stored in the value chain snapshot):
  - A database of projects in exploration with associated timelines
  - A catalog database with hyperlinks to all created sales materials
  - Pre-bibles
  - Sales pitches
  - Demos
  - Pilots
  - Best shows
  - Scripts
  - Budget templates for different genres and types of shows
  - Budgets of previous budgeted project
- Social networks (for idea exchanges and internal validation):
  - Social network applications prepared to support the discovery circle and to help find solutions across creative entities allowing anyone to post ideas, participate within the creative process, or validate an internal concept (These applications include software and online platforms to share ideas and classify them; to find solutions to problems and creative situations arising from casting questions; to look for specific ideas to solve a plot, evaluate scenarios, etc.; and to find vendors. Members of open social media platforms, such as LinkedIn, use these platforms to find solutions from other people who are members of these platforms or networks.)

Data Base: Proposals Submitted for Evaluation

Projects	Date Evaluation	Company	Locale	Writer	Evaluator	Genre	Sub-genre	Materials	Result	Synopsis	Comments
Project 1	8/1/14	AAA Productions	Mexico	FFF, GGG	GB	Variety	Late night	Episodes 1, 2, 3	Recommend		Working on bible
Project 2	7/1/14	BBB Writers	Spain/UK	GGGG, HHH	GB	Sitcom	Mock reality	Demo	Consider		
Project 3	10/17/14	Writer AAA	Spain/UK	AAAA, GGG	AI	Sitcom	Traditonal	Demo	Consider		
Project 4		BBB Productions	UK	BBBB, PPPP	AI	Drama	Anthology	Demo	Consider		
Project 5		CCC Productions	UK	JJJJ, III	AI	Drama	Telenovela	Scripts 1, 2, 3	Consider		
Project 6		DDD Productions	Ireland	FFFF, RRR	AI	Drama	Teleseries		Pass		
Project 7	10/30/14	EEE, FFF	USA	EEEE, CHH	GB	Reality	Franchise	Paper format, 2 pp	Pass		
Project 8	10/21/14	GGG, HHH	USA	NNNN, OOO	MR	Reality	Docu-soap	Demo	Pass		
Project 9	10/22/14	Writer AAA	USA	AAAA, GGG	MR	Reality	Competition	Paper format, 1–4 pp	Consider		
Project 10	10/21/14	KKK, HHH	USA	KKKK, UUU	MR	Reality	Competition	Demo	Consider		
Project 11	10/21/14	NNN Media	USA	DDDD, YYY	MR	Reality	Competition	Paper format, 1–4 pp	Consider		
Project 12	10/22/14	TTT Media	The Netherlands	ZZZ, VVV	MR	Game Show	Studio	Paper format, 1–4 pp	Pass		

Figure 19-11. Evaluations database for submitted projects.

Name	Skill	Specality	Relevant Work	Reference	Suitability
AAA BBB	Writer	Sicoms	*Frasier*	Worked with XXX	Any Sitcom
CCC DDD	Producer	Entertainment (Variety)		Newcomer	Project X
EEE FFF	Production Coordinator	Variety			Project A
GGG HHH	Writer	Game Shows	*Wheel of Fortune*		Project Y

Figure 19-12. Creative resources database.

- Sites offering solutions such as Imaginatik (http://imaginatik.com), HYPE (http://hypeinnovation.com), Brightidea (http://www.brightidea.com/fall2014), Kindling (https://www.kindlingapp.com), and Idea Connection (http://www.ideaconnection.com/software/)

LEGAL, FINANCIAL, AND ADMINISTRATIVE SUPPORT

Lawyers, accountants, and professionals in general who manage everything related to contracts, negotiations, intellectual property management, accounting, and finance are also part of innovation management teams. These professionals provide support on matters that a creative professional wants properly covered and managed.

Legal. The preparation of a contract, negotiations with a commissioning entity, and even negotiations with individuals who could eventually become part of your team are meticulous work that requires expertise. Moreover, the management of intellectual properties, the registration of ideas in the proper copyright instance, and format protection must be taken seriously and led by an attorney who ensures that all rights are properly secure or negotiated. These tasks can be onerous. They demand the incorporation of professionals whose time is costly. Make them part of your team. Work out a way financially to incorporate these professionals into your process. Find a way to eventually share the success of the project with them if you cannot pay upfront for their services. Publications such as those by Litwak (1998, 2012) provide templates of contracts and a comprehensive list of legal documents needed to be taken into consideration. Some deals you will be working during the different stages of the value chain of innovation include those shown in Figure 19-13. Deals to take into consideration include:

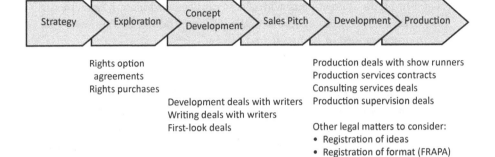

Figure 19-13. Deals in the value chain showing where resources could offer future project opportunities.

- Submission releases
- Non-disclosure agreements
- Option and literary purchase agreements
- Rights option agreements: Rights option agreements provide the buyer of content with the right to represent the format or the content itself within a market for a limited period of time. During this time, the buyer has an opportunity to work on a suitable version of the format or the content for a specific market. Restrictions in terms of what can be changed apply and are totally up to the owner of the rights. The rights holder can be a writer or a creative individual. Depending on the content's viability and the skill sets of the writer, the writer might be the right person to develop the concept for the market.
- Rights purchases: A rights purchase refers to the action of acquiring from a rights holder the rights of a property for a specific period of time or in perpetuity. Payments to the rights holder can occur up front when negotiation is complete or throughout the making of a show. Depending on the nature of the agreement, a rights purchase may include clauses that ensure revenue sharing of the net proceeds between the buyer and the rights holder.
- Development agreements with writers: Writing agreements concern either conceptualizing or developing a show "in the bubble" (pre-bible stage).
- Writing agreements with writers: Writing agreements with writers are for scriptwriting.
- First-look agreements: First-look agreements ensure the right of a company to look at the content the writer will produce within a specific time period.

- Production agreements with show runners: Production agreements with show runners ensure who the leading producer of a show will be, commissioned or being pitched.
- Production services agreements
- Licensing agreements
- Consulting services agreements
- Above-the-line professional agreements, production services contracts, joint venture agreements, music commissioning deals, TV music rights, synchronization/performer/master use and mechanical licenses
- Acquisition and distribution agreements
- Loan negotiations
- Soundtrack recording agreements
- Production supervision agreements
- Certificates of authorship
- Certificates of origin
- Registrations of idea and copyright protection
- Domain purchases
- Registrations of formats: International associations are especially dedicated to fighting format piracy and providing writers and producers with support to ensure the protection of formats. An example of these organizations is the Format Recognition Protection Association (FRAPA, http://www.frapa.org).

Financial. Accountants and other financial professionals help keep track of costs and resource controls and ensure that each property/project is given the proper business attention to ensure that a property will provide the group or the company with the revenue and profits necessary to ensure continuity and sustainability. Recommended is that each property/project be seen as a separate business unit with very clear objectives and financial expectations. Clarity in this matter will allow emphasis on the properties that really matter.

Administrative. Remember that innovation generates value for those involved and that entails both the creator of the innovation and the audience. For the creator of the innovation, value means an increase in the worth of their material, intellectual, and emotional assets. Material assets require financial, administrative, and operations professionals to come into play. Lawyers help with the protection of the patrimony (legal entitlements) and your personal intellectual properties.

STEP 5

EMBRACE THE ENTIRE METHODOLOGY THROUGH THE CIRCLE OF CONTENT INNOVATION

Chapter 20. The Full Circle of Innovation for Media Content Creation

After nineteen chapters, we have discussed the four steps required to implement a process of innovation for media content creation. We have discussed:

- The meaning of strategy, creativity, and innovation
- The importance of setting the strategic goals and conditions for innovation to occur
- How to adopt discovery as a core strategy by implementing the discovery circle of innovation
- How to implement a process to deliver—the value chain of innovation

Now that discussion of Steps 1 through 4 has been accomplished, we need to visualize the entire philosophy and methodology as one solid framework of continuous operation—the full circle of innovation for media content creation.

20

THE FULL CIRCLE OF INNOVATION FOR MEDIA CONTENT CREATION

The full circle of innovation derives from juxtaposition of the discovery circle, the value chain of innovation, and the different outputs that are subject to creative validation from the inception of an idea to its emission in any platform (Figure 20-1). The heart of the process is the discovery circle (discussed in Chapter 11, *The Discovery Circle*). The value chain of innovation (Chapter 12, *The Value Chain of Innovation*), the framework to deliver innovations, is presented in this chapter as a linear representation of the process composed of six processes, each delivering a very specific output. The different outputs are strategy, ideas, inventions, commissions, tailored content, and innovations (Figure 20-2). These outputs, however, cannot be seen as a *finite* linear process, instead they must be seen as a cyclical process that retro-sustains. The circle in Figure 20-3 shows the interconnection between all of the value chain activities and the nonlinear aspect of the process. The value chain in Figure 20-3 retro-feeds itself constantly while all of the activities occur simultaneously.

The circular representation of the value chain and its outputs surround the discovery circle, molding it into perfect harmony. Figure 20-4 presents the discovery circle as the heart of the value chain operation. As we can see, discovery holds the value chain together with an ultimate goal of discovering and generating insights within the processes of strategy generation, evaluation, concept development, sales, development, and production.

Figure 20-1. The discovery circle.

Figure 20-2. Linear representation of the value chain of innovation and its outputs.

ACTIVATION OF THE INNOVATION CIRCLE

Activation of the full circle of innovation occurs when the processes of creative validation of the different outputs of the value chain are integrated (Figure 20-5). Each output is validated by a different validating instance. These three validating instances are:

- The internal circle of validation within a company or a creative team,
- The validation provided by industry experts, clients, and commissioning entities, and
- The validation of the audience.

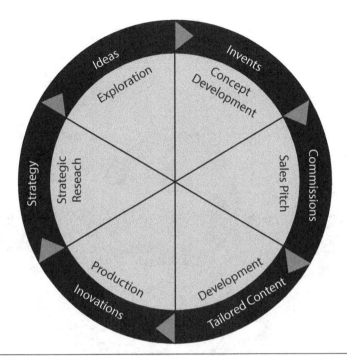

Figure 20-3. Cyclical representation of the value chain of innovation and its outputs.

Figure 20-5 presents a summary of the full circle of validation. The summary compiles the process of innovation for media content creation and becomes a valid representation of all the learnings presented in this book:

- The company validates the strategy, ideas, and inventions.
- Experts in the industry (including clients) validate the pitch and the content that has been tailor-made for the client.
- The audience ultimately validates the innovations.

Having a full circle is the "rule of the game," the method, the heart, and your compass. Even if you do not implement all of the processes with methodical precision and do not have a battalion of people to cover all of the activities, you now have a clear understanding of what you need to do and all of the different activities embedded in the process of content generation to create innovation.

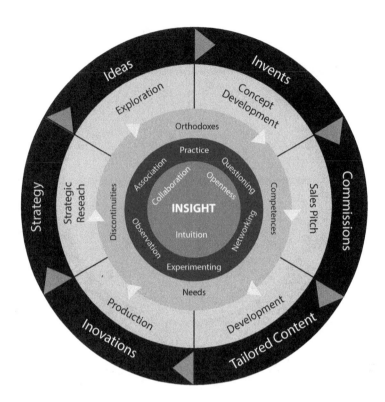

Figure 20-4. The discovery circle, the value chain of innovation, and their outcomes juxtaposed as one circle.

SUSTAINABILITY: KEEPING THE VALUE CHAIN OF INNOVATION FRESH

The process of innovation for media content creation is based on a framework of operation. The results and validation throughout keep the innovation process fresh and activated. Feedback is crucial because all results provide knowledge and intelligence for making the innovation process better in the future. Interaction of people facilitates not only anticipation that an idea is going to become an innovation but also the possibility of making the idea better, thus confirming the importance of staying connected within your context and staying organized based on the framework of operation for innovation in media content creation.

This connection within your context becomes the essence for building a sustainable model of innovation as a process that reinvents and nurtures itself in a cyclical way. People, resources, environment, time, willingness, and openness form a part of the key aspects you need to consider to bring the full circle

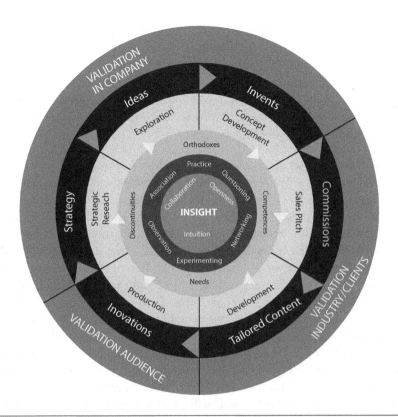

Figure 20-5. The full circle of innovation for media content creation.

of innovation to life. Throughout this book we have discussed how innovation depends on strategy, creativity, people, discovery, and organization. Innovation does not happen as an act of God but as a result of activities, interactions, and processes. Each person is creative within their personal realm of knowledge. It is the cross-pollination of know-how that makes innovative works come to life every day.

Guarantee sustainability. To guarantee sustainability, be prepared to create, filter, develop, sell, convert, and expose content. After exposing the content, involve an audience in the creative process. Listen to what they say. If the content is not working with this audience, think carefully. Try to find out what will directly add value for them and why your show or creative proposition does not add the value they are looking for. Identifying a problem with content could take a while and might not necessarily be spotted before the show is over. The importance of this action, however, is that it allows you gain experience and try again using the valuable propositions and suggestions received. All of this intelligence adds to the database of strategy research and provides orientation for how you can shift the course of the creative ship to find better ways to identify solutions for stories or shows that might bring a better experience to the audience than the one being provided. Sustainability needs strategy, creativity, and innovation—the three concepts explained as being the first step in implementing the process of innovation (*Step 1: Understanding Strategy, Creativity, and Innovation*). Understanding these three concepts ensures a healthy process.

Keep the circle of discovery and the circle of innovation alive. The circle of discovery must be active across the board—in all activities of the value chain of innovation. Acceptance of successes and failures can help reshape a creative strategy, build a better present, and keep an innovation process up to speed. The circle of innovation revolves around people who need to be motivated and encouraged to generate innovative ideas throughout everything they do. People are motivated in different ways. One way is related to recognition of the value of their ideas by participation in the monetary results, which could translate into participation-appropriate compensation or rewards that drive free thinking and a full commitment to an operation. This compensation aspect combined with the right environment—an atmosphere for acceptance of open innovation and the cross-pollination of ideas between partnerships and with clients and guests in which a creative individual could participate in specific projects—can constitute the right organizational context for the circle of innovation to exist and grow. Without this strong level of commitment, people will perform only what is necessary and will concentrate on the mere execution of their day-to-day tasks. The circle of innovation relies on skillful, happy, committed, encouraged people. Otherwise, the circle of innovation does not work.

Test organizational characteristics. Test your company (or group) constantly to ensure that you stay true to the circle of innovation approach. Every so often, use the checklist of organizational characteristics shown in Figure 20-6 to determine your support (and your company's support) of creativity and innovation. Assign a point value to each characteristic, for example, 1 through 10, to determine how strong or weak your support is. The stronger a creative team is the more sustainable the circle of innovation will be (Harvard Business Essentials, 2003, pp. 99-113).

There is no magic formula—just formulas to be broken. Audiences will always speak up and say what they think about a show. If they don't like it, you either fix it or change it—one of the two. Don't keep hitting the same wall over and over because that wall is a result of stubbornness that could turn into orthodoxy. If the orthodoxy is identified and challenged, the status quo could take a positive

Characteristic	Strong	Weak
Management takes risks.		
New ideas and new ways of doing things are welcomed.		
Information is free flowing and not controlled by managers.		
Employees have access to knowledgeable sources: customers, benchmarking partners, creative communities, etc.		
Good ideas are supported by top executives.		
Innovators are rewarded.		
Radical innovations have been brought to the market.		
Incremental innovations are made.		
Discovery over delivery is the heart of the operation.		

Figure 20-6. Sample checklist to determine level of support of creativity and innovation.

turn and allow a process or show to succeed. Challenging orthodoxy can happen anywhere—with stories, characters, shows, and channels.

Overall, breaking the mold, surprising audiences, and going against the rules in a significant strategic way are the essence of creating innovative programming. The objective is to give people an entertaining experience that brings value and fulfills a need that you have to discover. Using the full circle of innovation is the best possible way to stay grounded. The circle of innovation satisfactorily provides a path to follow to find triggers for insights and solutions for your quest to yield innovations in media.

Coming up with radical innovations consistently is, of course, difficult, but having the convenience of being able to make incremental innovations allows a company to participate in the process of diffusion of a formula and to develop the working capital necessary to ensure the incorporation of resources to continue gathering information and looking for the next blockbuster hit. Once that blockbuster occurs, it becomes the main revenue generator for a company. This revenue must then be used to strengthen the entire value chain to improve the new formula created and to find more new breakthroughs.

This has been an extraordinary journey and I really hope this book helps orient the search and development of new content. I am sure that while you read it, new examples, references, and ideas will come up that would reflect our innovative reality. Please feel free to connect with me and let me know if you would like to discuss these topics. I do not own the truth and this material is one of many approaches that can help establish a methodology and make the creative process smoother. I would love to hear about different approaches and understand how they are helping you. Please connect. I hope you enjoyed reading this book and forever will be thankful for having taken the time to do so!

APPENDIX 1. REFERENCES

Introduction

Aris, A. & Bughin, J. (2005). *Managing Media Companies: Harnessing Creative Value*. Chichester, West Sussex, England: John Wiley & Sons Ltd.

Chapter 1

Bilton, C. (2007). *Management and Creativity: From Creative Industries to Creative Management*. Malden, MA: Blackwell Publishing.

Grant, R. (2002). *Contemporary Strategy Analysis: Concepts, Techniques, Applications*. Malden, MA: Blackwell Publishing.

Johnston, E.R. & Bate, D. (2013). *The Power of Strategy Innovation: A New Way of Linking Creativity and Strategic Planning to Discover Great Business Opportunities*. New York: American Management Association.

Chapter 3

Bernardo, N. (Producer/Creator). *Beat Girl Nominated for the Kidscreen Awards as Best TV Movie* (December 2, 2013). [Online] Available: http://www.beactivemedia.com/beat-girl-nominated-for-the-kidscreen-awards-as-best-tv-movie/

Bilton, C. (2007). *Management and Creativity: From Creative Industries to Creative Management*. Malden, MA: Blackwell Publishing.

Chapter 5

Amabile, T. (1983). *The Social Psychology of Creativity*. New York: Springer-Verlag.

Amabile, T. (1998). How to kill creativity. *Harvard Business Review*, September-October (pp. 77-87). Watertown, MA: Harvard Business Press.

Bilton, C. (2007). *Management and Creativity: From Creative Industries to Creative Management*. Malden, MA: Blackwell Publishing.

Harvard Business Essentials (2003). *Managing Creativity and Innovation: Practical Strategies to Encourage Creativity*. Boston: Harvard Business Press.

Hayes, J.R. (1989). Cognitive processes in creativity. In Glover, J.A., Ronning, R.R. &. Reynolds, C.R. (Eds.). *Handbook of Creativity* (pp.135-146). New York: Plenum Press.

Kaufman, J. & Baer, J. (2004). Hawkin's Haiku, Madonna's Math: why it is hard to be creative in every room of the house. In Sternberg, R.J., Grogorenko, E. & Singer, J. (Eds.). *Creativity, From Potential to Realization* (pp. 3-19). Washington, DC: American Psychological Association.

Runco, M. (2004). Everyone has creative potential. In Sternberg, R.J., Grogorenko, E. & Singer, J. (Eds.). *Creativity, From Potential to Realization* (pp. 21-30). Washington, DC: American Psychological Association.

Sawyer, K. (2006). *Explaining Creativity: The Science of Human Innovation*. Oxford: Oxford University Press.

Sternberg, R.J. & Lubart, T.I. (1995a). *Defying the Crowd: Cultivating Creativity in a Culture of Conformity*. New York: Free Press.

Sternberg, R.J. & Lubart, T.I. (1995b). The concept of creativity: prospects and paradigms. In Sternberg, R.J. (Ed.). *Handbook of Creativity* (pp. 3-15). New York: Cambridge University Press.

Chapter 6

Abuhamded, S. & Csikszentmihalyi, M. (2004). The artistic personality: a system perspective. In Sternberg, R.J., Grogorenko, E. & Singer, J. (Eds.). *Creativity, From Potential to Realization* (pp. 3-19). Washington, DC: American Psychological Association.

Amabile, T. M. (1982). Social psychology of creativity: a consensual assessment technique. *Journal of Personality and Social Psychology*, 43: 997-1013.

Csikszentmihalyi, M. (1988). Society, culture, and person: a systems view of creativity. In Sternberg, R.J. (Ed.). *The Nature of Creativity* (pp. 325-339). New York: Cambridge University Press.

Gluck, J., Ernst, R. & Unger, F. (2002). How creatives define creativity: definitions reflect different types of creativity. *Creativity Research Journal*, 14(1): 109; as cited in Lubart, T. & Guignand, J. The generality-specificity of creativity: a multivariate approach. In Sternberg, R.J., Grogorenko, E. & Singer, J.

(Eds.). *Creativity, From Potential to Realization* (pp. 43-56). Washington, DC: American Psychological Association.

Lubart, T. I. (1994). Creativity. In Sternberg, R.J. (Ed.). *Thinking and Problem Solving* (pp. 289-332). New York: Academic Press.

Lubart, T. & Guignard, J. (2004). The generality-specificity of creativity: a multivariate approach. In Sternberg, R.J., Grogorenko, E. & Singer, J. (Eds.). *Creativity, From Potential to Realization* (pp. 3-19). Washington, DC: American Psychological Association.

Sawyer, K. (2006). *Explaining Creativity: The Science of Human Innovation.* Oxford: Oxford University Press.

Sternberg, R.J., Kaufman, J.C. & Pretz, J.E. (2002). The propulsion model of creative contributions applied to the arts and letters; as cited in Lubart, T. & Guignand, J. The generality-specificity of creativity: a multivariate approach. In Sternberg, R.J., Grogorenko, E. & Singer, J. (Eds.). *Creativity, From Potential to Realization* (pp. 43-56). Washington, DC: American Psychological Association.

Chapter 7

Aris, A. & Bughin, J. (2005) *Managing Media Companies: Harnessing Creative Value.* Chichester, West Sussex, England: John Wiley & Sons Ltd.

Bilton, C. (2007). *Management and Creativity: From Creative Industries to Creative Management.* Malden, MA: Blackwell Publishing.

Brooks T. & Marsh, E. (2007). *The Complete Directory to Primetime Network and Cable TV Shows.* New York: Ballantine Books.

dal Zotto, C. & Kranenburg, H. (2008). *Management and Innovation in the Media Industry.* Chetleman, UK: Edward Elgar.

Edgerton, G. & Rose, B. (2005). *Thinking Outside the Box: A Contemporary Genre Television Reader.* Lexington: The University Press of Kentucky.

Edwards, B. (2011). *The birth of the iPod.* [Online] Available: http://www.macworld.com/article/1163181/the_birth_of_the_ipod.html (October 23, 2011).

Harvard Business Essentials (2003). *Managing Creativity and Innovation: Practical Strategies to Encourage Creativity.* Boston: Harvard Business School Publishing Corporation.

Hayes, J.R. (1989). Cognitive processes in creativity. In Glover, J.A., Ronning, R.R. & Reynolds, C.R. (Eds.). *Handbook of Creativity* (pp.135-146). New York: Plenum Press; as cited in Kaufman, J. & Baer, J. (2004). Hawkin's Haiku, Madonna's Math: why it is hard to be creative in every room of the house. In

Sternberg, R.J., Grogorenko, E. & Singer, J. (Eds.). *Creativity, From Potential to Realization* (pp. 3-19). Washington, DC: American Psychological Association.

Lewisohn, M. (2003). *Radio Times Guide to TV Comedy*. London: BBC Worldwide Ltd.

Martin, R. (2009). *The Design of Business: Why Design Thinking Is the Next Competitive Advantage*. Boston: Harvard Business Press.

Perebinossoff, P., Gross, B. & Gross, L. (2005). *Programming for TV, Radio & the Internet: Strategy, Development & Evaluation*. Oxford, UK: Elsevier.

Chapter 8

Aris, A. & Bughin, J. (2005). *Managing Media Companies: Harnessing Creative Value*, Chichester, UK: John Wiley & Sons Ltd.

Brooks, T. & Marsh, E. (2007). *The Complete Directory to Primetime Network and Cable TV Shows*. New York: Ballantine Books.

Harvard Business Essentials (2003). *Managing Creativity and Innovation: Practical Strategies to Encourage Creativity*. Boston: Harvard Business School Publishing.

Jenkins, H. (2013). *Spreadable Media: Creating Value and Meaning in a Networked Culture*. New York: New York University Press.

Keller, R. (2008). *A History of Reality Television (Part Four): Show Me Your Talents*. [Online] Available: http://www.aoltv.com/2008/07/09/a-history-of-reality-television-part-three-show-me-your-talen/#

Chapter 9

Brooks, T. & Marsh, E. (2007). *The Complete Directory to Primetime Network and Cable TV Shows*. New York: Ballantine Books.

Cooper, D. (1997). *Writing Great Screenplays for Film and TV*. New York: Arco.

Lim, D. (2011). Reality-TV originals in drama's lens. *The New York Times*, April 15, 2011. [Online] Available as online print: p. AR22, April 17, 2011.

iMDb (2012). *Titanic Miniseries*. [Online] Available: http://www.imdb.com/title/tt1869152/?ref_=fn_al_tt_7.

McKee, R. (1997). *Story: Substance, Structure, Style and the Principles of Scriptwriting*. New York: HarperEntertainment.

Webber, M. (2005). *Television Scriptwriting: The Writer's Road Map*. Herndon, VA: GGC Publishing.

Zettl, H. (2013). *Sight, Sound, Motion: Applied Media Aesthetics, 7th ed.* (The Wadsworth Series in Broadcast and Production). Boston: Cengage Learning.

Chapter 10

dal Zotto, C. & Kranenburg, H. (2008). *Management and Innovation in the Media Industry.* Chetleman, UK: Edward Elgar.

Dyer, J., Gregersen, H. & Christiansen, C. (2011). *The Innovators DNA: Mastering the Five Skills of Disruptive Innovators.* Boston: Harvard Business Press.

Lehrer, J. (2012). *Imagine: How Creativity Works.* New York: Houghton Mifflin Harcourt.

Martin, R. (2009) *The Design of Business: Why Design Thinking Is the Next Competitive Advantage.* Boston: Harvard Business Press.

Meister, J. & Willyerd, K. (2010). *The 2020 Workplace: How Innovative Companies Attract, Develop, and Keep Tomorrow's Employees Today.* New York: HarperCollins.

Page, S. (2007). *The Difference: How the Power of Diversity Creates Better Groups, Forms, Schools and Societies.* Princeton, NJ: Princeton University Press; as cited in Skarzynsky, P. & Gibson, R. (2008). *Innovation to the Core: A Blueprint for Transforming the Way Your Company Innovates.* Boston: Harvard Business Press.

Skarzynsky, P. & Gibson, R. (2008*). Innovation to the Core: A Blueprint for Transforming the Way Your Company Innovates.* Boston: Harvard Business Press.

Trias de Bes, F. & Kotler, P. (2011). *Winning at Innovation: The A to F Model.* London: Palgrave Macmillan.

Chapter 11

Dyer, J., Gregersen, H. & Christiansen, C. (2011). *The Innovator's DNA: Mastering the Five Skills of Disruptive Innovators.* Boston, MA: Harvard Business Press.

Eberle, B. (2008). *SCAMPER: Let Your Imagination Run Wild!* Waco, TX: Prufrock Press.

Gordon-Levitt, J. (2010, January 1). HitRecord. [Online] Retrieved from: http://www.hitrecord.org

Johnston, E.R. & Bate, D. (2013). *The Power of Strategy Innovation: A New Way of Linking Creativity and Strategic Planning to Discover Great Business Opportunities.* New York: American Management Association.

Lehrer, J. (2012). *Imagine: How Creativity Works.* New York: Houghton Mifflin Harcourt.

Skarzynsky, P. & Gibson, R. (2008). *Innovation to the Core: A Blueprint for Transforming the Way Your Company Innovates.* Boston: Harvard Business Press.

Thomas, K. (2014, June 8). *Today's News: Our Take. Orphan Black's Creators on Their Newest Character, Being a "Feminist" Show, and More.* www.tvguide.com. [Online]Available: http://www.tvguide.com/News/Orphan-Black-New-Clone-1082659.aspx.

Trias de Bes, F. & Kotler, P. (2011). *Winning at Innovation: The A to F Model.* London: Palgrave Macmillan.

Zettl, H. (2013). *Sight Sound and Motion: Applied Media Aesthetics.* Boston: Wadsworth CENGAGE Learning.

Chapter 13

dal Zotto, C. & Kranenburg, H. (2008). *Management and Innovation in the Media Industry.* Chetleman, UK: Edward Elgar.

Friedrich, R., Peterson, M., Koster, A. & Blum, S. (March 2010). *The Rise of Generation C* (PDF). A Booz & Company white paper.

Nielsen (2014). *Solutions. Social TV.* [Online] www.nielsen.com. Retrieved from: http://www.nielsen.com/us/en/solutions/measurement/social-tv.html.

Todotvnews (2011). *Contenidos para la generacion C.* [Online] www.todotvnews.com. Available: http://www.todotvnews.com/scripts/templates/estilo_nota.asp?nota=10040062&numero=44503&newsletter_esp

TV Guide (2014, November 2). TV Listings. TV Listings for Eastern (ET). [Online] Retrieved from: http://www.tvguide.com/Listings/ (Sunday, November 2, 2014).

Chapter 14

Aris, A. & Bughin, J. (2005). *Managing Media Companies: Harnessing Creative Value.* Chichester, West Sussex, England: John Wiley & Sons Ltd.

Blumenthal, H. & Goodenough, H. (2006). *The Business of Television: The Standard Guide to the TV Industry.* New York: Billboard Books.

Bogart, L. (1995). *Commercial Culture: Mass Media System and the Public Interest.* New York: Oxford University Press; as cited in dal Zotto, C. & Kranenburg, H. (2008, p. xvi). *Management and Innovation in the Media Industry.* Chetleman, UK: Edward Elgar.

dal Zotto, C. & Kranenburg, H. (2008). *Management and Innovation in the Media Industry.* Chetleman, UK: Edward Elgar.

Fey, C. (2012). *Trading TV Formats.* Grand-Saconnex, Switzerland: European Broadcasting Union-Euroradio Eurosonic (EBU-UER).

Gans, H.J. (2003). *Democracy and the News.* Oxford: Oxford University Press; as cited in dal Zotto, C. & Kranenburg, H. (2008, p. xvi). *Management and Innovation in the Media Industry.* Chetleman, UK: Edward Elgar.

Harvard Business Essentials (2003). *Managing Creativity and Innovation: Practical Strategies to Encourage Creativity.* Boston: Harvard Business Press.

Kellison, C. (2009). *Producing for TV and New Media: A Real World Approach for Producers, 2nd ed.* Boston: Elsevier/Focal Press.

Litwak, M. (2002). *Deal Making in the Film & Television Industry from Negotiations to Final Contracts.* Beverly Hills/Los Angeles: Silman-James Press.

Perebinossoff, P., Gross, B. & Gross, L. (2005). *Programming for TV, Radio & the Internet: Strategy, Development & Evaluation.* Burlington, MA: Focal Press.

Skarzynsky, P. & Gibson, R. (2008*). Innovation to the Core: A Blueprint for Transforming the Way Your Company Innovates.* Boston: Harvard Business Press.

Trias de Bes, F. & Kotler, P. (2011). *Winning at Innovation: The A to F Model.* London: Palgrave Macmillan.

Chapter 15

Kellison, C. (2009). *Producing for TV and New Media: A Real World Approach for Producers, 2nd ed.* Boston: Elsevier/Focal Press.

McKee, R. (1997). *Story: Substance, Structure, Style and the Principles of Scriptwriting.* New York: HarperEntertainment

Webber, M. (2005). *Television Scriptwriting: The Writer's Road Map.* Herndon, VA: GGC Publishing.

Chapter 16

Newell, F. (2003). *Why CRM Doesn't Work: How to Win by Letting Customers Manage the Relationship.* Princeton, NJ: Bloomberg Press.

Chapter 18

Angell, D., Casey, P., Lee, D. (Creators, 1993, September 16). *Frasier.* Hollywood, CA: NBC. [Online] Retrieved from: http://www.imdb.com/title/tt0106004/episodes?ref_=tt_eps_yr_mr.

Cagle, J. (Ed.) (2013, July 5). The 100 all-time greatest movies. *Entertainment Weekly* (pp. 56-72). [Online] Available at: http://www.ew.com/article/2013/06/26/this-weeks-cover-100-all-time-greatest.

Chapter 19

Litwak, M. (2002). *Dealmaking in the Film & Television Industry from Negotiations to Final Contracts.* Los Angeles: Silman-James Press.

Litwak, M. (2012). *Contracts for the Film & Television Industry, 3rd ed.* Los Angeles: Silman-James Press.

Chapter 20

Harvard Business Essentials (2003). *Managing Creativity and Innovation: Practical Strategies to Encourage Creativity.* Boston: Harvard Business Press.

APPENDIX 2. GLOSSARY

Beat sheet. A method of sequencing a story that uses bullets instead of sentences that can later be further developed into an outline or sentences and paragraphs.

Binge viewing. Watching all episodes of a series season one after another.

Blue ocean market. A market with uncontested space.

Bible. A summary of all production, creative, and business aspects of a show.

Bread and butter. A show that can be produced with a large number of episodes and therefore have long run potential.

Blockbuster. An idea, concept, or product with global relevance, format potential, and the opportunity to establish a new business practice; a product having great commercial success.

B-story videos. A story that is subordinate to the main story; a subplot.

Business cycle for content generation. The interaction of service providers, procurers, distributors, sponsors, and platforms of exposition in the television industry.

Can. A finished product ready for distribution and viewing by audiences.

Capital assets. The overall infrastructure and profits of a studio.

Catalog. Keeps track of the different developed materials and serves as an inventory of scripts, pre-bibles, demos, and the pilot; contains information about the trailers, promos, and the best episodes to show clients for shows already produced.

CCR. Customers in charge of a relationship.

CMR. Customer management of relationships.

Conceptual blending. Mixing concepts that are not thought of as being compatible; using past concepts to create something new; combining trends to create a new solution; applying ideas in a different context to create a breakthrough.

CRM. Customer relationship management.

Cross-boarding. A shooting model in which several episodes are filmed at the same time based on a location.

Crowdfunding. A practice used by artists to obtain funding for a project by raising small amounts of money from many people, often using the internet.

Demo. A key selling tool also known as a promotional trailer; an audiovisual representation of a show that can be put together from original or existing footage.

Development in a vacuum. Development of an idea without a definite client or platform in mind.

Disruptive process. A process involving a format that helps create a new entertainment market; a term used for an innovation process that provides a new product and new competition format, usually for consumers in a new market.

Dramedy. A subgenre that combines the elements of comedy and drama, particularly in television.

Drivers. Aspects of content intrinsic to the generation process of a product that are related to the story, the characters, and aesthetics; aspects that are a consequence of cultural changes and industry context and are related to audience habits and behavior and technology and business.

Exposition windows: The different platforms to showcase content, with the platform being tied to geographic limitations and terms of use; film, theater, television, the internet, mobile devices, cable, hotel entertainment platforms, subscription video on demand, in-flight entertainment platforms, etc.

Final bible. A recipe-type book that details all production, creative, logistics, and business aspects that make an original show a hit.

Flashback. A storytelling device that breaks the chronological progression of a show with an event that happened in the past.

Flash forward. A storytelling device that breaks the chronological progression of a show with an event that will happen in the future.

Flash sideways. A storytelling device attributed to the producers of the television show *Lost* that presents timelines that appear to be parallel to what is actually happening in the current timeline.

Format distribution. A method to extend the life cycle of a show beyond the original series.

Franchise potential. The possibility a show has to be on the air for a long period of time.

Free TV. Traditional network television channels that can be seen on any television device without paying for a subscription.

Genius myth. Only a genius can come up with an outstanding creative idea.

Genre. A concept framework that generates a formula and a cluster or group of shows; a direct consequence of a successful or breakthrough concept that propels the proliferation of other similar shows.

Geo-filter. Geographically filtering television content to certain areas based on location; also called geo-blocking.

Idealization. A process in which scientific models assume facts that are false but which make another model easier to understand.

iMDb. Internet Movie Database; an online database related to films, television programs, video games, actors, production crews, biographies, plot summaries, and trivia.

IMDb Resume. A website designed for actors and crew members in the entertainment industry (available only through subscription to IMDbPro.com) that provides exposure to users of the database with name pages, résumés, and photo galleries.

Imitation. The evolution of an innovation that grows markets and generates variations of an existent innovation; the third stage of innovation evolution.

Incremental innovation. Small changes to an innovation that occur over time.

Innovation. A new product/idea/practice that serves a purpose, possesses commercial value, fulfills an unknown need, and generates a new market; the second stage of innovation evolution.

Innovation diffusion. When the market accepts an innovation, conditions are right for a new entrant to the market, and the innovation becomes widely used, leading to imitations; the third stage of innovation evolution.

Innovation evolution. Identification of an opportunity for improvement of an idea/product/practice that leads to an idea and then to an invention, which is validated and embraced by a market that turns the invention into an innovation.

Intellectual property. A legal term for an original creative work that refers to a creation of an individual's mind such as a concept, idea, script, etc.

Intellectual property rights. Protections that grant an owner of an intellectual property the exclusive rights to the use of that property; patents, copyrights, trademarks, etc.

Invention. A product with no proven utilitarian purpose; a product with potential, but still not any assurance of being relevant for a specific audience; the first stage in innovation evolution.

IPTV. Internet Protocol Television; a system delivering television services, using the Internet Protocol Suite, over the internet or a local area network (LAN) instead of delivery through traditional methods (satellite, cable television, etc.).

Media assets. The content library of a studio or media company.

Media content innovation. A new intellectual property that provides a new utilitarian experience for an audience, creates a new business model, opens a market, and increases the value and profit generation of a media firm.

Linear TV. Regular television programming presented sequentially following a time schedule.

Mobisode. An episode of a program made for mobile phone viewing that usually lasts from 1 to 3 minutes.

New media myth. Anyone can skyrocket to stardom with the support of internet viral social networks.

Niche. A product for specific audiences, thematic channels, or platforms.

Open-access TV. Television programs for the general public.

Open website. A website with no access restrictions.

OTT. Over-the-top; an app or service that delivers audio, video, or some other media product over the internet by bypassing traditional distribution models (no involvement with a system operator).

Orthodoxy. Conforming to generally accepted theories, practices, or rules.

Pilot. A full-length representation of the first episode of a show; also known as episode zero.

Platforms of exposition. Television, movies, magazines, smart televisions, HDTV, 3DTV, internet-enabled devices, mobile devices, mobile applications, online sites, OTT channels, mobile television, satellite television, digital cable, Amazon, Netflix, cable video on demand, pay television channels and services, iTunes, digital video recorders, free online video services (YouTube, Vimeo, Crackle, the Cloud), Short Message Service (SMS), email, and social media sites (Facebook, Twitter, Instagram, Google+, Pinterest).

Pre-bible. Documentation generated before a show is commissioned or produced; a document containing information about the creation of a show that has occurred in a vacuum because only the nature of the content, target market, and available resources are considered and no definite client or platform is in mind; a document that states the characteristics of a show and how to produce it; a document that contains all necessary information needed for a client during the sales process; documentation that becomes a bible when a show is produced.

Production hub model. A replication model using the same studio (e.g., a set or a house) or a similar locale so that many countries can produce the same show; a model that offers the same infrastructure so producers only need to bring in actors.

Roundtables. Quarterly or bi-monthly meetings with the purpose of selecting projects that will enter the conceptualization stage.

Screeners. An advance viewing of a television show sent to critics, awards groups, and industry professionals such as producers.

Second-screen initiative. A method of increasing television viewer access to shows that includes apps to enable viewers who watch television via connected devices such as smartphones and tablets.

Show runner. The leading creative engine (a person) for the production team of a show.

Synopsis. A brief summary; an outline of an episode of a television show.

Sound and video posts. Overall sound and video synchronization.

Spin-off. A derivative work based on a previous innovation that was successful; a formula used to extend the life cycle of a show or series.

Story killer. An event that eliminates the signature tension of a show or accomplishes the mission of a character(s).

Table reads. An activity involving reading fiction and non-fiction script(s), usually while seated at a table, that can include writers, creative producers, and actors; also known as read-throughs and table work.

Tag. A short mini-act of 1 to 5 minutes at the end of a show or episode but before (sometimes during) the end credits that is used to show the effects or aftermath of the episode.

Teaser. A technique for jumping directly into a show.

Telenovela. A Latin American television soap opera.

Teleseries. The merger of the telenovela genre with weekly drama series and miniseries formats to form a format that tells continued stories differently than telenovelas; a format that has a faster-paced season of 40 to 60 episodes.

Three-act structure. Standard writing structure; a proven dramatic storytelling model that uses three parts known as the setup (the beginning), the confrontation (the middle), and the resolution (the end); a form, but not a formula, that suggests the location of a story's main points.

360 multiplatform environment. Online, mobile, and social media sites and traditional platforms, e.g., the opportunity to activate an online platform related to a television show that allows downloads of music, episodes, extra footage, B-story episodes, behind-the-scenes interviews with the cast, and relevant information about a show.

Transmedia. Use of different media platforms to present a show or story.

Treatment. A short document of about ten pages that contains a summary of the major scenes in a proposed concept/idea and descriptions of significant characters (sometimes sample dialogue).

Up front. A meeting hosted by television network executives attended by major advertisers with the main purpose of allowing advertisers to buy television airtime "up front" or several months before a television season begins.

VCI. Value chain of innovation.

VCCI. Value chain of content innovation.

VOD. Video on demand.

Webisode. A television episode made for online viewing.

Widget. An app or component of an interface that enables access to a service.

Windows of exposition. The different platforms to showcase content, with the platform being tied to geographic limitations and terms of use; film, theater, television, the internet, mobile devices, cable, hotel entertainment platforms, subscription video on demand, in-flight entertainment platforms, etc.

INDEX